# The Biology of Psychism
## *from a Christian Perspective*

by

# Rev. Joseph Adam Pearson, Ph.D.

# Copyright

Paper Book Identifiers:
ISBN-10: 0996222464
ISBN-13: 9780996222464

Published by
Christ Evangelical Bible Institute
(SAN: 920-3753)
Dayton, Tennessee

Last edited on October 18, 2022

# Definitions for the Prospective Reader

## *Biology*

The author's definition of *biology* in the context of this book includes the scientific study of the structures and functions of individual living things and the interrelationships, interdependencies, and interactions of those individual living things with other living things.

## *Psychism*

The author's definition of the word *psychism* in the context of this book includes: (1) the doctrine that consciousness is the universal soul force that animates all living beings, corporeal or incorporeal (here, the term *soul force* should not be confused with the branding of any product or any political or religious movement); (2) the essential character or nature of consciousness that permits conceptual communication between and among all living beings, corporeal or incorporeal; (3) the eternality of the soul, reincarnation, astral projection (soul travel), and personal psychic abilities, including: hearing psychically, seeing psychically, spiritual healing, electromagnetic healing, "laying on of hands," telepathy, far-memory (recollection of past lives), far-seeing (clairvoyance), far-hearing (clairaudience), automatic writing, channeling, and other transcendent communications between extrabiological life forms (i.e., incorporeal beings) and biological life forms (i.e., corporeal beings); and (4) investigative research on, or study of, any one, any combination, or all of the previous topics.

In summary, the word *psychism* is descriptive of (1) universal consciousness (i.e., general psychism) as well as (2) the extrasensory abilities of individuals (i.e., specific psychism). In its narrowest sense, a *personal psychism* (i.e., a specific psychism in an individual human being) is a divine spiritual *charism* when it is operated by the Creator-God's Holy Spirit. For the sake of clarity, a *charism* is a gift from the Holy Spirit to be used for the glory of the God of the Holy Bible.

Author's Notes: The English words *charism* and *charisms* are derived from the Greek words *charisma* (singular) and *charismata* (plural) [χάρισμα and χαρίσματα], both of which are found in the Greek New Testament [referenced in *Strong's Exhaustive Concordance* as G5486].


## *Christian*

A *Christian* in the context of *The Holy Bible* and this book is: a person who believes in Jesus Christ as (1) the *only-begotten* Son of God; (2) God Incarnate (the Creator-God, or Word of God, in flesh); (3) the promised Messiah of Israel; (4) the one true Savior of the world; and (5) one's only personal Savior.

Author's Notes: The following names are synonymous — Jesus Christ, Christ Jesus, Jesus the Christ, Jesus the Messiah, the Messiah Jesus *(Christ* is derived from the Greek word for *Messiah)*


For the author of *The Biology of Psychism from a Christian Perspective*, psychism is normal and not paranormal.

# Dedication

*The Biology of Psychism from a Christian Perspective*

is dedicated to all who seek to reconcile Christianity with psychism.

# This Book's Purpose

With the guidance and approval of the Creator-God's Holy Spirit, this book has been written: (1) to establish a baseline of knowledge in *psychism* for people living at the end of *the pre-Millennium* and during *the Millennium*; (2) to credit the Creator-God as Author, Originator, and Evolver of all *psychism* as defined by this book (with the exceptions, of course, of demonic influences and possessions); (3) to confirm that the *divine Mind* of Jesus Christ and *personal psychism* in individual human beings are not mutually exclusive; (4) to prepare the human race for the continuous outpouring of the Creator-God's Holy Spirit throughout *the Millennium*; (5) to educate the human race as to the nature of the spiritual gifts given by, and operated through, the Creator-God's Holy Spirit; and (6) to please the Lord God Almighty.

Further, it is the purpose of this book to present an intelligible explanation of universal consciousness as it relates to *general psychism*. And it is the purpose of this book to articulate a coherent exposition on *specific psychism* in order to establish a baseline understanding of corporeal and incorporeal activities as they relate to hearing psychically, seeing psychically, astral projection (soul travel), spiritual healing, electromagnetic healing, "laying on of hands," telepathy, far-memory (recollection of past lives), far-seeing (clairvoyance), far-hearing (clairaudience), channeling, automatic writing, and other transcendent communications between and among physical beings and spiritual beings, including the Supreme Being *(the Creator-God)*.

It is the intention of the author of *The Biology of Psychism from a Christian Perspective* to help bring the Creator-God into the 21st century through this book. Of course, the Creator-God Himself does not need to be brought into the 21st century: It is human understanding about the Creator-God that needs to be brought into the 21st century. And part of bringing the Creator-God into the 21st century involves reconciling the seeming differences between psychism (both general and specific) and mainstream Christian biblical understanding.

# Introduction

Eternity is ageless. Temporality is not. Eternity is dimensionless. Temporality is not.

Based on the original emergence and success of various life forms on Earth as measured by their numbers and diversity, biologists might divide chronological time on Earth into the following ages: Age of Invertebrates, Age of Fishes, Age of Amphibians, Age of Reptiles, Age of Dinosaurs, Age of Birds, and Age of Mammals. Of course, there are scientific names as well as epoch divisions associated with each of the Ages, but this author will not burden this book's readers with that nomenclature.

Based on their understanding of events recorded in the Bible, Christians might divide time on Earth into at least three separate ages or dispensations. Indeed, Jesus Christ himself spoke of distinct ages:

> "And whoever may speak a word against the Son of Man it shall be forgiven him, but whoever may speak against the Holy Spirit, it shall not be forgiven him, neither in this Age nor in that which is coming."
>
> *Matthew 12:32 YLT*

In the previous quotation, the Greek word from which "age" has been translated is αἰών (ī-ōn´) [G165], from which the English word *eon* is derived. The Apostle Paul also used the plural of this Greek word to denote periods of time:

> {25} Whereof I am made a minister of the church, according to the dispensation of God, which is given to me for you, to

fulfill the word of God; {26} the mystery which has been hidden from ages [*plural* αἰώνων] and from generations, but now is made manifest to His saints.

*Colossians 1:25-26 KJV Paraphrase*

Regardless of the actual number of ages or dispensations to which individual Christians might subscribe, most Christians agree on at least the following two periods of chronological time in terms of sequence as well as length of time: (1) the Age of Grace (also known as the Church Age, the Ecclesial Age, the Gospel Age, and the Age of Salvation) from the time of the First Coming of Jesus Christ until the time of his Second Coming (approximately 2,000 years); and (2) the Millennial Kingdom (also known as *the Millennium,* the Kingdom Age, and the Zionic Age) from the time of the Second Coming of Jesus Christ until the formation of "a new heaven and a new earth" (Revelation 21:1 KJV) at the end of his earthly reign (approximately 1,000 years).

During the Church Age, many people interested in *psychism* appropriated the phrase *New Age* from biblical thinking that *the Millennium* would be a time of immense personal spiritual growth. Unfortunately, at the same time that many people tried to jump the spiritual gun to a *New Age,* they also ended up avoiding any traditional biblical understanding of who Jesus Christ is — namely, that he is: (1) the *only-begotten* Son of God; (2) God Incarnate (the Creator-God, or Word of God, in flesh); (3) the promised Messiah of Israel; (4) the one true Savior of the world; and (5) one's only personal Savior.

During the present author's lifetime, ignorance characterizes all three groups of people: modern scientists, Christians, and New Agers. Most modern scientists choose to ignore (1) spiritual consciousness, (2) psychic phenomena, and (3) the role of Jesus Christ in creation, salvation, and sanctification. Most Christians choose to ignore (1) credible astronomical and geological theories, (2) spiritual consciousness, and (3) psychic phenomena. And most *New Agers* choose to ignore (1) psychic fakery, (2) spiritual quackery, and (3) the role of the biblical Jesus in creation, salvation, and sanctification. In other words, most people from these three groups choose to be ignorant about certain concepts that are collectively very important to more fully understanding life on Earth.

During the Church Age: (1) many Christians have falsified and misused gifts of the Creator-God's Holy Spirit and falsified miraculous, supernatural events; (2) many New Agers have contrived and falsified psychic phenomena; and (3) many modern scientists have rejected the existence of supernatural events or sought to find only natural causes to explain them.

The author of this book, *The Biology of Psychism from a Christian Perspective,* acknowledges: (1) the role of the biblical Jesus in creation, salvation, and sanctification; (2) consciousness as the only real tangible substance in the entire universe; (3) the existence of authentic psychic phenomena; and (4) the credibility of most scientific methods, investigations, and findings in modern astronomy, biology, chemistry, geology, and physics.

The author of this book also acknowledges that the God of the Holy Bible is (1) the Author of miraculous supernatural events and spiritual gifts as well as (2) the Creator-Evolver of the entire universe and all life therein, corporeal (i.e., physical) as well as incorporeal (i.e., spiritual).

# Notes

As used in this book, *KJV* is an abbreviation for the public domain *King James Version* of the Holy Bible. To ensure their accuracy throughout this book, all paraphrases of the public domain *King James Version* of the Holy Bible were finalized only after first checking: (1) the Masoretic Hebrew text of the Tanakh (the Jewish Bible) for accuracy of passages from the *KJV Old Testament;* and (2) the earliest Greek text extant for accuracy of passages from the *KJV New Testament.* Additionally, to enhance readability of the public domain *KJV* text, the present author has changed words like *hath, thou,* and *ye* to their modern equivalents.

Most transliterated Hebrew and Greek words referenced within the text of this book are noted by their respective numbers [in brackets with a preceding "H" for Hebrew or "G" for Greek] from the *Dictionary of the Hebrew Bible* and the *Dictionary of the Greek Bible* found in *Strong's Exhaustive Concordance of the Bible* by James Strong (Copyright 1890), Crusade Bible Publishers, Inc., Nashville.

Although God the Father *(the Lord God Almighty)* and God the Son *(the Lord Jesus Christ)* are consubstantially united in the Godhead along with God the Holy Spirit, in order to distinguish *God the Father* from *God the Son,* an upper case "H" is used for personal pronouns specifically referring to *God the Father (He, His,* and *Him)* and a lower case "h" is used for personal pronouns specifically referring to *God the Son (he, his,* and *him).*

Whenever the titles *God* or *Creator-God* are used in this book, the reader should assume that they are referring solely to: (1) the God of the Holy Bible — who is the *Lord God Almighty* or *Yahweh* (YHWH);

(2) the one true and only real Creator-Evolver and Creator-Savior; (3) *His* tripartite nature; (4) *His* sevenfold Spirit; and (5) *His* various facets.

Although the Creator-God does not possess a human gender, there are no apologies for the use of the male pronouns *He, His, and Him* in this book when referring to the Lord God Almighty for the following reasons: In general, certain words in theology and philosophy are capitalized to show that they represent qualities and characteristics that transcend human understanding and experience. This includes the pronouns *He, His,* and *Him* and even the word *God* itself. *She* and *Her* are not used in this book when referring to the Creator-God because many people, if not most, tend to confuse the use of female pronouns with advocating Wicca and other pagan cults that worship the Mother-Goddess — such as those devoted to Cybele, Aphrodite, Hecate, Artemis, Magna Mater, Ma, Anaitis, Astarte, or their modern counterparts.

As a final note here, *demonic forces* (collectively known as *Evil* in this book) include: (1) Satan (the fallen Lucifer); (2) the messengers of Satan (Satan's fallen angels); (3) discarnates whose souls once resided in human bodies but are now beyond divine reclamation because of their active, willful, obdurate, and eternal rejection of Jesus Christ as Savior (also known synonymously as *unclean spirits, devils,* or *demons* in various translations and versions of the Holy Bible); and (4) current human beings who are irrevocably on the road to becoming unclean spirits by (a) blaspheming the Creator-God's Holy Spirit (in ridiculing or labeling the Holy Spirit's attributes, gifts, and operations as *evil)* and/or (b) actively, willfully, obdurately, and eternally rejecting the Holy Spirit's personal invitation for them to receive Jesus Christ as Savior (this does not include passively rejecting Jesus Christ out of ignorance of who he is nor does it include those Jews who have *Messianic expectancy).*

# About the Author

It seems to me that I have lived my entire life believing that thoughts are things and that things are thoughts. *For example,* I remember a recurring dilemma throughout most of my childhood concerning the meaning of "exit" and "entrance" signs. Often, I had to pause at a door with such signage and think: "Am I exiting the store in order to enter the world or am I exiting the world in order to enter the store?" I often needed to look at the direction in which the doors swung in order to solve the problem. This dilemma occurred regularly. As I saw it, life was *only* filled with conceptual puzzles that needed to be figured out. Now, as a senior adult (seventy-five at the printing of the 2022 edition of this book), door signage continues to pose similar questions that I must ask myself (and answer correctly) before I proceed.

As a child, I often laughed when I fell. I thought it funny that the cumbersome body in which I found myself could be so clumsy and unaware of its surroundings or that its nervous system could be so incapable of making right decisions relative to the direction of its movements. At the age of seventy-five, I still laugh for similar reasons. Although I could write at length about many related occurrences, it is sufficient for me to state at this juncture that, because I found the world to be an inhospitable place at a very young age, it was easy for me to learn to dissociate myself from it. I have always felt, and still feel, like a stranger in a strange land. I have always felt, and still feel, that physicality, or corporeality, is alien to me and that I am an alien in it. As a result, throughout my entire life, I have made a distinction between *physical existence (corporeal existence)* and *spiritual being (incorporeal being)*.

Throughout my life, words, phrases, and statements have come to me from out of nowhere. *For example,* I remember walking home one day in 1966 and inwardly hearing: *"Time is a sequence of related events."* Every word and image that I received over the years, I would ponder and reflect on, often for decades. As I matured, I came to understand and accept that I had a susceptibility, or sensitivity, to receiving external words and images from otherworldly sources. (Incidentally, although I am still maturing at the age of seventy-five, I believe that it is sometime during our 50th year that we truly begin to mature spiritually.)

I am very grateful for my mentoring as a young person by an aunt who had a substantial understanding of Christian metaphysics. She posed just the right questions to me about who I thought I am and who I really *am.* As a preteen, I remember her telling me to look at myself in her large living room wall mirror. She asked me if the image in the mirror represented who I really *am.* I remember her telling me that it did not and why it did not. We met regularly to explore together who and what I was, and am, in God through Christ Jesus. During her tutelage, I became very comfortable with the concepts and language of Christian metaphysics, comparing and contrasting such concepts as *corporeality versus spirituality, absolute truth versus relative truth,* and *statements of existence versus declarations of being.*

As a young person, I loved traditional children's Sunday school. And I was a Vacation Bible School (VBS) junkie: During the summers, I would attend the Baptist VBS, Lutheran VBS, Methodist VBS, and Presbyterian VBS for two weeks each to study the Bible, memorize Bible verses, and work on Bible-related crafts. I also attended Bible Camp in Mukwonago, Wisconsin during the summers. I loved — and still love — reading, studying, and comprehending the Holy Bible and using the spiritual truths that it contains as a filter through which to view the world, its reality, and its unreality.

I remember deciding as a sophomore in high school what I wanted to do with my life: I wanted to become a biology teacher, a pastor, and an author.

To help fulfill my goals, I majored in biology at Loyola University in Chicago. My favorite science courses included: comparative embryology of vertebrates, comparative anatomy of vertebrates, physiology, histology, genetics, physics, and organic chemistry. In addition to science courses, I took various elective courses in world religions, Aristotelian logic and ethics, and metaphysics. I distinctly remember that my metaphysics professor, an ex-Jesuit, hated my written compositions because I tried to link metaphysics to Christianity. I now understand that, although he believed in the existence of an invisible reality, he thought of it only as an intellectual reality and not a spiritual one.

I have always enjoyed reading books directly and indirectly related to metaphysics, like Immanuel Kant's *Prolegomena to any Future Metaphysics* (1783) and Walter Haushalter's *Mrs. Eddy Purloins from Hegel* (1936). Today, I still read such works. *For example,* I have recently finished reading Friedrich Nietzsche's *Also sprach Zarathustra* (1885). I read the German original side-by-side with an English translation *(Thus Spoke Zarathustra)* to see if they were the same book. Because the two languages do not possess the same nuances of word meaning, I concluded that they really are not *exactly* the same.

After earning my Bachelor of Science degree in biology at Loyola University (Chicago) in 1969, I remained at Loyola for an additional two years to earn a Master of Science in biology with an emphasis in cell biology. Serving as a graduate teaching assistant in the Department of Biology at Loyola permitted me to finance my graduate studies: I especially enjoyed teaching human histology laboratory sections while I was there. During my Junior and Senior years as an undergraduate, as well as during my graduate years at Loyola, I also worked as an electron microscopist in the Department of Oral Histology at the University of Illinois Dental School and in the Department of Anatomy at the University of Chicago.

After receiving my Master of Science degree in 1971, I became a high school biology teacher at a prestigious, all-boys college preparatory school where I taught for two years. I then served for two years on the faculty as a Research Associate in the Department of Ophthalmology at the University of Illinois Medical Center, where I first-authored and co-authored many scientific papers in reputable, refereed (i.e., peer-reviewed) journals under my birth name of Joseph Vlchek (J.K. Vlchek). While working as a Research Associate, I entered a doctoral program as a graduate student in the Department of Anatomy at the University of Illinois Medical School (the Abraham Lincoln School of Medicine). While in that program, I took advanced human anatomy, advanced human physiology, and advanced human histology. During that time, I also began to teach "Structure and Function of the Human Body," "Evolution, Genetics, and Development," and "Scientific Inquiry" as an adjunct faculty member in the Department of Natural Science at the Lewis Towers Campus of Loyola University.

Although I continued adjunct teaching at Loyola for many years, I left the University of Illinois Medical Center to take a full time teaching position with the City Colleges of Chicago in the Department of Biology at Kennedy-King College, where I taught human anatomy and physiology full time for eight years to students of medical education (primarily nursing students). Because, at that time, the Department of Anatomy at the University of Illinois permitted only full time status for its doctoral students, I matriculated into a doctoral program at the University of Chicago in its Department of Biology with the endorsement of the distinguished cell biologist, Dr. Hewson Swift, in whose laboratory I had conducted laboratory research for my Master's thesis while at Loyola. At the University of Chicago, I took courses in biochemistry, lipoproteins and enzyme kinetics, and cell biology. Incidentally, the biochemistry course at the University of Chicago was the most difficult course I have ever taken. We covered the 1,000-page eighth edition of *Principles of Biochemistry* by Albert L. Lehninger in nine weeks, and students were responsible for understanding and remembering all formulas, equations, and molecular structures in the book.

Eventually, I decided that I knew all that I needed to know for future independent learning in the content area of biology. I became more intrigued and challenged by the presentation of information to enhance its assimilation and accommodation by learners. So, in 1981, I left everything in Illinois to move to Arizona: (1) to enter a doctoral program in education at Arizona State University with an emphasis in teacher education, language, literacy, linguistics, and textual analysis as well as (2) to teach for the Maricopa County Community College District, where I served full time as: (a) biology and chemistry faculty at South Mountain Community College for five years; (b) lead professor in human anatomy and physiology (as well as Biology Department Chairperson) at Scottsdale Community College for ten years; and (c) founding instructional dean at the Red Mountain Campus of Mesa Community College (MCC) and director of MCC's Extended Campus for a total of ten years. Altogether, I was employed in the Maricopa County Community College District for twenty-five years. During that time, I earned my Doctor of Philosophy (Ph.D.) from Arizona State University in 1988 with a dissertation entitled *Testing the Ecological Validity of Student-Generated versus Teacher-Provided Postquestions in Reading College Science Text* (1988). I am pleased that my research findings were accepted in 1991 for publication in the highly respected, refereed *Journal of Research in Science Teaching*.

Throughout my life, I have always multi-tasked and led double professional lives. *For example,* during the last ten years of the time that I worked for the Maricopa Community College District, I also served as Senior Pastor for Healing Waters Ministries in Tempe, Arizona. Additionally, for the past twenty-six years (1996-2022), I have served as International President and Chief Executive Officer of Christ Evangelical Bible Institute (CEBI), which has thriving branch campuses in India, Pakistan, and Tanzania. In that capacity, I have been responsible for developing, designing, and deploying Bible curriculum as well as for in-servicing the various branch campus administrators, ministerial students, and local pastors. At the time of this writing (2022), I am still serving as International President and CEO of CEBI as well as teaching online Bible courses.

I believe strongly that after we are saved, and at the same time we are being sanctified, our individual actions on Earth are part of an "application" for the jobs that we will each hold during Christ Jesus' millennial reign on Earth. My greatest goal is to be one of the many committed Christian educators who will be teaching throughout *the Millennium*. It is my hope that I will be able to use this book as a textbook for students of Christian psychism during that period of time.

When I was three years of age, I remember someone from Heaven telling me during an afternoon nap what my specific purpose for being on Earth is. I was also told that when I awoke I would not remember the specific purpose but that I would remember that I had been told. When I awoke from my nap that day, it was exactly so: I did not remember my specific purpose, but I did remember that I had been told. I suspect that the writing of this book — as well as the other books that I have completed — is part of why I am here.

In closing this section, I will add that, throughout my entire life and from my earliest recollections, I have always heard and seen things that did not exist to most other people. I also learned how to conduct *thought experiments* in the laboratory of my mind and to regularly present my findings to the Creator-God's Holy Spirit for approval as well as for guidance and insights concerning refinement of my findings and subsequent investigations. *The Biology of Psychism from a Christian Perspective* is a product of my *thought experiments*. In fact, all of my published books are products of my nurture, training, education, employment, Bible study, and Christian ministry in conjunction with my thought experiments.

......

For the sake of clarity, when the author of *The Biology of Psychism from a Christian Perspective* uses the phrase *the present author* in this book, he is referring to himself.

# Table of Contents

## Chapter Two:

## Hindrances to Personal Psychism...........................111

# Chapter One:

# The Basics of Psychism

# The Etymology of *Psychism*

Because of their contemporary associations with (1) satanic witchery and (2) commercial charlatanism, the words *psychic* and *psychism* are not often viewed as suitable words for Christians or educated people to use in the early 21st century society. However, people who have a distaste for the words *psychic* and *psychism* are either ignorant of their etymology or have chosen to ignore the continued importance of these two words and their related variants and derivatives in academic theology, academic philosophy, and modern science.

Just as the Greek word *pneuma* was important to Aristotle and continues to be important to New Testament scholars, so does the Greek word *psuche* — from which the words *psyche, psychic, psychical, psychism, psychology,* and *psychiatry* are derived — continue to have importance in academic theology, academic philosophy, and modern science.

Based on the two Greek nouns most often used in the New Testament for a human being's "spirit" and "soul" — πνεῦμα *pnyü'-mä* [G4151] ("spirit" or "breath") and ψυχή *psü-khā'* [G5590] ("soul" or "mind") — one can define: (1) *spirit* as "the invisible essence of a human being characterized by one's unique personality;" and (2) *soul,* or *mind,* as "the seat of a human being's thoughts and feelings that impart individual consciousness." In modern scientific contexts (especially in biology, neuroscience, psychiatry, and psychology), ψυχή *psü-khā'* ("soul" or "mind") refers to consciousness that is associated with general regions and specific areas of the human brain. However, what is generally described by the words *psychic* and *psychical* is in contradistinction to what is generally described by the words *physics* and *physical.*

Highly educated biologists, historians, linguists, neuroscientists, philosophers, psychiatrists, psychologists, and theologians might spend a significant amount of time trying to elucidate and clarify the differences between the "spirit" and the "soul" of a human being. So, we will leave that worthy discussion to them. Yet it is important to note at this juncture that the combined "spirit" and "soul" of a human being are like dissolved sugar in distilled water: The water and sugar molecules are indivisible from one another under normal circumstances and conditions. Similarly, the combined "spirit" and "soul" of a human being are indivisible from one another under normal circumstances and conditions. To be sure, one's combined "spirit" and "soul" are distinguishable as well as divisible from one's somatic, or physical, identity at the same time that both spirit and soul can influence one's bodily form, likeness, appearance, physiognomy, and physiology.

Indeed, ψυχή *psü-khā´* is the Greek word from which the English nouns *psychic* and *psychology* have been derived. Thus, just as the word *psychology* means "the study of the *mind*" or "the study of the *soul*" so, in certain contexts, can the noun *psychic* mean *"mind* reader" or *"soul* reader" (i.e., telepathic discerner of another being's conscious or subconscious thoughts). In an extended sense, the adjective *psychic* goes well beyond describing functions of the brain as detected by human brain wave activity (i.e., electroencephalography or EEG). And, in its most transcendent sense, the adjective *psychic* describes detecting activity in the invisible, incorporeal, electromagnetic, and supernatural realm by gifted and talented "sensitives," "susceptible channels," "spiritual empaths," or "psychics." Metaphysically speaking, to be a *psychic* means that one "receives impressions telepathically from the soul, mind, or consciousness of another person" and/or that one "is able to transcend space-time to sense aspects of the past, present, or future."

Common 21st century cultural connotations of *psychic* activity include far-seeing (clairvoyance or knowing beforehand), far-hearing (clairaudience or perceiving what is inaudible to the natural ear), far-memory (remembering past events and circumstances outside of one's current lifetime and personal experience), spiritual healing, electromagnetic healing, "laying on of hands," telepathy ("reading" what is in another person's mind), channeling (including spiritual mediumship and automatic writing), and astral projection (soul travel).

For the sake of clarification, *automatic writing* has a different connotation in *psychism* than in psychology or psychiatry. *Automatic writing* in psychology or psychiatry assumes that the subconscious mind (i.e., unconscious mind) of the writer is directing the writing; in contrast, *automatic writing* in *psychism* assumes that an incorporeal entity is using a corporeal agent's psychomotor apparatus for writing.

The word *psyche* ("soul" or "mind") serves as the base or root for *psychism*. And, depending on its base or root word, the suffix "-ism" can denote: (1) a doctrine or an ideology; (2) a characteristic or an ability; (3) a body of knowledge or an investigative study; or (4) an act or a deed. To what the word *psychism* is specifically referring depends on the context of its use.

# *Psychism* as Used by Teilhard de Chardin

In Teilhard de Chardin's *The Phenomenon of Man*, the words *psychic, psychical,* and *psychism* are never used in reference to their common 20th or early 21st century cultural connotations. Rather, *psychic, psychical,* and *psychism* had very broad meanings to de Chardin that included everything and anything associated with (1) consciousness, (2) the *interiority,* or (3) *the Within* (as used by de Chardin, all three of these labels are synonymous):

> We shall assume that, essentially, all energy is *psychic* in nature… [italics mine]
>
> *Phenomenon, p. 64*

> It is generally accepted that we must assume psychic life to 'begin' in the world with the first appearance of organized life, in other words, of the cell.
>
> *Phenomenon, p. 88*

> From the moment we regard evolution as primarily psychical transformation, we see there is not one instinct in nature, but a multitude of forms of instincts each corresponding to a particular solution of the problem of life. The 'psychical' make-up of an insect is not and cannot be that of a vertebrate; nor can the instinct of a squirrel be that of a cat or an elephant: this in virtue of the position of each on the [phylogenetic] tree of life. [brackets mine]
>
> *Phenomenon, p. 167*

> Here, and throughout this book *[The Phenomenon of Man],* the term 'consciousness' is taken in its widest sense to indicate every kind of *psychism,* from the most rudimentary

forms of interior perception imaginable to the human phenomenon of reflective thought. [brackets and italics mine]

*Phenomenon, Footnote 1, p. 57*

For de Chardin, *psychism* (French singular *le psychisme* and plural *les psychismes*) includes cytoplasmic streaming, taxes (i.e., behavioral responses to stimuli [pronounced tak-seez´]), tropisms, instincts, self-reflections, intuitions, socializations, and metaphysical consciousness convergence by any and all living things.

From the biosphere to the species, [evolution] is nothing but an immense ramification [branching] of *psychism* seeking for itself [to be expressed] through different forms. [brackets and italics mine]

*Phenomenon, p. 151*

To de Chardin, *psychism* existed in the protoplasm of the very first primordial cells just as it exists in the physical centers of individual consciousness (e.g., cerebral hemispheres) of the most complex vertebrates living today. Extremely important to the present author's paradigm of *psychism*, de Chardin identified Christ Jesus as the principle of universal vitality responsible for all consciousness in primordial cells as well as in complex multicellular organisms:

Christ... put himself in the position (maintained ever since) to subdue under himself, to purify, to direct and superanimate the general ascent of consciousness in which he inserted himself. By a perennial [i.e., ongoing and everlasting] act of communion and sublimation [i.e., transformation], he aggregates to himself the total *psychism* of the Earth. [brackets and italics mine]

*Phenomenon, Epilogue, p. 294*

To express the role of Christ Jesus in subduing and gathering all things unto himself in the process of their ultimate unification and eventual collective presentation to God the Father at the end of *the Millennium,* de Chardin stated:

> And when [Christ Jesus] has gathered everything together and transformed everything, he will close in upon himself and his conquests [through the process of involution], thereby rejoining, in a final gesture, the divine focus he has never left. Then, as St. Paul tells us [in *1 Corinthians 15:24-28*], *God shall be all in all.* [brackets mine]
>
> Ibid.

Although the present author sees the formation of the *all in all* at the end of *the Millennium* of Jesus Christ's rule on Earth as an infusion of the physically knowable universe with the Totality of the Creator-God's Being and Fiery Presence, de Chardin's view is somewhat more immanent than transcendent:

> This [formation] is indeed a superior form of 'pantheism' without trace of the poison of adulteration or annihilation: the expectation of perfect unity, steeped in which each element will reach its consummation at the same time as the universe [reaches its consummation]. [brackets mine]
>
> Ibid.

Because of his bent toward Aristotelianism — as attested by his embracing "immanence within matter" *(Phenomenon, p. 88)*, de Chardin failed in his writing to provide an account of the biblical revelation that, when God the Son presents everything subdued under his feet (and, therefore, within his control and under his power) to God the Father at the time of the formation of the *all in all* referred to in 1

Corinthians 15:28 (KJV), all elements in the physically observable universe will be consumed by *fervent heat* in an atomic fission induced by the Creator-God:

> {10} But the day of the Lord will come as a thief in the night, at which time the heavens shall pass away with a great noise, and the elements shall melt with fervent heat, and the Earth also and the works that are therein shall be burned up. {11} Seeing then that all these things shall be dissolved, what manner of persons ought you to be in all holy conversation and godliness. {12} Looking for and hastening unto the coming of the day of God, wherein the heavens being on fire shall be dissolved, and the elements shall melt with fervent heat.
>
> *2 Peter 3:10-12 KJV Paraphrase*

For de Chardin, every physical thing has both a "Within" as well as a "Without." The "Without" (i.e., de Chardin's *le Dehors*) comprises a physical thing's external features and characteristics. The "Within" (i.e., de Chardin's *le Dedans*) of a physical thing is consciousness itself, which has urged and pushed physicality to grope toward hominization (for de Chardin, *hominization* is distinctly different from *humanization*). To de Chardin, reflection (i.e., self-reflection and *knowing that one knows*) has played the most important role in the beginning of the hominization of anthropoids. He believed, and rightfully so, that, when anthropoids crossed the threshold from simply *thinking* to *reflecting,* and from simply *knowing* to *knowing that they knew,* they had evolved into true man (i.e., hominized men and women or modern hominins). For de Chardin, the psychic advance of prehistoric true man from earlier anthropoids is evidenced by their: (1) increased cerebralization with correspondingly larger cranial cavities; and (2) behaviors associated with *self-reflection.* The aforementioned behaviors first appeared *as a complete package, or ensemble, of skills* somewhere between 80,000 and 48,000 years ago and included: (1) chipping and polishing stones; (2) making fire in hearths; (3) ritually burying the dead; (4) adorning the living or dead body with scars, inks, tattoos, and/or jewelry; (5) carving and painting on rocks and cave walls; (6) planting crops; (7) making artifacts associated with worship; and (8) producing functional pottery. In his *self-reflection*, the earliest modern man not only recognized his own physical, mental, emotional, spiritual, and social needs but also discovered or invented ways to meet those needs.

For the author of *The Biology of Psychism from a Christian Perspective*, just as *Homo neanderthalensis* and *Homo sapiens* coexisted and interbred in Eurasia for an overlapping 5,000 year period of time (from approximately 44,000 to 39,000 years ago), so also prehistoric modern man *(Homo sapiens* var. *sine anima)* and the descendants of Adam and Eve *(Homo sapiens* var. *cum anima)*[1] co-existed and interbred for an overlapping 1656 years (from approximately 4004 BC to 2348 BC), which duration is derived from the following two criteria:

> (1)  Calculations from Bible genealogies help us to conclude that Adam and Eve materialized on Earth in the form of *Homo sapiens* in approximately 4004 BC (when the two were evicted from the Garden of Eden); and

---

[1]  The author of *The Biology of Psychism from a Christian Perspective* has coined the following taxonomic names for two different categories of modern man: (1) *"Homo sapiens* var. *sine anima"* referring to "the variety of modern man without a soul" and (2) *"Homo sapiens* var. *cum anima"* referring to "the variety of modern man with a soul." Read the author's book entitled *Intelligent Evolution* for additional explanations concerning this nomenclature.

(2) Calculations from successive generations of various Antediluvians in the Bible — specifically Adam, Seth, Enosh, Kenan, Mahalelel, Jared, Enoch, Methusaleh, Lamech, and Noah — help us to calculate that Noah's flood occurred in approximately 2348 BC.

Although some *Homo sapiens* interbred with some *Homo neanderthalensis* from approximately 44,000 to 39,000 years ago, the species *Homo sapiens* ended up outlasting and replacing the species *Homo neanderthalensis*. Similarly, from the present author's perspective, although some *Homo sapiens* var. *cum anima* interbred with *Homo sapiens* var. *sine anima* from approximately 4004 to 2348 BC, the species *Homo sapiens* var. *cum anima* ended up outlasting and replacing *Homo sapiens* var. *sine anima,* resulting in physically-evolved human beings with souls.

For the sake of clarity, (1) Adam and Eve materialized in the flesh of hominids (specifically, in the flesh bodies of hominins or modern human beings) and (2) their immediate direct descendants (e.g., Cain and Seth) interbred with hominids (specifically, with the flesh bodies of hominins or modern human beings) who had evolved physically but did not have souls. Thus, contemporary members of the species *Homo sapiens* received their physical forms from the descendants of Adam and Eve who interbred — beginning approximately 6,000 years ago — with physically-evolved modern man.

In keeping with the Will of the Creator-God, all direct descendants of Adam and Eve received eternal souls (albeit fallen souls) from their birthright as descendants of Adam and Eve. *For example,* when Cain went to live with the people of Nod *(Genesis 4:16-17),* he ended up living with people who had no souls *(Homo sapiens* var. *sine anima).* However, because he himself had a soul, all of his offspring also would inherit souls *(Homo sapiens* var. *cum anima)*. There are no human beings today without souls because the subpopulation of people without souls were wiped out with Noah's flood.

In addition to a geosphere and a biosphere, de Chardin believed that the Earth possesses a surrounding noösphere, or *metaphysical sphere of human thought,* with an axis of increasing complexity that: (1) drove the evolution of humankind in the direction of self-reflection as well as socialization and (2) continues to drive its evolution toward higher heights through unification. In other words, de Chardin postulated that the Earth possesses a global human consciousness, or human collective consciousness, that moved humankind from possessing simple instincts to developing traits associated with self-reflection and, then, to developing traits associated with socialization. To de Chardin, traits associated with socialization are of a higher order than traits associated with self-reflection because they have allowed modern human beings to reach their current psychic heights and they will permit them to reach even higher heights in the future through collective unification (as human beings converge in the future, according to de Chardin, at the *Omega Point).*

To de Chardin, the future higher heights of human beings include reaching *the Omega Point.* To the author of *The Biology of Psychism from a Christian Perspective,* the higher heights of humankind along the way to this so-called Omega Point also include human beings developing spiritualized intuition in the form of (1) increased extrasensory sensation and perception, (2) heightened susceptibility to the thoughts and feelings of the Creator-God, and (3) enhanced sensitivity to the specific thoughts and feelings of others. The development of this spiritualized intuition is in keeping with the following Bible prophecy:

{17} "It shall come to pass in the last days," says the Lord God Almighty, "I will pour out My Holy Spirit upon all flesh: and your sons and your daughters shall prophesy, and your young men shall see visions, and your old men shall dream dreams; {18} And on my servants and on my handmaidens in those days I will pour out My Holy Spirit; and they shall prophesy."

*Acts 2:17-18 KJV Paraphrase (quoting Joel 2:28-29)*

To be sure, the Creator-God has not chosen any one human being to be the sole voice for truth during this "psychozoic era" *(Phenomenon, p. 183)*. Rather, the Creator-God has chosen His Holy Spirit to be the sole voice of truth for this age. How will humankind know when its *psychism* has arrived at its greatest heights? For the present author, humankind shall arrive — as well as recognize that it has arrived — when our thoughts in relative space-time are indistinguishable from thoughts in eternity. In other words, our *psychism* shall have arrived at its greatest heights when we live in a world without self-delusions and our "spirit man" has stepped in and taken over from our "natural man." (Derived from the Bible, the noun phrases "spirit man" and "natural man" are non-gender-specific.)

Like de Chardin, the author of *The Biology of Psychism from a Christian Perspective* believes that there is a role for our enemies to play in the development of higher psychisms in modern man. (Here, *higher psychisms* include all mental activities associated with *spiritualized intuition,* one's sixth sense.) So important is the role of this impetus for change, de Chardin asked: "What would we do without our enemies?" *(Phenomenon, p. 149)* In other words, our enemies provide the impetus for us to reach higher psychisms by helping us to move away from our "fundamental inertia" *(Ibid.)* — in conjunction, of course, with the outpouring of the Creator-God's Holy

Spirit, such outpouring first referred to in the Holy Bible by the Prophet Joel *(Joel 2:28-29)*. Our enemies play an important role in our arriving at higher heights because their potential, immanent, and actual intrusions and invasions force the development of our *spiritualized intuition* to help ensure our individual and collective survival. In other words, our individual specific psychism (i.e., personal psychism) is forced to germinate in adverse conditions.

The author of *The Biology of Psychism from a Christian Perspective* believes that the higher psychisms of: (1) increased extrasensory sensation and perception, (2) heightened susceptibility, and (3) enhanced sensitivity are examples of *spiritualized intuition* that accompany the higher consciousness provided to us by our Creator-God through His Holy Spirit. In contrast to de Chardin's requirement of an innate *"inner* principle" for increased psychogenesis *(Phenomenon, p. 149),* the present author views the human brain of modern man more as a channel, or conveyor, for heightened consciousness rather than as the originator of increased consciousness. As once told to me by a heavenly source: "The family of God increases by decreasing, includes by excluding, and often varies yet never changes." Metaphysically speaking, the family of God excludes its enemies at the same time that it sharpens its wits in spiritualized intuition through the Creator-God's Holy Spirit in order to protect itself from potential intrusions as well as imminent and actual invasions. Christ Jesus forewarned his disciples: "Understand that I send you out as sheep in the midst of wolves: therefore, be wise as serpents and harmless as doves" *(Matthew 10:16 KJV Paraphrase)*.

Spiritualized intuition mediated by the Creator-God's Holy Spirit is an integral part of being wise and providing an effective witness of one's sixth sense in addition to surviving.

Much ado has been made about de Chardin's *Omega Point* by all sorts of people who want to make his psychogenesis concept more complicated than it is. To de Chardin, physical and mental evolution is simply the rise of consciousness, and the rise of consciousness eventually effects a psychic union of all human beings, whose psychic union is named by de Chardin as *the Omega Point*. For de Chardin, "no evolutionary future awaits [human beings] except in association with all other [human beings]" *(Phenomenon, p. 246, brackets mine).* In the elaboration of his *Omega Point,* de Chardin placed hope in mankind by developing his own peculiar brand of religious humanism; to be sure, he believed that "the crown of [human] evolution" is situated "in a supreme act of collective vision obtained by a pan-human effort of investigation and construction" *(Ibid., p. 249, brackets mine).* Unfortunately, de Chardin's ideal human government consists of an elite intelligentsia dominating the masses *(Ibid., Footnote 1, p. 245).* Although de Chardin decried the injustices of Communism and National Socialism, he might not have condemned the most modern form of totalitarianism (i.e., the Beast of Islam under the control of the final end-time Antichrist). To be sure, de Chardin's fascination with populist unanimity and mechanization is seen in his comment about perverted idealism:

> Monstrous as it is, is not modern totalitarianism really the distortion of something magnificent, and thus quite near to the truth?
>
> *Phenomenon, p. 256*

The previous quote from de Chardin is equivalent to saying that Stalin and Hitler were geniuses. Although one can argue for the genius status of those despots, it is not expedient to do so because their cunning was a perversion of the Creator-God's nature of intelligence that He intended for humankind.

For those who might erroneously assume that de Chardin's *Omega Point* is equivalent to *the Mind of Christ, Christ Consciousness, the Supraconsciousness of the Creator-God's divine Mind,* or a *Cosmic Christ,* de Chardin provides clarification that there is still "a supreme Someone" who supersedes his human-based *Omega Point:*

> To be more exact, "to confirm the presence at the summit of the world of something in line with, but still more elevated than, the Omega point." This is in deference to the theological concept of the "supernatural" according to which the binding contact between God and the world, *hic et nunc* inchoate [here and now not fully formed], attains to a super-intimacy (hence also a super-gratuitousness) of which man can have no inkling and which he can lay no claim by virtue of his "nature" alone. [brackets mine]
>
> *Phenomena, Epilogue, Footnote 1, p. 298*

Thus, Christ Jesus himself is "already on high" *(Phenomenon, p. 298)* — at a summit far beyond the locus in which a saved, unified, and evolved human consciousness can, and will, converge — which locus is called *the Omega Point* by de Chardin. Unfortunately, without reading one footnote in his Epilogue (see the previously indented quote), the student of de Chardin's *The Phenomenon of Man* might dispute the existence of the actual truth to which de Chardin subscribed (i.e., that there remains something beyond *the Omega Point*).

In summary, the title of this book could have been *The Biology of Consciousness from a Christian Perspective.*

# The Author's Definition of *Psychism*

Having considered the meanings of the base word (i.e., root word) *psyche* and the suffix *-ism* as well as uses of the word *psychism* by Teilhard de Chardin, the present author's definition of the word *psychism* in the context of this book includes: (1) the doctrine that consciousness is the universal soul force that animates all living beings, corporeal or incorporeal (here, the term *soul force* should not be confused with the branding of any product or any political or religious movement); (2) the essential character or nature of consciousness that permits conceptual communication between and among all living beings, corporeal or incorporeal; (3) the eternality of the soul, reincarnation, astral projection, and personal psychic abilities, including: hearing psychically, seeing psychically, spiritual healing, electromagnetic healing, "laying on of hands," telepathy, far-memory (recollection of past lives), far-seeing (clairvoyance), far-hearing (clairaudience), automatic writing, channeling, and other transcendent communications between extrabiological life forms (i.e., incorporeal beings) and biological life forms (i.e., corporeal beings); and (4) investigative research on, or study of, any one, any combination, or all of the previous topics.

In summary, the word *psychism* is descriptive of (1) universal consciousness (i.e., general psychism) as well as (2) the extrasensory abilities of individuals (i.e., specific psychism). In its narrowest sense, a *personal psychism* (i.e., a specific psychism in an individual human being) is a divine spiritual *charism* when it is operated by the Creator-God's Holy Spirit. For the sake of clarity, a *charism* is a gift from the Holy Spirit to be used for the glory of the God of the Holy Bible. As a footnote here, the English words *charism* and *charisms* are derived from the Greek *charisma* (singular) and *charismata* (plural) [χάρισμα and χαρίσματα], both of which are found in the Greek New Testament [G5486].

It is the purpose of this book to present an intelligible explanation of universal consciousness as it relates to *general psychism*. And it is the purpose of this book to articulate a coherent exposition on *specific psychism* in order to establish a baseline understanding of corporeal and incorporeal activities as they relate to: hearing psychically, seeing psychically, astral projection, spiritual healing, electromagnetic healing, "laying on of hands," telepathy, far-memory (recollection of past lives), far-seeing (clairvoyance), far-hearing (clairaudience), channeling, automatic writing, and other transcendent communications between and among physical beings and spiritual beings, including the Supreme Being, the *Creator-God*.

# *Psychism* as it Relates to Universal Consciousness

Every *thing* is a thought and every thought is a *thing*. Understood in its metaphysical context, a *thing* can be seen or unseen, visible or invisible, living or nonliving, animate or inanimate, corporeal or incorporeal, conceptual or nonconceptual, real or imaginary, and spiritual or physical. However, regardless of its individual attributes, every *thing* is a function of consciousness.

Often, when people discuss consciousness, it is either (1) wakefulness or (2) awareness that they are thinking about. Of course, there are different levels of wakefulness as well as different levels of awareness. In general, wakefulness is more objective than awareness because wakefulness is mainly brain-driven. Except for the awareness of phantom limbs or phantom pain (both of which are mainly brain-driven), awareness is more subjective than wakefulness, not only because it is demonstrated to different degrees in different people (and at different levels and times in the same person), but also because it is dependent on both the visible brain as well as the unseen mind. For human beings, awareness includes, but is not limited to:

(a)  awareness of one's environment
(b)  awareness of one's self
(c)  awareness of others
(d)  awareness of one's responsibility to change incorrect thinking and wrongdoing
(e)  awareness of imagined things and possibilities
(f)  awareness of extrasensory sensations
(g)  awareness of the presence of the Creator-God through His Holy Spirit
(h)  awareness of the need to please the Creator-God
(i)  awareness of pleasing the Creator-God

From a Christian metaphysical perspective, "mind" for human beings is somewhat nebulous because it involves one's soul: the soul inhabits the human body and expresses itself through that body. To be sure, there is a linkage between the soul and human brain; generally speaking, the soul inhabits a human body because the human brain is sufficiently well-developed enough to allow for thinking, planning, and decision-making. Although "I think, therefore I am" ("cogito, ergo sum") is a popular philosophical and theological proposition, perhaps "I am aware that I am, therefore I am" might be more accurate. There are no other mammals and no other great apes that possess such a unique sense of individuality and self as human beings. In summary, the basis of consciousness for a human being is its soul, which expresses itself through a bihemispheric brain whose architecture is uniquely well-developed to facilitate self-awareness and self-reflection. It should be noted that sometimes the human body is unfit to house a soul — *for example,* when a developing embryo, fetus, or neonate is missing parts of its brain (i.e., anencephaly).

Although wakefulness and awareness are subsumed within the general topic of consciousness, wakefulness and awareness do not delineate the full extent of consciousness, especially when consciousness is viewed in the context of Christian metaphysics and general psychism.

In the context of Christian metaphysics and general psychism, consciousness is *true substance.* Yes, matter is the substance of the physical universe, but consciousness is the true substrate of the entire universe (i.e., *das gesamte Universum* or *das ganze Weltall).* Everything everywhere is a function of universal consciousness. Consciousness is the only real substance of the entire universe. Within the entire universe, spiritual things collectively constitute one domain and physical things collectively constitute their codomain. Both things and thoughts are inputs as well as outputs of consciousness.

As used here, "the entire universe" includes the so-called spiritual universe and the so-called physical universe because the two are interdependent, interwoven, and interdigitated throughout all-space and all-time. Even though one may speak or write about the spiritual universe and the physical universe as if they were separate, there really is only one universe. Mathematically speaking, the *entire universe* constitutes one whole and complete *set* that includes the spiritual universe and the physical universe as its *subsets*. In other words, the *entire universe* includes everything spiritual as well as everything physical and is synonymous with the expression *all-that-is*.

The spiritual universe is a subset of the entire universe and the physical universe is a subset of the entire universe. The spiritual universe and the physical universe intersect as subsets to the highest order of $E = mc^2$, where $E$ represents unbound energy and $m$ represents bound energy. For human onlookers, the image of the domain of the spiritual universe is completely obscured by the image of its codomain, the physical universe. In other words, corporeality masks incorporeality. That is why, for human beings, the spiritual universe can only be seen — that is, apprehended and perceived — metaphysically through one's understanding of concepts related to general psychism.

(In the previous five paragraphs, the signification of the terms *function, domain, codomain, inputs, outputs, sets, subsets,* and *order* are drawn from a traditional academic study of mathematics.)

In the context of Christian metaphysics and general psychism, consciousness as true substance is the fabric of *all-that-is*. Consciousness constitutes every thing and every thought. Consciousness provides the substrate upon which everything spiritual or physical is constructed. Although every object is not self-aware, everything that exists in the entire universe is a manifestation of consciousness.

What is presented here should not be confused with *pantheism*. *Pantheism* is the belief that the Creator-God inhabits every physical thing, including inanimate objects as well as animate beings. In a way, pantheists view all physical objects as transient emanations of divinity — regardless of the different verbiage they might use to express what is perceived as the Creator-God's connectedness to physicality. Pantheists often conclude that the Creator-God can actually be found in physical things — not just in their design or essence but in the things themselves. (The common grammatical construction "things themselves" just used is distinctly different from the traditional metaphysical expression "things-in-themselves.")

The statement "every *thing* is a function of consciousness" is not meant to be pantheistic. It is meant to convey the idea that consciousness manifests every spiritual thing as well as every physical thing. And the statement "every *thing* is a function of consciousness" is not meant to convey the idea that everything is consciousness-in-itself or that the Creator-God inhabits physical objects or living things — the only exception, of course, is for people still in flesh bodies who have accepted Christ Jesus as their personal Savior and, therefore, have the Creator-God's Holy Spirit indwelling their souls. (The Holy Spirit indwells each saved soul at the same time that each saved soul in corporeality resides in its own physical body.)

In the context of Christian metaphysics and general psychism, consciousness is the pulsating substance from which everything is created or made. Consciousness provides the matrix upon which each spiritual thing is constructed. And consciousness provides the matrix upon which each physical thing, inanimate or animate, is constructed. Although everything physical is a manifestation of consciousness,

consciousness-in-itself is tangible only to the metaphysical sense, which is part and parcel of *the sixth sense* of personal psychism. Consciousness itself is not tangible to the physical senses; it is only through the metaphysical sense that we perceive consciousness. In other words, it is only our metaphysical sense that can become conscious of consciousness. Although the metaphysical sense can be translated into brain neural activity so that human beings can become knowledgeable of and discuss metaphysical truths, our metaphysical sense originates independently of our brain neural activity. Although our physical senses can detect physical elements that might lead us to make metaphysical conclusions about the physical creation's intelligent design, our metaphysical sense of *causality* is independent of our physical senses.

Consciousness can only stimulate the sense that it comes directly in contact with. Consciousness does not come directly in contact with our physical senses. (However, consciousness does come directly in contact with specific neural networks in our brains through its electromagnetic dimension.) Thus, our knowledge of consciousness is generally limited to our psychic, sixth, or metaphysical sense (all three adjectives are synonymous here). I write "generally" because, when the Supraconsciousness of the Creator-God's divine Mind surrounds, enshrouds, or envelopes human beings, their thinking and understanding are elevated beyond their own psychic, sixth, or metaphysical abilities to more fully apprehend and perceive the things and thoughts of the Creator-God.

*Consciousness* in the context of general psychism includes the Supraconsciousness of the Creator-God's divine Mind that is accessible to: (1) unfallen created beings who are incorporeal, (2) saved fallen created beings still in flesh bodies, and (3) spiritually-restored created beings who have returned to incorporeality (i.e., redeemed souls who have already transitioned back to Heaven).

*Consciousness* even includes, albeit obliquely, the vampiric semi-consciousness of Satan's mortal mind that permanently owns the personal space of fallen created beings whose souls are beyond redemption or divine reclamation.

It is the vampiric semi-consciousness of Satan's mortal mind that seeks to encroach on the personal space of: (1) unsaved fallen created beings whose souls are not yet beyond redemption or divine reclamation (this includes some discarnate souls as well as some incarnate souls) and (2) redeemed fallen created beings still in flesh bodies. Concerning the latter category, as long as redeemed fallen created beings remain in corporeality, they retain dual natures (i.e., physical and spiritual natures). However, when they transition from corporeality to incorporeality (i.e., from an incarnate state to a discarnate, or heavenly, state), redeemed souls become immune to temptation because their old carnal natures have ceased to exist (i.e., they no longer possess a fleshly component).

Spiritual warfare exists in the universe between the Supraconsciousness of the Creator-God's divine Mind and the vampiric semi-consciousness of Satan's mortal mind. This warfare is entirely spiritual. However, in the earth plane of consciousness, this warfare primarily takes place on the battlefield of the human mind. Daily, each human being is tempted by the vampiric semi-consciousness of Satan's mortal mind to consciously yield to it. Lamentably, even when the battle is over at the end of one day, the war continues the next day. Although particular daily battles may be won, the war between Good and Evil will never be completely over until Satan and all of his minions are finally cast into the Lake of Fire at the end of Christ Jesus' millennial reign on Earth.

Because Satan and his minions seek to control human beings through their fear of the uncertainties associated with the human condition, human beings can only maintain their individual certainty through their steadfast acceptance of, and trust in, Jesus Christ as their personal Savior.

All of the inanimate and animate objects in the physical universe provide evidence of a creation that has been cursed by the Creator-God in response to the errant actions of created beings who fell because they consciously (i.e., willfully and knowingly) stepped outside of the Creator-God's Will. Even though their Fall was the cause of the Creator-God's curse, (1) consciously stepping outside of His Will and (2) the imposition of His resultant curse were metaphysically concomitant — that is, *inseparably simultaneous.*

In the physical universe, matter represents the "thickened consciousness" of spiritual darkness conceived (i.e., manifested) by errant created beings at the time of their spiritual fall — which, because it was instantaneous, was really more of a *crash.* (Because the word *fall* can erroneously imply a drifting downward or slow descent, the author of *The Biology of Psychism from a Christian Perspective* prefers *crash* over *fall* for the downward spiral of beings who willfully and knowingly stepped outside of the Creator-God's Will.)

*Consciousness* excludes nothing but does not include everything. *For example,* the Supraconsciousness of the Creator-God's divine Mind actively sequesters itself from the vampiric semi-consciousness of Satan's mortal mind. The Supraconsciousness of the Creator-God's divine Mind is capable of such an active exclusion because it possesses all-power (i.e., the only real power) and all-reality (i.e., the one true reality). Coincidentally, at the time the vampiric semi-consciousness of Satan's mortal mind originated, it passively excluded itself from the Supraconsciousness of the Creator-God's divine Mind because its nature is antithetical to the Nature of the Creator-God. From a Christian metaphysical standpoint, Good and Evil are no yin and yang of universal consciousness; Good and Evil belong to separate domains, each with different orders.

Satan's mortal mind has no *real* power (i.e., no eternal power). Satan's mortal mind can only tell lies and create illusions to get created beings to turn their own power and dominion over to it. Metaphysically speaking, Satan's mortal mind seeks parasitic dominion over the consciousness of all life forms throughout the entire universe. Satan's mortal mind seeks parasitic dominion because it is in competition with the Supraconsciousness of the Creator-God's divine Mind. The impetus for such competition was, and is, Satan's jealousy, envy, and hatred of the Creator-God's omnipotence, omnipresence, and omniscience. Satan, his fallen angels, and his unclean spirits, demons, or devils are in competition with the Creator-God, His angels, and His redeemed souls.

What imparts self-awareness to created beings with free will? Only the Supraconsciousness of the Creator-God's divine Mind imparts self-awareness. Only the Creator-God is the author of all true life and all real being. The vampiric semi-consciousness of Satan's mortal mind is a perversion of the original consciousness with which the Archangel Lucifer was endowed. The consciousness that Lucifer possessed was eternally poisoned when jealousy, envy, and hatred of the Creator-God originated within him.

Can consciousness in the context of Christian metaphysics and general psychism be observed empirically from a human standpoint? Yes, by observing the actions, reactions, and interventions of various forms of consciousness, including actions, reactions, and interventions within the physical universe from: (1) the Supraconsciousness of the Creator-God's divine Mind, (2) angelic consciousness, (3) human individual and collective consciousness, and (4) the vampiric semi-consciousness of Satan's mortal mind.

For the sake of clarity, the vampiric semi-consciousness of Satan's mortal mind manifests itself through the actions, reactions, and interventions of Satan himself, his fallen angels, and his unclean spirits, demons, or devils (all three of which are biblically synonymous labels).

Unfortunately, many students of psychism (regardless if they have the word *psychism* within their active vocabularies or not) are not aware that the noun *Christ* and the noun phrase *Christ Consciousness* have been trivialized by those who entertain certain inaccurate concepts from Eastern religions, New Age philosophy, Theosophy, and Christian metaphysics.

*For example,* the Hindu deity Krishna, the supposed earthly incarnation of the Hindu deity Vishnu, is worshiped by seeking to propagate his consciousness as revealed in various Hindu scriptures. (For the sake of clarification, the Holy Bible is the one true and only real Scripture.) This concept of *Krishna Consciousness* has been imported to Christianity as the ill-defined *Christ Consciousness.*

To be sure, when used alone, the word *Christ* may accurately imply a spiritual state of mind and a heightened level of consciousness; unfortunately, however, when used alone, the word *Christ* can also inaccurately imply that this spiritual state of mind and heightened level of consciousness can be achieved without accepting the biblical Jesus as: (1) the *only-begotten* Son of God, (2) the promised Messiah of Israel, (3) the one true Savior of the world, (4) one's only personal Savior, (5) the Word of God, and (6) the Creator-God Incarnate (i.e., God-in-flesh). Indeed, one cannot have "the Christ," "the Mind of Christ," "divine Mind," "universal Mind," "Christ Consciousness," or "the Supraconsciousness of the Creator-God" without accepting the shed blood of the only-begotten Son of God as the only sacrifice acceptable to God the Father for the remission of our sins and the cancellation of the debt we owe to Him for those sins.

One of the earliest representations of codification in the separation of *Jesus* from *Christ* and *Christ* from *Jesus* is seen in the writings of Phineas Parkhurst Quimby (1802-1866), whose errant ideas helped serve to form related false doctrines propagated by religious movements such as *Christian Science, Unity,* and *Religious Science* (i.e., *Science of Mind).*

In this book, the expression *Christ Consciousness* is synonymous with *the Supraconsciousness of the Creator-God's divine Mind* as well as *the Mind of Christ.* Indeed, *Christ Consciousness* is the consciousness that is found in the mind of Christ Jesus. But no human being can have Christ Consciousness without first recognizing Christ Jesus as the only-begotten Son of God as well as accepting him as one's personal Savior.

Because every *thing* is a function of consciousness, thoughts, images, concepts, and ideas can *bleed through* from one plane of consciousness to another. *For example,* thoughts, images, concepts, and ideas can *bleed through* from spiritual beings in a heavenly plane of consciousness to human beings in the earth plane of consciousness. And, within the earth plane of consciousness itself, thoughts, images, concepts, and ideas can *bleed through* from one human being to another.

For redeemed souls in Heaven, the phrase "bleed through" is ironic because, living fully in the shed blood of Christ Jesus (metaphysically, of course), they are able to communicate with one another without hindrance. (When we live, move, and have our being fully in the shed blood of Christ Jesus, all communications between and among souls who belong to the Creator-God are crystal clear.)

Although redeemed souls in Heaven can communicate with redeemed souls on Earth, such communication is more difficult because of the constraints placed upon human beings by their corporeality as well as by the Creator-God. The Creator-God places constraints on communication from souls in Heaven to souls on Earth because He wants human beings to develop their individual faith and trust in Him as the source of all Life and not shift their dependence on Him to dependence on angels and saints in Heaven (or on Earth, for that matter).

The present author was once told by a mentor from Heaven that *"anyone* who claims that they can initiate contact with those who have passed on is perpetrating a hoax. Such Earth-initiated contact would be unseemly." So-called *mediums* are just using their own psychic abilities to fool others. And fooling others is very easy to do, especially by people who can pick up information psychically. And being fooled is very easy, especially for people who are willing to believe almost anything. Although some people are more gifted psychically than others, no one on Earth initiates contact with those in Heaven. If anyone reading what I have just written cannot accept its validity, I would attribute their nonacceptance to gullibility, wishful thinking, and naiveté.

What is a *plane of consciousness* and what *planes of consciousness* exist?

As used by this author, a *plane of consciousness* is a layer, level, stratum, or band of consciousness. Major planes of consciousness include: (1) the heavenly plane, (2) the terrestrial plane, (3) the interim plane, and (4) the hellish plane. (Each of these four major planes contains various substrata.)

(1) The heavenly plane is the highest, deepest, and greatest plane of consciousness; the totality of the Creator-God's divine Mind indwells this plane of consciousness. (The consciousness of the Creator-God's divine Mind can also be referred to as *the Supraconsciousness of the Creator-God* and the spiritual space that it fills may be referred to as the *Creator-God's spiritual universe*.) (2) The terrestrial plane is the plane of consciousness in which sentient beings live in physicality; for human beings, this plane may also be referred to as *the earth plane of consciousness*. (3) The interim plane of consciousness is the state of being in which souls await their physical rebirth as human beings. And (4) the hellish plane of consciousness is the state of being in which souls beyond divine reclamation await their final judgment.

What is the dimensionality of consciousness?

Consciousness transcends dimensionality although consciousness can *insert* its substantive reality into multi-dimensional states of being. *For example,* when the Creator-God speaks in acts of physical creation or in acts of physical judgment, He *inserts* His reality onto the axes, or dimensions, that are associated with physicality. The axes of physicality include these five vectors: (1) length, (2) width, (3) depth, (4) time, and (5) unified spatial force. (Because it is still debatable what to call the fifth dimension, the author of *The Biology of Psychism from a Christian Perspective* has chosen to call it "unified spatial force." As I see it, "unified spatial force" unites quantum mechanics, wave theory, electromagnetism, and gravity.) These five vectors constitute physical *space-time,* which is subsumed within the all-space and all-time (i.e., *eternity)* of the entire universe. For the sake of clarity, eternity is dimensionless and ageless.

As indicated previously, the spiritual universe and the physical universe are subsets to the highest order of $E = mc^2$, *where E* represents unbound energy and *m* represents bound energy. Together, these subsets constitute *all-that-is* — which is to say, *the entire universe*. Since they are subsets of the entire universe, one can think of consciousness as the function that unites the spiritual universe to the physical universe. Every element in the spiritual universe has at least one corresponding element in the physical universe, and every element in the physical universe has at least one corresponding element in the spiritual universe.

What is the difference between *structured* consciousness and *unstructured* consciousness?

The present author uses the qualifiers *structured* and *unstructured* to help distinguish (1) creative consciousness in human beings that utilizes deductive and inductive reasoning (i.e., structured or analytical thinking) from (2) creative consciousness that utilizes discernment (i.e., unstructured awareness).

Is it necessary to use the qualifier *creative* in conjunction with *consciousness* (i.e., *creative consciousness*)?

Using the qualifier *creative* in conjunction with *consciousness* helps to distinguish true consciousness from the altered consciousness of Satan, his fallen angels, and his unclean spirits, demons, or devils. Although the eternally fallen may devise cunning plans, such beings are not genuinely creative nor can they ever be (even though they were creative before they consciously decided to oppose the Creator-God). Eternally fallen beings can only cast illusions and spin lies; they cannot actually create. It is impossible for anyone evil to actually create.

What is an *altered consciousness* or *altered state of consciousness?*

Relative to individual human beings, an *altered consciousness* or *altered state of consciousness* refers to changes in wakefulness and/or awareness due to specific factors such as astral projection, biofeedback, concussion, delusion, electroconvulsive therapy, fasting, hypoxia, hypercapnia, infection, meditation, organic brain syndrome, overeating, psychosis, schizophrenia, stages of sleep, stroke, trance (ἔκστασις [G1611])[2], and various drugs 'and medications — *for example,* alcohol, amphetamines, anesthetics, antidepressants, antihistamines, antipsychotics, opioids, psychedelics/hallucinogens, and sedatives.

Relative to general psychism, an *altered consciousness* or *altered state of consciousness* refers to dynamic changes in universal consciousness. *For example,* the Supraconsciousness of the Creator-God's divine Mind before Lucifer's *crash* (i.e., the Luciferian Fall) was the only consciousness that existed within the entire universe. However, that consciousness became altered in Lucifer and in his fallen angels and, eventually, in the entire Adamic race after their fall (i.e., the Adamic Fall) from succumbing to Satan's temptations. Although that consciousness is permanently altered for the eternally damned (Lucifer, his fallen angels, and members of the Adamic race who have consciously — that is, willingly and knowingly — rejected Christ Jesus as their personal Savior), that consciousness is only temporarily altered for members of the Adamic Race who eventually accept Christ Jesus

---

[2]  *Ecstasis* comes from the Greek word ἔκστασις (ek´-sta-sis) [G1611] that refers to a trance-like state induced by the Holy Spirit. This Greek word is specifically translated as "trance" in the King James Version of the Holy Bible, denoting the state into which both the Apostle Peter and the Apostle Paul fell *(Acts 10:10; 11:5; 22:17)* when they each had visions induced by the Creator-God's Holy Spirit as they were praying.

as their personal Savior while they are still in corporeality. The operative words here are "while they are still in corporeality" because it is the Creator-God's Will that eternal salvation can only be received and experienced during one's sojourn in corporeality. Salvation cannot be received and experienced when a discarnate is in either an interim state or a hellish state.

To understand how we become one with the Creator-God, it is important for students of Christian metaphysics and psychism to recognize that the Creator-God abides in us and we abide in the Creator-God through the universal consciousness we share. (The meaning of the verb *abide* here includes "to live, dwell, reside, continue, and remain" in each other.) It is through the consciousness we share that the Creator-God becomes our universal Self. And it is through the consciousness we share that we are not only made one with the Creator-God but also made one with each other.

Throughout the entire universe, every holy thing is a function of the Supraconsciousness of the Creator-God's divine Mind and every holy thought in His creation is built on the matrix of His creation's desire to please Him by worshiping Him in spirit and in truth as well as by accomplishing His Will. Here, it is important to understand that the Creator-God is sublimely pleased with human beings when we (1) worship Him in spirit and in truth and (2) fulfill His Will for us individually and collectively on Earth. Such worship and fulfillment are the real indicators of true success.

# Identity and Consciousness

There is a para-equivalence among all individual mammals and marsupials because each of these creatures has an individual identity and an individual consciousness in addition to a group identity and a group consciousness. All other biological groups of living beings *(for example,* fish, amphibians, reptiles, and birds) only have a group identity and a group consciousness; their members do not have an individual identity or an individual consciousness. For this reason, saved human beings can expect to spiritually see and know the individual identities of every mammal and marsupial in Heaven just as they can expect to see and know the individual identities of every saved human being in Heaven. Of course, mammals other than human beings and marsupials are neither saved nor unsaved on Earth or in Heaven. There is no requirement for them to be saved in order for their spirits or personalities to go to Heaven. Although mammals other than human beings and marsupials have individual spirits and personalities, they do not have souls made in the complete image and perfect likeness of the Creator-God. Therefore, mammals other than human beings and marsupials are not held accountable for their actions on Earth. Our Creator-God recognizes them and loves them in His special way as the created building blocks He used in His biological evolution of human beings.

Human beings who are saved and still on Earth have their group identity and group consciousness (i.e., collective consciousness) in Christ Jesus along with all other saved human beings who are now in Heaven. All saved human beings on Earth and in Heaven not only have individual identities, they also are one in Christ Jesus. In Christ Jesus, each saved soul is part of an *us all.* Altogether, we are of one mind and one collective consciousness. Altogether, we have one collective Self (i.e., one supraself or higher self) in addition to an individual personal self.

Although some biological organisms other than mammals and marsupials function instinctively as one social unit either temporarily or permanently, their individual members do not have an individual identity or an individual consciousness. *Examples* of those that function temporarily as one social unit include schools of fish, flocks or murmurations of birds, and dens of snakes. *Examples* of those that function permanently as one social unit include colonies of insects such as ants, bees, and hornets. Such units can be thought of as metaphysical *ripples* in the sea of universal consciousness that manifest as biological group social identities. The ripples represent complex textures in the Supraconsciousness of the Creator-God's divine Mind.

Biological organisms in seasonal migrations orient themselves according to the Earth's magnetic field. Their orientation to magnetic field functional guidelines serves as an allegory for how saved souls willingly and instinctively orient themselves toward the intersecting vectors of the Creator-God's electromagnetic Will. (Although the Creator-God's Will is spiritual, it has an electromagnetic dimension in the physical universe.) In contrast, demonic beings orient themselves in directions away from the Creator-God's Will. For saved human beings, pain and suffering help us to reorient ourselves to the vectors of the Creator-God's electromagnetic Will whenever we get off track. This includes emotional, mental, physical, and spiritual pain and suffering. Simply stated, we learn to depend increasingly on the Creator-God when we experience pain and suffering.

# The Author's Synonyms for *Personal Psychism*

The present author's expressions for the phrase *personal psychism* as it relates to the specific consciousness of an individual human being include: extrasensory ability, extrasensory sensation, extrasensory perception, electromagnetic sensitivity, spiritual intuition, psychic intuition, spiritualized intuition, spiritual empathy, psychic empathy, spiritual discernment, supraself communion, *the sixth sense,* susceptibility to receiving the thoughts and ideas of others, ability to spiritually discern the motives and intents of others, apprehending one's supra-consciousness, and impartation of special knowledge from one's higher self through a spiritual infilling (i.e., *eine geistliche Einfühlung).*

*Simple intuition* in a human being can come solely from an individual's ability to be cognitively and emotionally aware of the possible thoughts, feelings, and actions of others based on the intuitive person's life experiences, past interactions with others, and intelligence. Indeed, *simple intuition* is a useful tool for *personal psychism,* but not all people that possess *simple intuition* are gifted *psychically.* Some people with *simple intuition* have high levels of intellectual and emotional intelligence and have had many life experiences in dealing with others. Their combined intelligence and experiences enable them to assess other people and predict what they might do, or what they might intend to do, given a specific set of circumstances and situations. For *simple intuition,* one does not need to be *psychic* to predict actions and reactions based on high degrees of probability. *Simple intuition* is not *spiritual intuition* (i.e., *psychic intuition or spiritualized intuition)* from a sixth sense perspective.

*Simple empathy* in a human being can come solely from an individual's ability to be emotionally sensitive to the thoughts, feelings, and actions of others based on an empathic person's life experiences, interactions with others, and intelligence. Some people have *simple empathy* because they have had to navigate through difficult life experiences. And it is from those difficult life experiences that they become increasingly sensitized to the difficult conditions and circumstances of others, especially those who have had experiences similar to their own. *Simple empathy* reflects shared life experiences. For *simple empathy*, one does not need to be *psychic* to understand the sorrow or joy that others are experiencing. *Simple empathy* is not *spiritual empathy* (i.e., *psychic empathy*) from a sixth sense perspective.

In contrast to *simple intuition* and *simple empathy*, *spiritual intuition* or *spiritual empathy* is a true higher order personal psychism that moves beyond mere cognitive and emotional sensitivities to the extrasensory sensation and perception of specific information that is new or foreign to the recipient. In *spiritual intuition* or *spiritual empathy*, one has access to information beyond the scope of one's personal experiences. In *spiritual intuition* or *spiritual empathy*, one senses and perceives the actual sorrow or joy in others and knows (1) what they are thinking and feeling generally as well as (2) a measure of their specific thoughts and feelings.

# Personal Psychism as the Sixth Sense

Thinking of *personal psychism* as *the sixth sense* provides one key to understanding a neurological paradigm for *specific psychism*. If *personal psychism* is a genuine sense (and it is), then it should be analogous to the other five senses — with certain exceptions, of course.

Like sensations from the five senses, *extrasensory sensation* is the conscious or subconscious awareness of external and internal stimuli. And, like perceptions of the five senses, *extrasensory perception* is the conscious awareness and interpretation of threshold stimuli that are received by groups of specific brain neurons — in this case, brain neurons sensitive to extrasensory sensations that are electromagnetic in nature. Without sensory and extrasensory threshold sensations, it would be impossible for us to initiate proper responses to changes in either our sensory environments or in our extrasensory environments. To be sure, like the five senses, the so-called *sixth sense* also receives some input that is not consciously perceived because: (1) some extrasensory input never reaches the thalamus and/or the cerebral cortex due to the subliminal, or subthreshold, nature of the stimuli; and (2) some extrasensory input that does reach the thalamus and/or cerebral cortex is filtered out by the subconscious mind. (Note: The thalamus is the major relay center in the brain and the cortex, or outer layer, of the cerebrum is where we become consciously aware of specific stimuli.)

Additional explanations follow:

(1) The subconscious mind filters out some extrasensory sensations as well as some sensory sensations so that we are neither overloaded nor overwhelmed by their inputs. Just as

autonomic functions, including respiratory and cardiac rates, are monitored continuously by the brain regardless of our conscious awareness of them so are extrasensory sensations monitored continuously by the brain regardless of our conscious awareness of them. And, just as specific neurons in the retina (i.e., photoreceptors) continuously monitor changing patterns of electromagnetic energy in the visible electromagnetic spectrum (i.e., visible light), and just as specific neurons in the skin (i.e., thermoreceptors) continuously monitor changing patterns of electromagnetic energy in the invisible electromagnetic spectrum (i.e., heat or thermal energy), so do specific groups of neurons in the brain continuously monitor changing patterns of electromagnetic energy in various bands of the invisible electromagnetic spectrum that are related to extrasensory sensations.

(2) The subconscious mind also filters out some extrasensory sensations as well as some sensory sensations that are not easily interpretable (i.e., intelligible). Like some dreams, some extrasensory sensations lack elements that are understandable to the conscious mind. When those elements are received by the conscious mind, the conscious mind tries to impose a rational order, sequence, and structure upon what may have no familiar rational order, sequence, or structure in order to grant them a status that is interpretable by the conscious mind. In other words, extrasensory sensations must have a familiar rational order, sequence, and/or structure to be accommodated, assimilated, and integrated by the conscious mind. Accommodation, assimilation, and integration by the higher brain centers require interpretation, even if the interpretation is incorrect, biased, prejudiced, erroneous, and/or intellectually dishonest. (Readers should put forth an effort to research the

differences between empiricism and rationalism in order to better understand the last statement.) To aid memory and learning, the conscious mind of the human brain requires either (1) an already-familiar conceptual structure or (2) an unfamiliar conceptual structure that becomes familiarized (i.e., made familiar) through cerebral interpretive processes that involve imposing rational order, sequence, and structure on it, often by associating it with already-known objects, concepts, qualities, and quantities. (Sometimes the rational order imposed is correct and sometimes it is incorrect. Sometimes the human mind uses insubstantial arguments to support its conclusions.) Many extrasensory sensations that are not interpretable are filtered out by the subconscious mind or they are perceived as nonsensical.

For the five senses, each specific type of sensation is called a *modality*. The sensory environment is established by (1) both visible and invisible physical external and internal environments and (2) the reception of stimuli by sense organs or individual sense receptors specific for a certain modality.

For the five senses, each specific type of *modality* includes a variety of sensory circuits that are categorized either as (1) general body senses (i.e., somatic senses) or (2) special senses:

(1) General body senses mediate modalities via individual receptor neurons that do not compose specific sense organs although some of the individual receptor neurons are highly distinctive histologically (i.e., microscopically). Somatic senses include pain, pressure, proprioception (i.e., central nervous system conscious and unconscious detection of body

position, movement, velocity, and force), temperature, stretch, and touch.

(2) The special senses are often categorized as special senses because they depend on specific sense organs to mediate modalities that are specific to each organ: vision (the visual sense), taste (the gustatory sense), smell (the olfactory sense), hearing (the inner ear cochlear sense), and equilibrium (the inner ear vestibular sense). Each special sense apparatus carries only one modality. Although five separate special senses or modalities have just been listed, they are often subsumed within four categories based on the existence of their four anatomically distinct sense organs (i.e., eye, tongue, nose, and ear). As the reader will learn shortly, initiation of *the sixth sense* is also associated with specific brain-related circuits whose various nerve pathways are as diffuse within the brain as each special sense organ and its various nerve pathways. *For example,* the visual special sense and its associated nerve pathways are distributed to many places within the brain just as the sixth sense and its associated nerve pathways are distributed to many places within the brain.


Because the origination of extrasensory sensations is in the brain (the stimuli are outside the brain), and because extrasensory sensations are *not* somatic senses (i.e., general senses), the sixth sense may be regarded as a special sense and not a general sense. In some ways, the sixth sense is not only extrasensory but also a special sense because it shares brain circuitry that imparts awareness of, and meaning to, sensory inputs from the five special senses.

It should be noted that the sixth sense is not associated with a specific pair of cranial nerves, unlike the five special senses:

## Olfaction

The olfactory sense requires (1) normally functioning olfactory receptors at the base of the cerebrum as well as (2) atoms, ions, molecules, and compounds that are odiferous to human beings (i.e., odorants). The olfactory sense is dependent on Cranial Nerve I. The conscious awareness of smell is in the medial aspect of the cerebral temporal lobe and impacts many nerve pathways throughout the entire brain. (Here, the word *medial* is defined as "toward the imaginary axis of the body or toward the imaginary vertical plane that bisects the body.") (See Figure One for the location of the temporal lobe.)

## Vision

The visual sense requires (1) at least one eye with normally functioning neurons (i.e., photoreceptors) in its retina in order to see as well as (2) objects that emit or reflect electromagnetic energy that can be seen. The visual sense is dependent on Cranial Nerve II. The conscious awareness of vision is in the medial surface of the cerebral occipital lobe and impacts many nerve pathways throughout the entire brain. (See Figure One for the location of the occipital lobe.)

## Audition

The auditory sense requires (1) at least one middle ear and normally functioning neurons in the cochlea of its associated inner ear in order to hear as well as (2) a vibratory pattern that is within a human being's audible range for decibels. The auditory sense is dependent on the cochlear branch of Cranial Nerve VIII. The conscious awareness of hearing is in the superior part of the cerebral temporal lobe and impacts many nerve pathways throughout the entire brain. (See Figure One for the location of the temporal lobe.)

## Equilibrium

The major sense of equilibrium requires (1) a normally functioning vestibular apparatus in each inner ear as well as (2) its detection of body position relative to gravity and movement. The sense of equilibrium is dependent on the vestibular branch of Cranial Nerve VIII. The subconscious awareness of equilibrium — in the cerebellum, the pons of the brainstem, the thalamus, and the basal ganglia of the cerebrum — impacts many nerve pathways throughout the entire brain. (See Figure Two for the location of the cerebellum and pons and see Footnote 18 on pages 129 and 130 for a description of the *basal ganglia*.)

## Gustation

The gustatory sense requires (1) normally functioning taste buds in the tongue and pharynx (throat) as well as (2) things that taste sweet, sour, salty, bitter, and/or umami. (The molecules that cause taste sensations are called *tastants*. *Umami* is the sensation that is linked with amino acids that commonly provide savory flavors, especially of meats — such as glutamic acid.) The gustatory sense is dependent on Cranial Nerve VII and Cranial Nerve IX. The conscious awareness of taste is in the cerebral parietal lobe and impacts many nerve pathways throughout the entire brain. (See Figure One for the location of the parietal lobe.)

## Somatic Senses

The somatic senses (i.e., general, or non-special, senses) require (1) normally functioning neurons sensitive to touch, cold, heat, movement, stretch, pressure, and pain as well as (2) specific stimuli that can be experienced by at least one of the following different categories of receptors: mechanoreceptors (sensitive to touch), thermoreceptors (sensitive to temperature), proprioceptors (sensitive to stretch), and nociceptors (sensitive to pain). Depending on location, innervation for the somatic senses relies on various individual cranial or spinal nerves. The conscious awareness of most somatic senses is in the cerebral parietal lobe and impacts many nerve pathways throughout the entire brain. As in the case of equilibrium, the subconscious awareness of somatic senses is in the cerebellum, the pons of the brainstem, the thalamus, and the basal ganglia of the cerebrum. (See Figure One for the location of the parietal lobe and refer to Footnote 18 on pages 129 and 130 for a description of the *basal ganglia*.)

## The Sixth Sense

During the state of wakefulness, the sixth sense of *personal psychism* requires: (1) at least some hypersensitive serotonergic neurons in the raphe (pronounced *ray'-fee)* nuclei of the brainstem (Figure Two); (2) at least some hypersensitive cholinergic neurons in the reticular activating system (RAS) at the midbrain-pons junction (Figure Three); and (3) changing patterns in invisible electromagnetic energy from extrasensory stimuli that can be detected by these hypersensitive neurons and by many second-order and third-order neurons radiating throughout the brain that are stimulated by axons from them (i.e., from the serotonergic neurons of the raphe nuclei and from the cholinergic neurons of the reticular activating system).[3]

During the state of rapid eye movement sleep (REM sleep), the sixth sense of *personal psychism* requires: (1) at least some hypersensitive cholinergic neurons in the reticular activating system (RAS) at the midbrain-pons junction; and (2) changing patterns in invisible electromagnetic energy from extrasensory stimuli that can be detected by these hypersensitive neurons and by many second-order and third-order neurons radiating throughout the brain that are stimulated by axons from them (i.e., from the cholinergic neurons of the reticular activating system).

Author's Notes: (1) Although additional brainstem nuclei — other than those mentioned in Chapter One of this book — are involved in a state of wakefulness, the author has chosen to discuss only those brainstem nuclei and neurotransmitters that, in his estimation, best facilitate a discussion and understanding of the sixth sense in relation to wakefulness without overtaxing the reader. (2) It should also be noted that the role of the neurotransmitter dopamine, dopaminergic

---

[3] Generally, first-order neurons are the specialized receptors that receive a specific stimulus, second-order neurons are stimulated by first-order neurons, and third-order neurons are stimulated by second-order neurons.

neurons, brainstem nuclei involved in dopamine production, and dopamine neural pathways will be discussed in Chapter Two of this book in the section entitled *Dopamine as a Hindrance to Personal Psychism.*

## Definitions and Clarifications

The word *serotonergic* refers to neurons that either produce and secrete the neurotransmitter *serotonin* or utilize it at the receptor level in postsynaptic neurons. The word *cholinergic* refers to neurons that either produce or secrete the neurotransmitter *acetylcholine* or utilize it at the receptor level in postsynaptic neurons. (See Figure Four.)

*Raphe nuclei* are specific groups of neuron cell bodies in the brainstem. From rostral to caudal [i.e., from the anterior part of the brain toward its tail], the *brainstem* is composed of the midbrain (mesencephalon), pons, and medulla oblongata.[4] Raphe nuclei are found in all three regions of the brainstem; and most raphe nuclei possess at least some *serotonergic* neurons.

The reticular activating system (RAS) is a specific group of neuron cell bodies at the midbrain-pons junction.

The subconscious and conscious awareness of extrasensory sensations is shared by various parts of the forebrain. The forebrain consists of cerebrum and diencephalon; and the diencephalon contains the epithalamus, thalamus, subthalamus, hypothalamus, and third ventricle. (See Figure Six for the location of the thalamus and the hypothalamus.)

---

[4] Some neuroscientists include the diencephalon as part of the brainstem. In this book, the present author includes the diencephalon as part of the forebrain (along with the cerebrum).

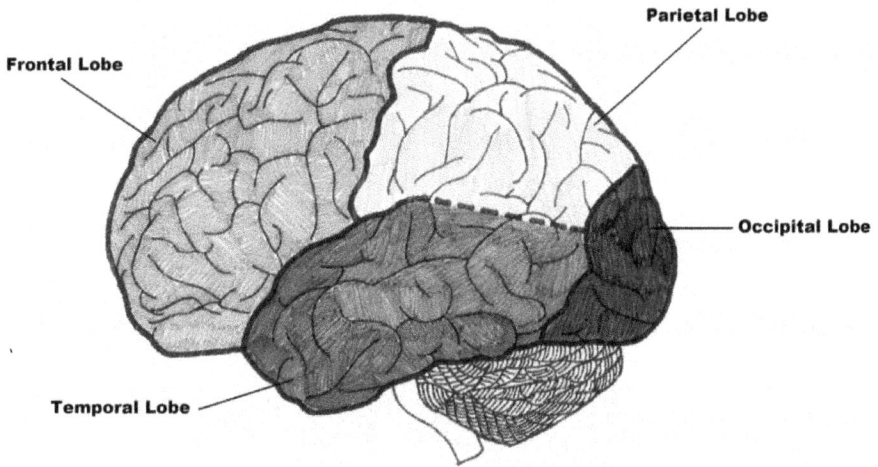

**Left Lateral View of the Cerebrum**
**Figure One**

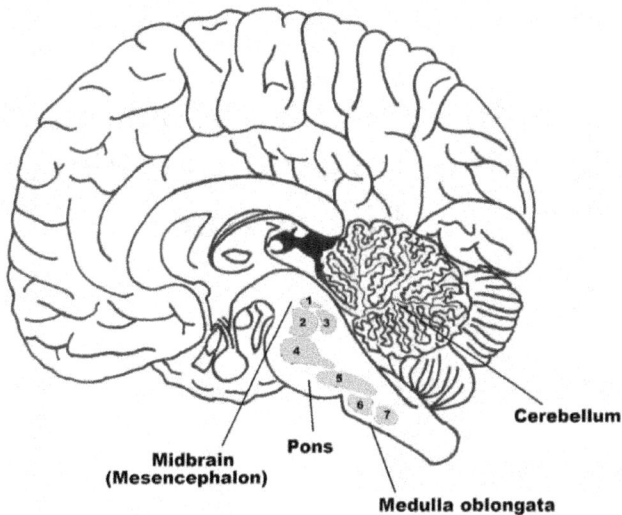

**Medial View of the Seven Raphe Nuclei Locations**
**Figure Two**

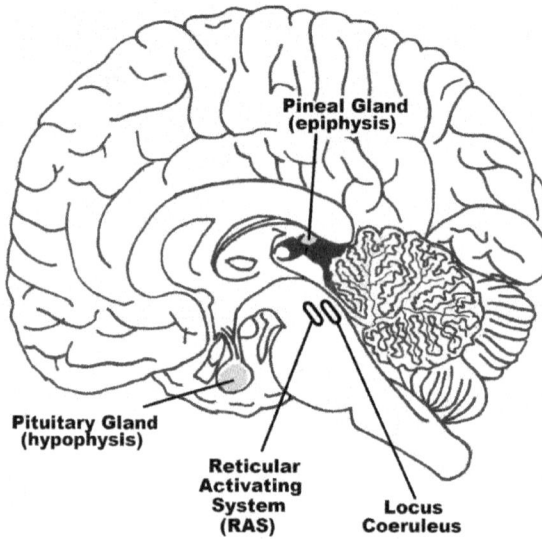

**Medial View of the Reticular Activating System, Locus Coeruleus, Pineal Gland, and Pituitary Gland**
**Figure Three**

# Understanding Neurotransmission

The following key vocabulary are important for understanding neurotransmission: *neuron, perikaryon, perikarya* (plural for perikaryon), *nucleus, nuclei* (plural for nucleus), *nucleoplasm, dendrite, dendritic* (adjective for dendrite), *axon, axonal* (adjective for axon), *action potential, neurotransmitter, synapse, synaptic* (adjective for synapse), *neurotransmission, presynaptic neuron, postsynaptic neuron, vesicle, exocytosis, axon terminal (bouton), serotonin, acetylcholine, norepinephrine, neurotransmitter receptor, reuptake, monoamine oxidase, acetyl-cholinesterase,* and *catechol-O-methyltransferase.*

A neuron is an individual nerve cell. The *perikaryon* of a neuron consists of that portion of the neuron containing its cellular nucleus and the neuroplasm (cytoplasm) surrounding the nucleus. (The *perikaryon* is also referred to as a *nerve cell body.*) Generally, a nerve impulse is transmitted toward the perikaryon by the dendritic portion (i.e., dendrite) of the neuron and transmitted away from the perikaryon by the axonal portion (i.e., axon) of the neuron. In addition to "the control center of a cell," the word *nucleus* — when used for brain neuroanatomy — refers to a cluster of nerve cell bodies (i.e., perikarya). Examples of brainstem nuclei include (1) the raphe nuclei, (2) the reticular activating system, and (3) the locus coeruleus (also spelled *ceruleus).* (See Figures Two and Three for the general locations of these three brainstem nuclei.)

The stimulation of a neuron results in an electrochemical phenomenon known as an action potential. Because an action potential does not jump from one neuron to the next sequenced neuron, the nerve impulse from one neuron to the next sequenced neuron depends on the movement of a neurotransmitter substance between the two neurons at the level of a synapse (i.e., junction). The movement of the neurotransmitter substance across the synaptic cleft (i.e., a space or gap at the junction) between two sequenced neurons is known as *neurotransmission*. The neuron before the synapse is called a presynaptic neuron and the neuron after the synapse is called a postsynaptic neuron.

There are many different neurotransmitters in the human body, including serotonin (5-hydroxytryptamine or 5-HT), acetylcholine (ACh), dopamine (D), and norepinephrine (NE). [Norepinephrine is also known as noradrenaline (NA).] Neurons that produce or utilize serotonin are referred to as *serotonergic;* neurons that produce or utilize acetylcholine are referred to as *cholinergic;* neurons that produce or utilize dopamine are referred to as *dopaminergic;* and neurons that produce or utilize norepinephrine are referred to as *noradrenergic.* (Because of biochemical structural and functional similarities between norepinephrine and epinephrine, sometimes both of their associated neuron receptors are referred to as *adrenergic.*)

Most neurotransmitters are packaged in specific, individual vesicles within neurons. Cellular vesicles are membrane-bound, fluid-filled sacs. From a submicroscopic standpoint, and depending on which neurotransmitter they are storing, vesicles are either large or small, regular or irregular, and have a dense core or clear core. Serotonergic vesicles are large, regular, and dense. Cholinergic vesicles are small, regular, and clear. And dopaminergic vesicles as well as noradrenergic vesicles are variable in size and regularity and are dense. Release of vesicular neurotransmitters occurs by the process of exocytosis. The processes of exocytosis and synaptic transmission are schematically represented in Figure Four.

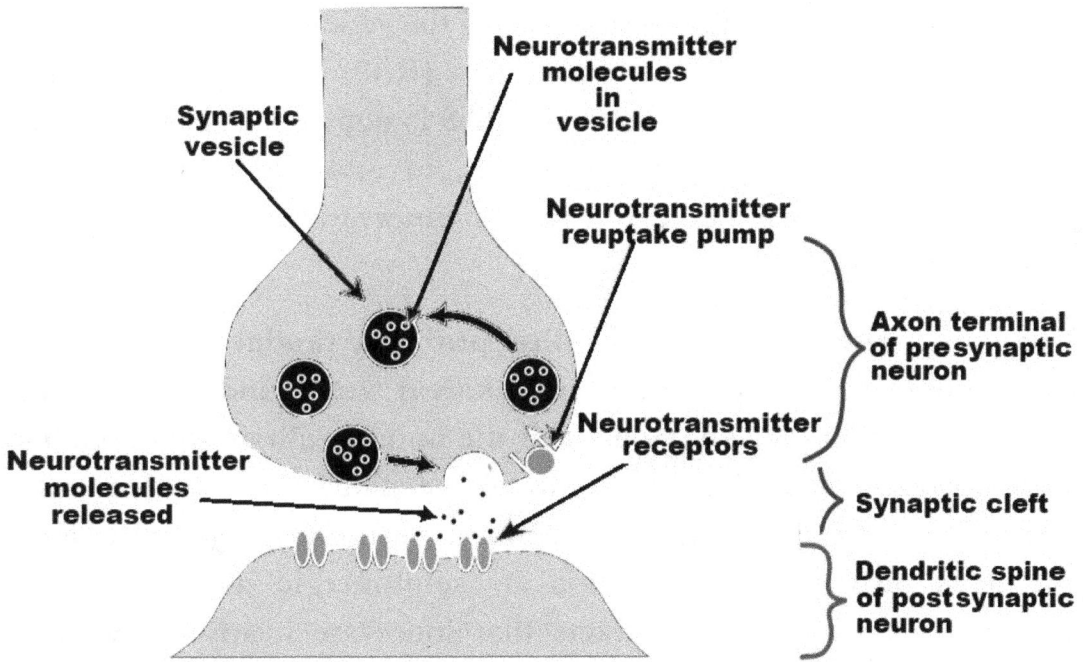

**Exocytosis and Synaptic Transmission**
**Figure Four**

Serotonin is a neurotransmitter primarily produced by neurons in the brain whose cell bodies (perikarya) are found in *raphe nuclei* (pronounced ray´-fee), which are on or near the median plane of the brainstem. The *raphe nuclei* are depicted as seven modified ovoid masses in Figure Two. Not all the neurons in the *raphe nuclei* produce serotonin, but those that do produce serotonin have axonal projections that innervate nearly every major region of the brain, especially the forebrain, which consists of cerebrum and diencephalon. (The diencephalon contains the epithalamus, thalamus, subthalamus, hypothalamus, and third ventricle.)

Acetylcholine is a neurotransmitter produced by many different types of neurons throughout the human body. One brainstem nucleus of cholinergic neurons is found in a part of the reticular formation that is known as the reticular activating system (RAS) at the pons-midbrain junction. The relative location of the RAS is depicted in Figure Three. All the neurons in the RAS also (i.e., in addition to serotonergic neurons) are part of nerve tracts that innervate nearly every major region of the brain.

Norepinephrine is a neurotransmitter primarily produced in the brain by neurons whose cell bodies (perikarya) are found in the locus coeruleus, which is in the pons near the pons-midbrain junction. The locus coeruleus is depicted in Figure Three. The locus coeruleus is the principal noradrenergic site in the brain. All the neurons in the locus coeruleus also (i.e., in addition to serotonergic and cholinergic neurons) are part of nerve tracts that innervate nearly every major region of the brain. Norepinephrine is also produced by the adrenal medulla and the sympathetic nervous system — both of which are covered in Chapter Two of this book.

In synaptic transmission, neurotransmitter molecules released by exocytosis travel across the synaptic cleft and become bound to neurotransmitter receptors that are specific for each type of neurotransmitter. It is in this way that a postsynaptic neuron is stimulated (either excited or inhibited). Serotonin molecules are released from their specific neurotransmitter receptors and are either catabolized (degraded) by the enzyme *monoamine oxidase* or returned to the presynaptic neuron through a neurotransmitter reuptake pump that is specific for serotonin. When acetylcholine molecules are released from their specific neurotransmitter receptors, they are all catabolized (degraded) by the enzyme *acetylcholinesterase* into acetate and choline; only the choline molecules are returned to the presynaptic neuron through a neurotransmitter reuptake pump that is specific for choline. When norepinephrine molecules are released from their specific neurotransmitter receptors, they are either (1) catabolized (degraded) by the enzyme *monoamine oxidase* or the enzyme *catechol-O-methyltransferase* or (2) returned to the presynaptic neuron through a neurotransmitter reuptake pump that is specific for norepinephrine as well as epinephrine and dopamine (all three are *catecholamines*).

# Melatonin, the Locus Coeruleus, and Sleep

Nerve tracts from serotonergic neurons of the raphe nuclei and nerve tracts from cholinergic neurons of the reticular activating system impactfully modulate states of wakefulness and sleep by way of their projections radiating throughout the thalamus and cerebral cortex (i.e., via thalamocortical projections). Nerve tracts from the noradrenergic neurons of the locus coeruleus in the pons of the brainstem (Figure Three) also contribute to the modulation of states of wakefulness and sleep by the norepinephrine inhibition of melatonin production in, and secretion from, the pineal gland (epiphysis) during states of wakefulness, especially during periods of prolonged exposure to sunlight. (Again, *noradrenergic* neurons are neurons that produce or utilize the neurotransmitter *norepinephrine.* And the locus coeruleus is the principal noradrenergic site in the brain.)

During periods of prolonged exposure to sunlight, decreased melatonin production and secretion result in a lack of sleepiness. During periods of darkness, decreased activity of noradrenergic neurons results in increased melatonin production in, and secretion from, the pineal gland. (See Figure Three for the location of the pineal gland.) Together, inactivity of serotonergic neurons in raphe nuclei and inactivity of noradrenergic neurons in the locus coeruleus during periods of darkness contribute to a state of sleep.

Serotonin (5-hydroxytryptamine or 5-HT) is produced from its precursors, tryptophan and 5-hydroxytryptophan (5-HTP). And serotonin serves as a precursor for the hormone melatonin produced by the pineal gland (epiphysis) in the epithalamus of the diencephalon. (See Figure Five for this biosynthetic pathway.)

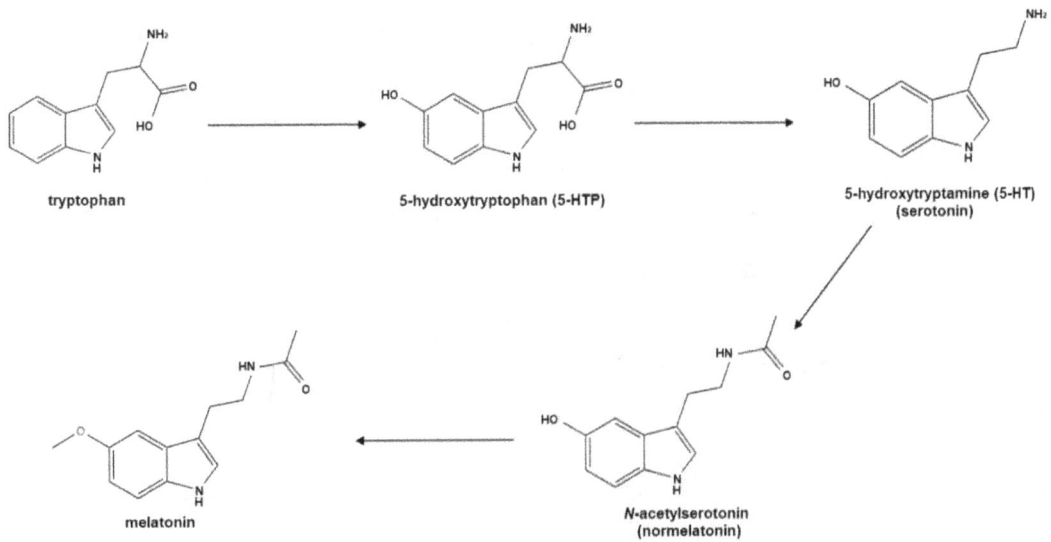

## The Biosynthesis of Melatonin
## Figure Five

The hormone melatonin is produced during darkness and enhances sleep. During exposure to sunlight and other forms of visible light, the electromagnetic energy of the light is transduced to electrochemical action potentials produced in neurons associated with the retina (but not the photoreceptors directly responsible for vision), whose impulses are then propagated along nerve tracts that eventually reach the pineal gland via the locus coeruleus. During periods of light, the axon terminals (boutons) of nerve tracts that travel from the locus coeruleus to the pineal gland release norepinephrine, which inhibits the production and secretion of melatonin. However, during periods of darkness, norepinephrine production slows, allowing for the production and release of melatonin. In combination with neuronal fatigue (most measurably in the forebrain), the presence of melatonin in the brain enhances sleep by stimulating sleepiness.

# Stages of Sleep and the Sixth Sense

Although the sixth sense is operational during wakefulness, it is less fettered during rapid eye movement sleep (REM sleep). Indeed, sleep is a state of altered consciousness, semi-consciousness, or partial unconsciousness that is comprised of non-rapid eye movement sleep (non-REM or NREM sleep) and rapid eye movement sleep (REM sleep).

Non-rapid eye movement sleep consists of four main stages:

Stage I (drowsiness or very light sleep) is the period during which EEG alpha waves wane and EEG theta waves appear.

Stage II (light sleep) is the period during which short bursts of EEG waves occur.

Stage III (moderately deep sleep) is the period during which short bursts of EEG waves occur along with EEG delta waves.

Stage IV (deep sleep) is the period that consists primarily of EEG delta waves.

Rapid eye movement sleep (REM sleep) occurs intermittently during sleep as the brain ascends from Stage IV to Stage III to Stage II and then to a level that not only has similarities to Stage I but also to an awake state. It is during REM sleep that psychic dreams, psychic visions, and psychic faux auditory and olfactory phenomena occur. Telepathic communications from other-worldly sources can also occur during REM sleep. (To be sure, non-psychic dream scenarios are also generated during REM sleep.)

When high intensity psychic dreams, visions, and faux auditory and olfactory phenomena occur, they usually occur during **REM** sleep. One reason that they are high intensity is because dream-related phenomena during **REM** sleep (i.e., psychic as well as non-psychic) involve increased activity in parts of the limbic system — such as the anterior cingulate cortex, amygdala, and the parahippocampal gyrus — that are associated with emotions, emotionality, and emotional memory. Indeed, the limbic system has often been referred to as *the emotional brain* (or *the emotional-visceral brain)* for understandable reasons. (See Figure Six for representative structures associated with the limbic system.)

A major difference between the sixth sense during wakefulness and during **REM** sleep is one's vulnerability during **REM** sleep to: (1) self-imagined sinful scenarios *(for example,* those that are sexual or criminal in nature); (2) emotion-laden telepathic attacks from other human beings who are using harmful psychic energy; and (3) psychic attacks from unclean spirits, demons, or devils fabricating sinful or fear-engendering scenarios. Although sinful scenarios, emotional attacks, and psychic attacks can occur randomly during wakefulness, the prefrontal cortex (PFC) of the cerebrum is more active during wakefulness and, thus, more able to consciously dismiss sinful scenarios as well as counter emotional and psychic attacks.

Among its other functions, the prefrontal cortex is involved in:

    (1) coordinating and adjusting complex behavior
    (2) controlling impulses
    (3) controlling emotional reactions
    (4) refocusing attention
    (5) ignoring distractions
    (6) prioritizing competing and simultaneous information
    (7) complex planning and decision-making

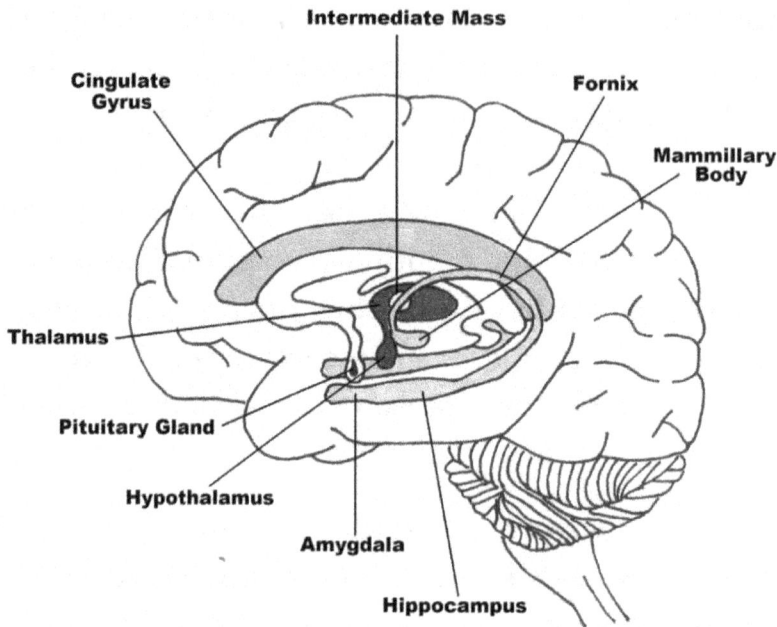

Limbic-Related Structures
Figure Six

During sleep, certain areas of the prefrontal cortex — such as the dorsolateral prefrontal cortex — are relatively inactive and, thus, less able to control thoughts and feelings generated by the limbic system. One way for individuals to counteract this is to decide during wakefulness that their prefrontal cortex will reawaken (i.e., become more active) during the times that their limbic system is being used in ways that are against their conscious desires. Although the reprogramming of one's prefrontal cortex may take some time (years even), one can learn to nip undesirable thoughts and feelings in the bud. However, while one is still in a flesh body, undesirable thoughts and feelings will never disappear completely, but one can cognitively trash (i.e., delete) them earlier — before the thoughts and feelings eventually take hold, possess the victim, and cause the victim to act on them subconsciously and/or consciously.

It is dangerous to allow unholy thoughts and feelings to act themselves out in our minds. Why? Allowing unholy thoughts and feelings to act themselves out in our minds makes it that much harder to rid ourselves of such thoughts and feelings the next time they arise. Although this is dangerous for everyone, it is especially dangerous for susceptible channels (i.e., people whose sixth sense is especially vulnerable to telepathic attacks from other people and psychic attacks from demonic forces).

High intensity psychic dreams, psychic visions, and psychic faux auditory and olfactory phenomena often stimulate one's arousal to wakefulness, thereby enhancing recollection of the extrasensory sensations experienced during REM sleep. In addition to high intensity psychic experiences, other stimuli can rouse one to wakefulness during REM sleep, including a pressing need for micturition (urination) or the presence of pain, bright light, or loud noises; therefore, the recollection of extrasensory sensations experienced during REM sleep can be enhanced because of these events, too.

......

*Depressants* are drugs that impair the central nervous system. They include: (1) alcohol (ethyl alcohol), (2) sedative-hypnotics (barbiturates and benzodiazepines), and (3) opioids (opium-derivatives and their synthetic analogs). Although depressants reduce anxiety, induce sleep, and relieve pain, they also impair one's psychic abilities at the same time. (Read the section entitled *Chemical Dependence as a Hindrance to Personal Psychism* in Chapter Two of this book.)

# Relationships between the Limbic System and Personal Psychism

*Assumptive beliefs* determine the direction that analytical thinking takes. That is why two or more intelligent and rational people, or two or more groups of intelligent and rational people, can be widely divergent in their views on emotionally-charged issues, each person or group claiming that the other person or group is "not thinking clearly" or accusing the other person or group of not being rational or disregarding certain "self-evident" and "obvious" truths.

*Assumptive beliefs* are convictions, or positions, of rationalism that are held to be true regardless of the existence or nonexistence of supporting or contradictory empirical evidence. When they are negative and inaccurate, assumptive beliefs prejudice their holders deleteriously because they taint objectivity and critical analysis. Negative assumptive beliefs interfere with (that is, *bias* or *slant*) deductive and inductive reasoning as well as interpretations of extrasensory sensations. And, because assumptive beliefs are grounded in emotions as well as provide for emotional grounding, those beliefs that are negative and inaccurate *bind* intellectual processes and extrasensory perceptions too tightly. On the other hand, positive and accurate assumptive beliefs *tether* intellectual processes and extrasensory perceptions but do not constrain them.

Because assumptive beliefs are related to emotions, emotion-engendering experiences, emotional memories, and emotional behaviors, the physical "seat" of assumptive beliefs is found in the so-called limbic system of the brain, also known as "the emotional brain" or "the emotional-visceral brain" (portions of which are illustrated in Figure Six). I write "so-called" to simply acknowledge that there is academic debate among neuroscientists concerning what is included and excluded in this system as well as the appropriateness in using the words "limbic" and "system." Regardless, many neuroscientists would include certain structures of the forebrain (i.e., cerebrum and diencephalon) as parts of the limbic system that form a central core of the brain, which core is mostly deep to (that is, below and inside) the neocortex of the cerebrum and above the brainstem. (The *neocortex* is the outermost layer and the largest part of the cerebral cortex.)

Cerebral regions and structures that constitute the most important parts of the limbic system include the: cingulate gyrus, parahippocampal gyrus, amygdala, olfactory cortex, olfactory bulb, orbital and medial prefrontal cortex, and ventral parts of the basal ganglia. The hippocampus is not as important to emotional experience and expression or the integration of emotional behaviors as was once thought. Rather, the hippocampus is more important in establishing new declarative (i.e., explicit) short-term memories. *Declarative memories* are those that are expressible in language (as opposed to, *for example,* learned motor skills).

Diencephalon regions and structures that constitute the most important parts of the limbic system include the hypothalamus and thalamus. The mammillary bodies of the hypothalamus are not as important to emotional experience and expression or the integration of emotional behaviors as was once thought.

Metaphysically speaking, the limbic system represents the spiritual-emotional self not only of unfallen, original Man (capitalized here to distinguish the Creator-God's original creation as spiritual and not physical) but also of the Creator-God Himself. (Remember, we were originally created in the complete image and perfect likeness of the Creator-God.)

Physically speaking, the limbic system in the human being also represents the *fallen* spiritual-emotional self, which must be overridden, or consciously redirected, by the prefrontal cortex in conjunction with the Holy Spirit if the restored spiritual self (i.e., *saved soul)* is to rein in, and reign over, potentially harmful conscious and subconscious thoughts, feelings, and actions. The prefrontal cortex represents the seat of free will, self-control, decision-making, planning, and individual volition.

In the etheric body double of every unsaved human being, the *fallen* spiritual-emotional self "hovers" over the physical limbic system: (1) misdirecting emotional-visceral responses and (2) driving inappropriate thinking, feeling, and behavior in the natural, corporeal, or carnal self. The *fallen* spiritual-emotional self is (1) responsible for our believing demonic delusions as well as (2) responsible for the invention of our own delusions. Only the Holy Spirit of the Creator-God that lives in the restored spiritual self of each saved soul has the power to override or consciously redirect emotions *away from* spiritually-unhealthy desires and responses *toward* spiritually-healthy ones. *For example,* only the Holy Spirit can override (i.e., repress) and replace the desire to indulge sinful and addictive behaviors with the desire to please the Creator-God in prayer, praise, and holy living. Indeed, the Holy Spirit is the prime mover in our taking captive every thought and emotion.

The Holy Spirit of the Creator-God has the power to "bump" the *fallen* spiritual-emotional self out of its position of control and replace it with the higher identity of the spiritual self that has been metaphysically restored by the shed blood of Jesus Christ. If the restored spiritual self has control over the emotions of the etheric body double in the electromagnetic counterpart to the physical limbic system, then this energy pathway in the human body is cleared for the supraself of the individual — which is subsumed within the Supraconsciousness of the

Creator-God's divine Mind — to be in the position of controlling the conscious and subconscious functioning self vis-à-vis its prefrontal cortex. The conscious and subconscious functioning self simply steps aside in acquiescence to control by one's higher self.

In individuals especially compromised by certain mental disorders or active addictions,[5] demonic forces also have the power to "bump" the spiritual-emotional self out of its position of control. In this case, however, a vampiric semi-consciousness is then in control — to what degree and at what interval and duration depends on the nature of each person's susceptibility and the kind and level of mental disorder and/or active addiction. When demonic possession of a human body occurs, it begins at the level of the limbic system.

When a human body is possessed, it is possessed by one or more discarnate entities whose souls belong to the hellish plane of consciousness. These discarnates are beyond divine reclamation (i.e.,

---

[5] As used in this book, addiction not only includes the abuse of external agents absorbed after their ingestion, inhalation, or injection but also chemical agents naturally produced by the body in response to danger, fear, alarm, pain, hunger, satiety, sexual arousal, and olfaction of odorants that are pheromones or pheromone-like. These naturally-produced, internal addictive agents include certain neurotransmitters and hormones as well as less complex chemicals such as glucose, oxygen, carbon dioxide, and various ions. In other words, human beings can become addicted to changing levels of their own naturally-occurring internal chemicals as well as external chemicals ingested, inhaled, or injected. To be sure, all sin is addicting and all addiction is sin. Addictions can only be completely overridden by the Creator-God's Holy Spirit. Unless the Holy Spirit indwells them and is in operation, human beings indulge their addictions without restraint.

beyond redemption). They are also known as unclean spirits, demons, or devils. Although they are members of the fallen Adamic race, unclean spirits are no longer permitted by the Creator-God to incarnate for the possibility of salvation. Because these discarnates still crave physical sentiency, demonic possession is their only option to satisfy that craving.

The seat of fear is also found in the limbic system and is, thus, greatly related to the level at which one experiences pain, sorrow, suffering, anger, rage, pleasure, satiety, affection, memory, and affect (i.e., mood). Because fear has great relevance to the spiritual-emotional self and the accuracy of extrasensory perceptions, and because fear is often defined too simplistically, I will discuss it at this juncture.

Too often, spiritually-minded people think of fear as being universally negative. That is not true. Some forms of fear have a survival advantage and some forms of fear accompany reverence for the Creator-God and awe of things divine.

Fears can be rational, irrational, or supernatural. When rational fears become uncontrolled, they can become irrational fears; and when irrational fears are consciously controlled, they can become rational fears. And some irrational fears can be influenced by demonic forces to become supernatural fears. To be sure, not all supernatural fears are demonic. Supernatural fears also include a reverence for the Creator-God and an awe of the magnificent things He has created.

Rational fears influence us to take protective measures and proactive steps against possible harmful events. In contrast, irrational fears, or phobias, can: (1) incapacitate us, (2) keep us from doing what needs to be done in successful daily living, and (3) hinder our accuracy in interpreting extrasensory sensations. As already indicated, the category of supernatural fear includes both reverence and intense respect for the Creator-God, as well as awe of spectacular events and majestic views of the Creator-God, and things created, designed, and orchestrated by Him; supernatural fear also includes the intense foreboding that is either demonically-engineered and satanically-engendered or the result of extrasensory sensations that foretell imminent danger or danger in the far future.

The following phrase of unknown origin is sometimes used to represent *fear* as an acronym: *F*alse *E*vidence *A*ppearing *R*eal. Although the phrase is useful to describe irrational fears that are of organic origin and supernatural fears that are of demonic origin, the statement does not represent rational fears necessary for practical daily living or the supernatural fear of the Creator-God or legitimate awe of things divine, divinely inspired, or majestically created. In other words, the phrase's *F-E-A-R* acronym is too simplistic.

Antidotes for fear include: (1) practical preparations for successful daily living by responding to rational fears; (2) medication, psychological therapy, and education in counteracting irrational fears; and (3) understanding and applying biblical truth in counteracting supernatural fears introduced by demonic forces. Trust in the Creator-God should be the major ingredient that accompanies the application of each of these antidotes. Trust in the Creator-God includes abiding faith, abiding hope, and abiding confidence in the Creator-God. It also includes fleeing to the Creator-God to take refuge even during times of seeming peace in addition to times of open attack. (Refer to the section entitled *Trusting in our Lord Jesus Christ with Certitude* in this chapter.)

If the tiny ungerminated mustard seed represents faith in the Creator-God,[6] then the huge mustard tree represents trust in the Creator-God that is fully rooted, flourishing, and producing fruit in Him. Trust in the Creator-God does not include the "name-it-and-claim-it," "blab-it-

---

[6]    Matthew 17:20; Luke 17:6

and-grab-it," or "confess-it-and-possess-it" types of super silly and supercilious belief systems so often endorsed by prosperity and "word-of-faith" Christian preachers that emerge in every generation. Rather, trust in the Creator-God includes affirmations that declare His goodness and righteousness as well as His Providence even during the direst circumstances.

Understanding the Creator-God's Providence begins in embracing Romans 8:28 *(NKJV)*:

> All things work together for good to those who love God, to those who are the called according to His purpose.

Christians are taught to "not be anxious about anything, but in every situation, by prayer and petition with thanksgiving, present their requests to God."[7] This directive presupposes that we place our trust in the Will of the Creator-God to do good always for those who belong to Him and are, therefore, "the called according to *His* purpose."

What sits enthroned in the spiritual-emotional self of the etheric body double determines our reactions to fear. Either the Spirit of God sits enthroned in our spiritual-emotional self or the spirit of Satan (i.e., his mortal mind) sits enthroned in our spiritual-emotional self. (Either one or the other sits enthroned but not both at the same time.) If the Spirit of God sits enthroned in our spiritual-emotional self, then the supraself (i.e., the higher self) of the individual directs the conscious and subconscious functioning self to relinquish control, allowing the supraself to direct our thinking and feeling as well as our reactions based on them. If the spirit of Satan sits enthroned in our spiritual-emotional self, then an emotionally-depraved "lower self" (i.e., a

---

[7]  Philippians 4:6 King James Version (Paraphrase)

primitive, carnal *archiself* or *paleoself*) directs the emotions, emotional memories, and emotional behaviors associated with the limbic system.

When the Spirit of the Creator-God is in control of the spiritual-emotional self, spiritually intuitive and empathic people are able to be precise and accurate in their extrasensory sensations and perceptions of the invisible. In contrast, when the spirit of Satan is in control, any intuited or discerned information is jumbled, mismatched, misperceived, and imprecisely understood by these gifted people. In other words, psychically-gifted people are easily deluded and confused when demonic forces are in control.

It is important to point out that pain and suffering are processed and interpreted on a subconscious level primarily in the diencephalon and processed and interpreted on a conscious level primarily in the cerebrum.

Sometimes, we erroneously interpret that pain and suffering constitute punishment from God when they do not. Of course, pain and suffering *can* be punishment from God, but they do not always constitute such punishment.

Earlier in this section, I wrote that "the limbic system represents the spiritual-emotional self not only of unfallen, original Man (capitalized here to distinguish the Creator-God's original creation as spiritual and not physical) but also of the Creator-God Himself." Thus, because unfallen, original Man was created in the complete image and perfect likeness of the Creator-God, the Creator-God's emotions are also seated, metaphysically speaking, within His nonphysical limbic system. This is where the Creator-God experiences and expresses love, joy, affection, pleasure, satiety, and patience as well as hatred, anger, disaffection, displeasure, dissatisfaction, and wrath. As you may have already concluded, the only emotion that the Creator-God does not experience or express is fear. (The Creator-God withdraws from places where evil abounds not out of fear but out of respect and reverence for His Own Holy Name.) However, the Creator-God understood, and still understands, human fear experientially, *for example,* through the palpable fears felt and shared throughout the Godhead by Christ Jesus in the Garden at Gethsemane. (For the sake of clarity, Christ Jesus was never afraid of evil; Christ Jesus was fearful of what he would experience on the cross at Calvary.)

Eternal hope, and not despair, springs within the emotional brain of the human being when the Creator-God is in control through His Holy Spirit. Eternal hope is irrational and unrealistic optimism. Eternal hope is irrational and unrealistic because it exists despite one's currently poor human conditions and the seemingly certain consequences of those conditions.

When metaphysically understood, our memories of the past heighten our imagination of the future. In the world of the Creator-God, not only are all good things possible, they are inevitable. Moreover, in the world of the Creator-God, not only are all good things inevitable, they already *are* (that is, they already exist in His reality). Divine metaphysics seeks to bring into human reality what already exists in the reality of the Creator-God, which is a supernatural reality. The world of the Creator-God is a world without delusion or confusion.

Depression and despair, and not optimism, are engendered by negative thinking. However, not all so-called negative thinking is really negative. Some so-called negative thinking helps us to avoid making the same mistakes in the future as well as avoid various forms of disruption, pain, and suffering in our lives. The Creator-God understands that we will make mistakes, but He wants us to learn from those mistakes. As we learn from our mistakes, we please the Creator-God. (Pleasing the Creator-God involves doing His Will as well as seeking to do His Will.)

# Susceptible Channels

A susceptible channel is a spiritually empathic human being who is more vulnerable to demonic attack than other people (i.e., other people who are not spiritually empathic or who are less spiritually empathic). A susceptible channel is more vulnerable because the combined functioning of its limbic system and certain brainstem nuclei uniquely creates a physical portal for supernatural electromagnetic energy to be more easily transduced to neuronal electrochemical energy with accompanying flow changes in the neurotransmission of sequenced neurons, radiating nerve tracts, and brain circuits. Henceforth in *The Biology of Psychism from a Christian Perspective,* the present author will refer to this unique physical portal as *the psychic apparatus.*

Metaphorically and metaphysically, *the psychic apparatus* is like a living trumpet: (1) with its mouthpiece located in the vicinity of the pertinent brainstem nuclei, (2) with its various slides and pistons regulating and modulating extrasensory sensations located in the sequenced neurons of afferent and efferent nerve tracts travelling toward and away from the pertinent brainstem nuclei, and (3) with its narrower portion of the trumpet's bell or horn located in the limbic system and its broader portion located in the radiating circuits that communicate extrasensory sensations throughout the brain, especially in the cerebrum. Unlike a brass trumpet, *the psychic apparatus* as a living trumpet carries no sound but, instead, conveys extrasensory sensations.

*The psychic apparatus* of a susceptible channel is more easily compromised in the following conditions: (1) when the susceptible channel is still in childhood and lives in a household where its guardians are: (a) ignorant of demonic influences and demonic possessions, (b) have not yet made a family commitment to put the God of the Holy Bible first in their lives, and (c) have not learned how to properly discipline a child; (2) when the susceptible channel begins to act out sinful scenarios created in its imagination by demonic forces; (3) when the susceptible channel suffers from mental disorders that initiate psychotic breaks with reality; (4) when the susceptible channel is addicted to thrill seeking and/or substance abuse; (5) when the susceptible channel suffers from organic brain syndrome or dementia; (6) when the susceptible channel suffers from sustained selfishness, pridefulness, and arrogance; (7) when the susceptible channel regularly entertains ideations related to immoral or unlawful activity; (8) when the susceptible channel clings to hatred, unforgiveness, resentment, revenge, retaliation, and paranoia; and (9) when the susceptible channel is given to jealousy, envy, and covetousness. One or more of the previously mentioned conditions opens the psychic apparatus to entrance by one or more unclean spirits. Although possession first occurs at the level of the psychic apparatus, all brain activities are eventually impacted.

Unless a susceptible channel is protected spiritually by the shed blood of God's only-begotten Son metaphysically applied to its psychic apparatus, a susceptible channel is especially vulnerable to demonic influence, attack, and control. As alluded to earlier, not all people are equally vulnerable to demonic influence, attack, or control because not all people are susceptible channels; moreover, not all people who are susceptible channels are equally susceptible.

The *majority* of people who wander the streets muttering to themselves, or who have been long-term residents in psychiatric institutions, are susceptible channels possessed (that is, inhabited) by unclean spirits. They are subject to demonic direction and control and may even attack others physically or harm themselves. To be sure, some diagnosable psychiatric conditions are entirely organic; some are entirely demonic;

and some are a combination of both organic and demonic in varying degrees. Medical practitioners, mental practitioners, and metaphysical practitioners should work together jointly concerning diagnosis and treatment of susceptible channels who are under demonic influence, attack, and control. All healing practitioners should receive education and training in this subject.

In closing this section on susceptible channels, it is important to include that, just as a specific mental disorder, disease, or propensity to drug addiction can be inherited genetically, so also can a uniquely susceptible psychic apparatus be inherited genetically. That is why more than one susceptible channel may be found in a genetically-related family, regardless of the family's or channel's awareness of (1) their own susceptibility or (2) specific activity by evil discarnates. A few susceptible channels in my own biological family have been influenced, possessed, and/or harassed by evil discarnates. The present author himself was harassed (harassed, but not influenced or possessed) by one messenger of Satan for many decades, especially during daydreams and REM sleep. This evil messenger was permanently removed from my presence by the Lord God Almighty in January of 2017. The evil discarnate and I spoke briefly before he departed. He communicated that he was sorry that he had been unable to control me or get me to turn to unclean things (i.e., unholy behaviors). I did not feel any rage toward him. I felt only pity for him because I knew what his ultimate end would be. This personal story of spiritual harassment is one example of what it means to have "a thorn in the flesh" *(2 Corinthians 12:7-10 KJV)*.

When I was vacationing in Oahu, Hawaii in 1983, I encountered a somewhat disheveled woman walking down the street. She approached me and asked me for money. I replied that I would give her a small amount of money in the name of Jesus Christ. She responded: "I thought you were going to try to give me something in *that* name!" She then declined the few dollars that I offered her. Later, in my hotel room, I asked the Lord to help me understand why she declined the offer. He told me that she was possessed and that the unclean spirits who resided within her would not allow her to accept anything in the name of Jesus for fear of her eventually accepting salvation in that name. If she had, then they would be undomiciled.

# The Importance of Imagination

Imagination should be important to human beings because it is through our imaginations that we communicate with the Creator-God. In fact, it is our imaginations that make our minds most like the Creator-God's divine Mind: The Creator-God is creative and communicative through His imagination and we are creative and communicative through our own imaginations. The Creator-God can express His imagination spiritually, mentally, emotionally, physically, and/or psychically. Similarly, we can express our imaginations spiritually, mentally, emotionally, physically, and/or psychically.

Specific brain regions related to imagination include: the prefrontal cortex, the cingulate cortex, the insular cortex, and the basal ganglia. (See Footnote 18 for a description of the basal ganglia.) However, although these and other brain regions are important to imagination, the prefrontal cortex is the primary region for initiating, experiencing, and directing the expression of imagination.

Although it was once thought that the prefrontal cortex was proportionately larger than other cerebral areas when compared to and contrasted with other primates, it is now known that the prefrontal cortex in humans is only larger in terms of its absolute size but not much larger in terms of its size relative to the rest of the cerebrum when compared to other primates: For most primates, including human beings, the proportional size of the prefrontal cortex to the rest of the cerebrum is between 35 and 40 per cent. It is true, however, that the prefrontal cortex is more developed in human beings than other primates because of the number and extent of its convolutions, internal circuits, and connections to other regions of the brain. (The prefrontal cortex of a human being needs to be well-developed for the brain to house a soul and allow that soul to learn how to express itself through the human body it inhabits.)

Imagination utilizes thinking, planning, weighing options and flexibility, evaluation of possible rewards and punishments, short-term and long-term memory storage and retrieval, emotions, and language. Human beings can choose to act, choose not to act, or choose to procrastinate (the three choices of decision-making).

Imagination is important to enacting our free will. How do we know that we have free will? We know that we have free will because we have the ability to override desires, temptations, lusts, and stubbornness. The existence of free will is indicated by our ability to choose to control ourselves, our thinking, our planning, and our flexible behaviors. We can imagine what it would be like: (1) to indulge ourselves or not indulge ourselves, (2) to reap a reward or a punishment, and (3) to live in heavenly bliss or hellish torment.

Our prefrontal cortex enables us to make and accept rules for ourselves, encode the rules in our brains, and employ the rules to override powerful emotions and powerful emotional memories from the limbic system. Through our Creator-God's Holy Spirit, our prefrontal cortex enables us to take captive every thought, feeling, idea, image, affiliation, association, desire, memory, word, attitude, motive, and action — spoken or unspoken, conscious or unconscious, declarative or nondeclarative. (*Declarative* memories are expressible in language; *nondeclarative* memories are not expressible in language except for describing them.)

Our prefrontal cortex enables us to adapt to changing environments. However, our abilities to adapt to changing environments are compromised by addictions, psychiatric disorders, and permitting others (human beings or evil discarnates) to manipulate, exploit, and control us.

# Far-Memories

Far-memories are autobiographical memories from one's past lives. Some of the memories are *declarative* (i.e., expressible in language) and some of the memories are *nondeclarative* (i.e., not expressible in language). *For example,* some children are prodigies (1) in writing musical scores based on their declarative memories from a past life or (2) in playing a musical instrument based on their nondeclarative memories of motor skills from a past life. Regardless, far-memories are carried within the mind of a soul from its past lives. (Remember, this book distinguishes between *brain* and *mind* in that the brain serves as a physical conduit for the electromagnetic mind of an individual.)

Far-memories are generally not available at a conscious level to the brain because they are suppressed and inhibited by the posterior cingulate cortex to allow the soul to focus on its present life without distractions or hindrances from the remembered events of its past lives. (The posterior cingulate cortex is the posterior half of the cingulate gyrus, the part of the limbic system shown in Figure Six.)

The posterior cingulate cortex is activated to retrieve memories from one's past lives: (1) in rare instances during wakefulness (especially at times of daydreaming, major distractions, and déjà vu experiences); (2) in some instances during hypnosis induced by oneself or a hypnotherapist; (3) in some instances during meditation; and (4) in some instances during astral projection (soul travel) and non-REM sleep. In these instances, the prefrontal cortex (in particular, the dorsolateral prefrontal cortex) opens a gateway in the posterior cingulate cortex to permit its increased activity, allowing it access to far-memories. The posterior cingulate cortex then makes the far-memories available subconsciously and/or consciously to the rest of the forebrain.

# Awareness of Extrasensory Sensations

(1) *Subconscious* awareness of extrasensory sensations during wakefulness and non-REM sleep is primarily associated with various ventromedial structures of the brain in its limbic system; and (2) *conscious* awareness of extrasensory sensations during wakefulness, and *semiconscious* awareness of extrasensory sensations during rapid eye movement sleep (REM sleep), are associated with various sensory, integrative, and association pathways in the cerebrum receiving nerve impulses (primarily but not solely) from its left insular lobe[8] and from the anterior cingulate cortex in its limbic lobe.[9] (See Figure Six for

---

[8] More specifically, in the left ventral anterior insula. It is important to note that some neuroscientists would not refer to the insular cortex of the cerebrum as a separate cerebral lobe. Instead, they would specify that the insular cortex is that part of the cerebrum that lies deep within the lateral sulcus, which is the fissure in the cerebrum that separates the temporal lobe from the frontal and parietal lobes. (Although not labeled, the lateral sulcus is depicted in Figure One.) Although not formally part of the limbic system, the insula is certainly limbic-related.

[9] More specifically, in Area 33 of the pregenual anterior cingulate cortex. (The cingulate gyrus of the cerebrum is shown in Figure Six.) It is important to note that some neuroscientists assert that the so-called limbic lobe of the cerebrum is composed of specific innermost portions of the frontal, parietal, and temporal lobes and is, therefore, not technically a separate cerebral lobe. In *The Biology of Psychism from a Christian Perspective,* the present author distinguishes the limbic *lobe* as the cerebral portion of the limbic *system*. To be sure, the limbic system is not a true system but, rather, a collection of

some of the structures commonly associated with the limbic system.) It should be noted that the serotonergic raphe nuclei in the brainstem (areas active only during wakefulness) as well as the arousal center in the pons[10] (active during REM sleep) have nerve pathways that travel to the left insular lobe, the anterior cingulate region, the parahippocampal gyrus, and the amygdala. It should also be noted that somewhat different regions of the limbic system are more active during wakefulness than during REM sleep.

Extrasensory sensations are experienced in the brain during wakefulness or sleep as: (1) *faux audition* or the sensation of hearing without actually involving sound waves or using the external, middle, or inner ears; (2) *faux olfaction* or the sensation of smell without actually involving odorants or using the olfactory bulbs and olfactory tracts; (3) remembering reconfigured familiar information and personal experiences from one's current life in prophetic visions and dreams; (4) learning new information (i.e., information previously unknown to the recipient) and having new experiences in prophetic visions and dreams; (5) remembering information and experiences from one's past lives (i.e., far-memories); and (6) learning new information and having new experiences during astral projection (soul travel) either by momentarily stepping into a different relative time in the space-time continuum or momentarily stepping into eternity (i.e., timelessness) and ascending into higher spiritual realms.

---

specific structures from the cerebrum and diencephalon that aid and assist in memory, emotions, and learning.

[10] More specifically, the arousal center is in the rostral dorsolateral pontine tegmentum. *(Pontine* is an adjective referring to what is of, or belonging to, the brainstem region known as the *pons.)*

Like all other senses, nerve impulse generation, conduction, and transmission are required for the sixth sense to operate through one's psychic apparatus (that is, for the brain to receive extrasensory sensations through its living trumpet). Like all other senses, these neural activities do not interpret the signification of the extrasensory impressions; specific brain regions interpret meanings of the extrasensory sensations based on: (1) the brain's past experiences, (2) patterns of brain development, (3) mental intelligence, (4) emotional intelligence, (5) spiritual intelligence, (6) established brain circuitry, (7) brain neural connections established through past learning, (8) levels of nutrients, and (9) associated degrees of cognitive, emotional, and spiritual maturity.

Intelligibility of extrasensory sensations is supplied by the brain in association with what is already familiar to the receiver. Sometimes, intelligibility of extrasensory sensations is immediate and sometimes intelligibility only comes (1) after specific extrasensory sensations are pondered in the brain and/or (2) when insights are provided to the brain by spiritual intercession from other-worldly sources *(for example,* by the Holy Spirit, angels, or redeemed souls in Heaven).

Over time and through experience, the receiver who is maturing in the practical use of his or her sixth sense becomes increasingly able to discern differences between unfamiliar extrasensory sensations and interference from (1) wishful thinking and daydreaming; (2) recollecting traumatic events; and (3) receiving irrelevant and random thoughts, ideas, associations, images, affiliations, desires, words, and attitudes (i.e., *psychic noise*).

# Receiving Extrasensory Sensations during Wakefulness (Part One)

(1) The entire brainstem plays an important role (a) in cardiac and respiratory rates as they relate to arousal from sleep as well as (b) in initiating brain awareness (i.e., waking consciousness and wakefulness) by stimulating myriad nerve tracts that radiate from the brainstem to the cerebral cortex, beginning with specific raphe (pronounced ray'-fee) nuclei in the brainstem and portions of the forebrain that are innervated by the arousal center in the pons.

(2) An increased production, secretion, availability, and utilization of serotonin by serotonergic neurons in specific raphe nuclei of the brainstem contribute to a heightened sense of well-being in the forebrain. This sense of well-being results in the enhanced sensitivity of, susceptibility to, and awareness of extrasensory sensations in many places throughout the cerebrum as well as other forebrain regions. (Some of these extrasensory sensations are readily intelligible and some of these extrasensory sensations are not readily intelligible.)

(3) During wakefulness, the human brain is primed to receive extrasensory sensations by the neurotransmitter serotonin.

The effects of serotonin are inhibited, suppressed, modulated downward, overridden, antagonized, and/or prevented by other neurotransmitters *(for example,* dopamine) and some hormones *(for example,* dihydrotestosterone). (See the sections entitled *Dopamine as a Hindrance to Personal Psychism* and *Sex Steroid Hindrances to Personal Psychism* in Chapter Two of this book.) In contrast, serotonin interactions with other neurotransmitters that are co-localized at serotonergic synapses and pathways *(for example,* endogenous opioids [opioid peptides] and gamma-aminobutyric acid [GABA] through their analgesic and anti-anxiety actions) augment the effects of serotonin on feelings of well-being in a kind of neural staircase phenomenon. (Previous to *The Biology of Psychism from a Christian Perspective,* the noun phrase *staircase phenomenon* has been used exclusively by biologists in reference to nerve-muscle interactions rather than nerve-nerve interactions.)

Physical factors that especially trigger the production, secretion (release), and continued synaptic presence of serotonin in the brain include: (a) the availability of its precursors (see Figure Seven); (b) ultraviolet light; (c) massage; (d) appropriate periods of rest; (e) healthy physical activity; and (f) low glycemic index carbohydrates. (Consuming low glycemic index carbohydrates causes lower and slower rises in blood sugar levels. Such carbohydrates include most soy products, beans, fruit, vegetables, minimally processed grains, pasta, low-fat dairy foods, and nuts.)

Emotional and spiritual factors that especially trigger the production, secretion (release), and continued synaptic presence of serotonin in the brain include: (a) gratitude; (b) remembering pleasant events; (c) meditation; (d) trusting in the Lord Jesus Christ with certitude (see following titled section); and (e) seeking his approval for every thought, feeling, idea, association, image, affiliation, desire, deed, attitude, word, motive, and action — spoken or unspoken, during wakefulness or sleep, and in solitude or in front of others.

In sum, stimuli for the production, secretion (release), and utilization of serotonin are related to diverse factors — some correlated and some not — and are, therefore, multivariate in nature.

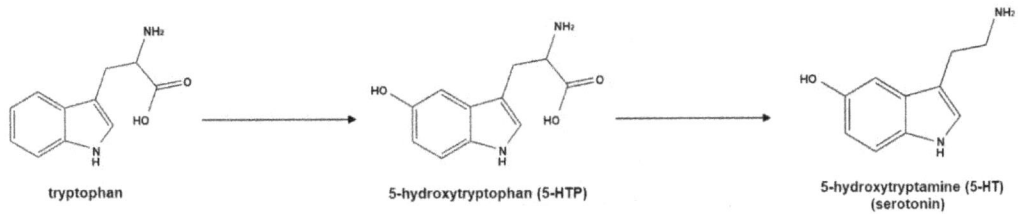

## The Biosynthesis of Serotonin
## Figure Seven

# Trusting in our Lord Jesus Christ with Certitude

Although you may have good friends and family members, you cannot trust them completely because one day (maybe even this very day) they may lie to you, they may steal from you, they may insult you, or they may take advantage of you. Likewise, your good friends and family members cannot trust you completely because one day (maybe even this very day) you may lie to them, you may steal from them, you may insult them, or you may take advantage of them. For each of us, there remains only one person who will never lie to us, never steal from us, never insult us, and never take advantage of us. That person is our Lord and Savior, Jesus Christ. We can trust him completely with certitude. "With certitude" means "with certainty," "without reservation," and "fully and completely." Our Lord Jesus Christ will never disappoint us, never forsake us, and never take advantage of us.

We know that our Lord Jesus Christ will never leave us because he proved his words with "works." What kind of "works?" The miraculous works that he accomplished while he was on Earth, including his work on the cross at Calvary. At the end of his life while he was on that cross, Jesus said: "It is finished." Jesus meant that the work for our redemption and salvation was accomplished through the sacrifice of his life for us. Jesus also proved his words with works by being raised from the dead.

Yes, we can trust in our Lord Jesus Christ with certitude. He will never leave us. He will never disappoint us. And he will never forsake us. Before the return of Jesus Christ to Earth, Satan fights to control us through the uncertainty in this world. What uncertainty? The uncertainty of not knowing what will happen tomorrow. Even after the return of Jesus Christ to Earth, our flesh will continue the fight to control us through the uncertainty of this world. (See the section entitled *Involuntary Physiologic Responses to Horribly-Stressful Incidents, Accidents, and Emergencies* in Chapter Two of this book.) However, if we maintain our certainty in Jesus Christ, neither Satan nor our flesh will be successful in causing us to fear uncertainty. We do not need to fear our future because Jesus Christ is our future.

Before the return of Jesus Christ to Earth, there have been many false doctrines taught in Christian churches. Some Christian churches in poor countries have been forced to teach false doctrines to receive money from the various religious denominations that support them. Some Christians have even been taught that the God of the Holy Bible wants them each to be financially wealthy and have many material goods. Unfortunately, people believing in this prosperity message have been shocked when they are murdered for believing in Jesus Christ.

In verses 9 through 11 of the Sixth Chapter in the Book of Revelation, we read:

> {9} And when he [the Lamb of God] had opened the fifth seal, I saw under the altar the souls of them that were slain for the word of God, and for the testimony which they held: {10} And they cried with a loud voice, saying "How long, O Lord, holy and true, will you not judge and avenge our blood on them that dwell on the Earth?" {11} And white robes were given unto every one of them; and it was said unto them that they should rest yet for a short season until their fellow servants also and their Christian brothers and sisters, who should be killed as they were, should be fulfilled. [brackets mine]

People who believe in false doctrines are often uncomfortable with the truth from the Bible that the followers of Jesus Christ will have tribulation, difficulties, and suffering and may even be murdered as a witness of their faith in him.

It is recorded that our Lord Jesus Christ said:

> These things I have spoken unto you, that in me you might have peace. In the world you shall have tribulation: but be of good cheer; I have overcome the world.
>
> *John 16:33 KJV Paraphrase*

Trusting in our Lord Jesus Christ with certitude includes believing *in* him and believing *on* him even during the most difficult of times — even as we are being molested or executed for trusting in him.

Here, the lesson for us all is that we should each teach and share the gospel of Jesus Christ with simplicity in spirit and in truth. We should not share false doctrines with others because such sharing is popular or because that is what someone else has required us to do.

We should read and study the Bible for ourselves and we should encourage others to read and study the Bible for themselves. We should serve as a resource to others but we should not think that we know everything. We are all students of the Bible. And we remain students of the Bible even as we teach the Bible to others.

As the author of *The Biology of Psychism from a Christian Perspective* reviews his entire life to answer why he has had it so easy, the answer comes to him in the recollection that he learned as a child to trust with certitude in our Lord Jesus Christ from attending: (a) weekly Sunday School in churches of various Christian denominations, (b) annual vacation Bible schools in those same churches, and (c) yearly residential summer Bible camps. For those reasons, he developed a love for Bible study and remained childlike throughout his entire life by trusting with certitude in our Lord Jesus Christ. This does not mean that he did not face hardships or difficulties. It means that the hardships and difficulties had minimal deleterious effects on his spiritual well-being because (a) he always ran to tell Jesus everything and (b) he always asked Jesus to explain complex topics and complicated situations to him in simple ways for the purpose of (a) his own personal understanding as well as (b) sharing that understanding with others. (He still does this as a senior adult.)

# Receiving Extrasensory Sensations during Wakefulness (Part Two)

Understanding one major mechanism of the sixth sense during wakefulness requires: (1) understanding that hypersensitive neurons in the brain become hyperactive when stimulated by changing electromagnetic energy patterns that are related to extrasensory stimuli; and (2) understanding that their hyperactivity causes an increased functioning of serotonergic neurons associated with specific *raphe nuclei* of the brainstem. (See Figure Two for the location of the raphe nuclei.)

An increased functioning of serotonergic neurons results in increased availability of serotonin from one or more of the following conditions: (1) an increase in serotonin production by presynaptic neurons, (2) an increase in serotonin release by presynaptic neurons, (3) a decrease in serotonin reuptake by presynaptic neurons, and (4) a decrease in monoamine oxidase activity in the synaptic clefts between presynaptic neurons and postsynaptic neurons (enzymes belonging to the family of monoamine oxidases catabolize, or break down, serotonin as well as a few other monoamine neurotransmitter substances, including epinephrine, norepinephrine, and dopamine). (See Figure Four for a schematic representation of synaptic transmission.)

There is cognitive and emotional processing of extrasensory stimuli through *raphe nuclei* and the axonal processes of their various serotonergic neurons that terminate in many cognitive and emotional sensory areas of the forebrain. In the sixth sense, the brain makes sense of changing invisible electromagnetic patterns that convey extrasensory thoughts, feelings, ideas, images, sounds, smells, tastes, tactile sensations, attitudes, words, associations, and/or desires to specific sensory awareness areas of the forebrain. Ultimately, the changes of specific patterns in electromagnetic fields impinge upon specific sensory awareness areas of the forebrain that make cognitive and emotional sense of the changing electromagnetic patterns. As a result, extrasensory sensations are received by the conscious mind of the individual, which then imparts meaning *to* them (i.e., derives meaning *from* them).

In summary, neuronal hyperactivity with increased serotonin production provides the single most important platform for *personal psychism* during wakefulness by priming the forebrain to receive extrasensory sensations (i.e., psychic impressions).

Does neuronal hyperactivity with increased serotonin production cause psychic impressions, or do psychic impressions cause neuronal hyperactivity with increased serotonin production? Although people with a well-developed sixth sense are truly impressionable (i.e., susceptible to receiving extrasensory stimuli), an external electro-magnetic stimulus must be present for a neuron to receive it — except when random biochemical events in the brain mimic the presence of extrasensory stimuli when there are none or when normal biochemical diurnal changes are responsible for an increased production of various neurotransmitters associated with extrasensory sensation and perception. Because random thoughts and feelings can be self-generated in the brain, it is important for the person sensitive to external electromagnetic stimuli to learn to discern differences between (1) random self-generated thoughts and feelings (i.e., *psychic noise)* and (2) authentic, externally-generated thoughts and feelings induced by electromagnetic stimuli. Susceptible people with a sixth sense must eventually become cognitively, emotionally, and spiritually mature enough to distinguish between meaningless self-generated psychic noise and true psychic impressions with important, underlying meanings. The question at the beginning of this paragraph is accurately answered by the following two statements: (1) Neuronal hyperactivity with increased serotonin production *permits* psychic impressions to be received more easily during wakefulness throughout the recipient's psychic apparatus. And (2) electromagnetic psychic impressions themselves cause neuronal hyperactivity accompanied by increased serotonin production during wakefulness.

Sensitivity in a channel (i.e., human being) susceptible to psychic impressions presupposes that the channel has an electromagnetic body double with energy vortices that are attuned to changes in invisible electromagnetic energy patterns. This body double is immediately outside of, and congruent with, its associated physical body. Sensitivity in a channel susceptible to psychic impressions also presupposes that there are neurons in the channel's brain that are hypersensitive to electromagnetic energy changes and, as a result, initiate ion flow in those neurons in response to those changes and to the increased production and availability of serotonin. In extrasensory sensations associated with the sixth sense, electromagnetic energy is transduced into neuronal action potentials in the brain and, then, propagated to postsynaptic neurons via synaptic transmission that is aided by the neurotransmitter serotonin.

The presence of serotonin in the brain helps to mitigate psychic interference during wakefulness. Any and all antagonists to serotonin and its actions result in the decreased sensitivity of the recipient to psychic impressions. In other words, any and all antagonists to the recipient's cognitive, emotional, physical, and spiritual well-being result in an impaired psychic apparatus during wakefulness. Therefore, the recipient must remain spiritually-focused as well as cognitively- and emotionally-centered throughout periods of grief, frustration, threat, attack, anxiety, and sickness if he or she is to continue receiving interpretable extrasensory sensations.

Serotonin is not necessary for the psychic apparatus to receive extrasensory sensations during REM sleep because there is less cerebral dissonance and interference during REM sleep. Why? There are unique functional disconnections for much of the cerebrum (but not all of the cerebrum) from the limbic system during REM sleep. Consequently, there are fewer impediments to receiving extrasensory sensations during REM sleep.

# The Impact of Diet on Serotonin Levels

Ingesting serotonin (5-hydroxytryptamine or 5-HT) has no effect on the sixth sense because serotonin does not pass through the blood-brain barrier (BBB). The blood-brain barrier is primarily established by (1) the tight junctions of endothelial cells that line brain capillaries and (2) the presence or absence of specific carrier molecules associated with those cells. Although 5-hydroxytryptamine (5-HT) does not pass through the BBB, serotonin's two immediate precursors do pass through the BBB (i.e., tryptophan and 5-hydroxytryptophan [5-HTP]). (See Figure Seven for the structural formulas of tryptophan, 5-HTP, and 5-HT.)

Ingesting either or both of these two precursors will not impact levels of serotonin in the brain unless one has a deficiency in either or both of the precursors. Thus, except for treating malnutrition, tryptophan-related nutritional supplements do not increase one's sixth sense. For some people, normal diurnal changes in serotonin levels (and inversely-related melatonin levels) enhance their sensitivity to psychic impressions (melatonin is a hormone synthesized in the pineal gland from tryptophan, 5-hydroxytryptophan, and serotonin). (See Figure Five for the molecular relationships of melatonin to its precursors.)

Because of the complex nature of (1) serotonin-mediated psychic impressions during wakefulness and (2) acetylcholine- and melatonin-mediated psychic impressions during REM sleep, everyone needs to identify for himself or herself optimal daily times to rest, meditate, sleep, and engage in physical activity to maximize awareness of psychic impressions.

Although increased melatonin levels in the brain do not increase one's sixth sense, increased melatonin levels in the brain do cause both mundane and extrasensory images during sleep to become more vivid and, therefore, easier to recollect during arousal from sleep and wakefulness.

One final note relative to taking dietary supplements is that, although serotonin does not pass through the blood brain barrier, melatonin does pass through. Thus, if you desire to maximize serotonin availability in your brain, take tryptophan or 5-hydroxytryptophan; if you desire to maximize melatonin availability in your brain, take melatonin.

# The Inverse Relationship between Selfishness and Personal Psychism

The author of *The Biology of Psychism from a Christian Perspective* was once told by someone from Heaven that "the purity of the channel depends on the purity of the channel." This means that the clarity and accuracy of someone with extrasensory abilities depends on the degrees of their individual selfishness and selflessness. The more selfish, or less selfless, an individual with extrasensory abilities is, the less clear and less keen are those abilities. Conversely, the more selfless, or less selfish, an individual with extrasensory abilities is, the clearer and keener are those abilities. Selfishness causes distortions of psychic impressions and impairs the ability to interpret psychic impressions accurately. In other words, the more selfish a person is, the more that person lives in a world of delusions; the less selfish a person is, the more that person lives in a world without delusions. Selfishness increases one's susceptibility to believing delusions no matter how rational one's beliefs might seem. Empiricism is at a disadvantage in selfish people.

Based on the present author's personal experience, perhaps the most difficult form of selfishness to identify in oneself is *benevolent selfishness*. *Benevolent selfishness* is an oxymoronic noun phrase coined by the present author to describe *a position of being* in which an individual's actions are seemingly benevolent to other people at the same time that the individual seeks to control or manipulate them, paradoxically, for their own benefit. Religious and political leaders often use *benevolent selfishness*. To be sure, this is not an endorsement for anyone to use *benevolent selfishness*. In fact, we should steer clear of it unless we are responsible for the care of people who are severely retarded and/or have significant mental disorders.

Our model, or template, for ideal spiritual motivation and behavior is the behavior of the Creator-God Himself: The Creator-God is always benevolent, but the Creator-God is never benevolent to the degree that He robs His created beings of their individual free will. Although the Creator-God laments the harmful decisions that we make, He never seeks to control our thoughts, emotions, or actions. The Creator-God may seek to influence us to help us make choices that are to our spiritual advantage, but He does not force a choice upon us or try to protect us from the ramifications of our poor choices and bad behaviors — especially if we have not repented of those poor choices and bad behaviors. The Creator-God wants us to learn how to control our own thoughts, emotions, and actions by depending on His Holy Spirit.

Unless we live in a society that legally safeguards medically-assisted suicide, we should always intervene in the intended suicide of a depressed person so that the person can live for another day to make better choices for himself or herself. We should always intervene in the actions of anyone who intends to physically harm himself or herself unless doing so would threaten our own physical well-being. However, we should not try to control others so that they do not suffer the consequences of their own poor choices or harmful behaviors. We may offer blunt, objective advice to them, but we should not seek to control them — even if it is painful for us to watch them suffer the consequences of their poor choices and harmful behaviors. We really cannot save others from themselves. It is the responsibility of individuals to acknowledge their own poor choices and harmful behaviors. It is the responsibility of their friends and loved ones to accept that they cannot decide personal choices and behaviors for other adults.

To be sure, it is painful for the Creator-God to watch us make the same mistakes over and over again, but the Creator-God does not save us from the consequences of our poor choices and harmful behaviors. Of course, He may intercede concerning those consequences after we repent or after someone else has prayed for us, but He also may not. He decides when to exercise His grace and mercy. He decides when, how, where, and for whom He wishes to intercede. Sometimes the Creator-God does not intercede because He wants the lessons that we learn to be indelible.

In the final analysis, we cannot protect others from the poor choices they make and the harmful consequences they suffer because of those poor choices. In some cases, we are not even able to protect ourselves from the poor choices of others or their harmful consequences. In those situations, the best we can do is to be grateful that their impacts make us flee to the Creator-God for solace and comfort in the knowledge that He is always in control despite circumstances, situations, and appearances that might suggest otherwise. Daily consequences can be vastly different from eternal outcomes.

# The Inverse Relationship between Lying and Personal Psychism

In the Book of Revelation, the Creator-God reveals the eternal divide between those who love lies, love to lie, and lie habitually and those who do not lie. Liars are prevented from entering the heavenly city called New Jerusalem. Liars are kept outside of that city's gates:

> And there shall in no way enter into the city anything that defiles, neither whoever is involved in idolatrous practices or lies: but only they that are written in the Lamb's Book of Life.
>
> *Revelation 21:27 KJV Paraphrase*

> For outside of the city are dogs, and sorcerers, and adulterers, and murderers, and idolaters, and whoever loves lies and loves to lie.
>
> *Revelation 22:15 KJV Paraphrase*

*Liars* in the New Testament are not just people (1) who tell untruths to protect themselves and those they love or (2) who suffer from a pathological condition of fanciful confabulation. *Liars* in the New Testament are idolaters. Idolaters: (1) do not honor the commandments of the Creator-God, (2) reject Jesus Christ as the *only-begotten* Son of God, and (3) say that they love God but demonstrate hatred toward other human beings:

> Whoever says "I know God" and does not keep His commandments is a liar, and the truth is not in him.
>
> *1 John 2:4 KJV Paraphrase*

> Who is a liar but the person that denies that Jesus is the Christ? That person is antichrist who denies the Father and

the Son.

*1 John 2:22 KJV Paraphrase*

If someone says "I love God" and hates his brother or sister, he is a liar: for he that does not love his brother or sister whom he has seen, how can he love God whom he has not seen?

*1 John 4:20 KJV Paraphrase*

People with natural psychic abilities who reject the God of the Holy Bible cannot be trusted to demonstrate their personal psychism without errors, biases, and flaws. They are like radios tuned to a particular station or channel that receive so much static along with the transmission that the broadcast can no longer be accurately understood or conveyed to others. People with natural psychic abilities who reject the God of the Holy Bible are not credible channels because the Holy Spirit of the Creator-God is not the one operating their spiritual gifts.

We each live in a "body of sin" *(Romans 6:6 KJV)*. This corporeal, sinful body attracts external thoughts and feelings that challenge us to live hedonistic lifestyles. But we must learn not to give in to carnal thoughts and feelings. We must take every sinful thought and feeling captive and place them under the Will of the Creator-God. We must discipline our thoughts and feelings in Christ Jesus. We must become prisoners of Christ Jesus to experience true spiritual freedom.

The most accurate and keenest psychics are those who have learned to discipline their own thoughts and feelings in Christ Jesus and, thereby, have victory over carnal thoughts and feelings. To achieve victory, each person should daily seek the approval of the Creator-God for every thought, feeling, idea, association, image, affiliation, desire, deed, attitude, word, motive, and action.

# A Paradigm of Disordered Personal Psychism from Schizophrenia

Schizophrenia is a mental disorder whose major characteristics help us to construct a practical paradigm for illustrating demonic influences in psychic human beings. People with schizophrenia hear voices, hallucinate, and are deluded and confused. Their personalities and behaviors are erratic and abnormal. They have psychotic episodes, lose their grasp of reality, and are unable to accurately sense and correctly interpret their environments. They are paranoid and hold false beliefs. They are unable to distinguish between demon-initiated thoughts and feelings and their own self-generated thoughts and feelings.

Although not all schizophrenics are demon-possessed, schizophrenics tend to become demon-possessed because (1) they more easily hear demonic voices mixed in with their own imagined voices and (2) they more easily receive demonic images and ideations mixed in with their own imagined images and ideations. Many schizophrenics are genuine psychics, spiritual empaths, sensitives, and susceptible channels who are neither able to discipline their own thoughts and feelings nor able to distinguish their own thoughts and feelings from the thoughts and feelings they receive from other-worldly sources. These inabilities are partly due to the abnormal physiologies of schizophrenics as well as their unique spiritual pathologies.

There is an earlier onset of schizophrenia in males than in females because testosterone and its derivatives are more potent drivers of schizophrenia than estrogens. Although testosterone and its derivatives are found in females, their concentrations are proportionately less than other steroid-based hormones. (How sex steroids specifically hinder extrasensory abilities is discussed in the section entitled *Sex Steroid Hindrances to Personal Psychism* in Chapter Two of this book.)

Because schizophrenics are often not able to discipline their own thoughts and feelings, they end up concluding that the demonic voices they hear and the demonic images and ideations they receive from other-worldly sources are generated by their own minds. As they increasingly entertain the thoughts and feelings of demonic personalities, schizophrenics become increasingly demon-possessed in terms of numbers of demons as well as degrees of entrenchment of those demons. Often, the more susceptible, sensitive, spiritually empathic, or psychic a schizophrenic is, the more demons become housed within its physical body and the more entrenched they become. Casting out demons from possessed individuals is more difficult than from those who are only mildly influenced by demons; as Christ Jesus has instructed us, such casting out requires considerable prayer and fasting *(Matthew 17:21 and Mark 9:29)*.

Before the twenty-first century, most schizophrenics were hospitalized in municipal, county, and state sanatoria. By the early 21st century, most schizophrenics have been either housed in community shelters and group homes or they faced homelessness. Today, many homeless schizophrenics encountered on the street are demon-possessed.

Biologically, schizophrenia is best understood in terms of abnormal synaptic neurotransmission.

# Personal Psychism Properly Anchored

Rather than read and study the Holy Bible and seek to comprehend its multiple layers of meaning at literal, figurative, interpretive, inferential, and metaphysical levels, most people who fancy that they are psychics, spiritual empaths, sensitives, or susceptible channels would rather study esoteric, gnostic, theosophical, philosophical, and non-Christian religious literature. They fail to realize that — unless they are properly anchored in Jesus Christ as (1) the *only-begotten* Son of God; (2) God Incarnate (the Creator-God, or Word of God, in flesh); (3) the promised Messiah of Israel; (4) the one true Savior of the world; and (5) one's only personal Savior — they will remain spiritually untethered. To close the door to schizophrenic and demonic hallucinations, delusions, and psychomotor control (i.e., control of neuromuscular actions), all people who have any measure of personal psychism must be grounded in a biblical way of thinking about Jesus Christ and about who they are in him and why they are on Earth. People with extrasensory abilities should daily submit for approval to the Creator-God every one of their thoughts, feelings, ideas, associations, images, affiliations, desires, deeds, attitudes, words, motives, and actions. Without such grounding, people with spiritual sensitivities open themselves up to disjointed, chaotic, jumbled, inaccurate, fanatical, fantastical, and impure thinking and feeling.

# Interpreting Extrasensory Sensations

## The Role of Cerebral Structure and Function

Just as the normal structures and functions of the brain are important for receiving and processing sensory information, no less are they important for receiving and processing extrasensory information (i.e., psychic impressions). As a reminder to its reader, *The Biology of Psychism from a Christian Perspective* makes a distinction between receiving psychic impressions as *extrasensory sensations* and interpreting psychic impressions as *extrasensory perceptions*.

Of the six major regions of the brain (i.e., cerebrum, diencephalon, cerebellum, midbrain, pons, and medulla oblongata), the cerebrum is the most important for processing new information, assigning meaning to new information, and integrating new information with the rest of the brain's cognitive framework. Although everything in the cerebrum is not connected directly to everything else in the cerebrum, *almost everything* in the cerebrum is connected to *almost everything* else in the cerebrum either directly or indirectly. Connectivity in the cerebrum is primarily established through association cortices (*cortices* is the plural for *cortex*), including: (1) the frontal association cortex, (2) the parietal association cortex, (3) the temporal association cortex, and (4) the occipital/parietal/temporal association cortices. Primary sensory and motor areas make up relatively small portions of the cerebrum in comparison to its combined association areas. Altogether, the association cortices constitute the seat of human cognitive ability.

Human cognitive ability can be impaired by torture, torment, trauma, victimization, oppression, persecution, dehydration, and malnutrition as well as abuse emotionally, mentally, physically, spiritually, sexually, socially, and economically. *For example,* post-traumatic stress syndrome (PTSD) and endogenous depression are each associated with decreased levels of the brain neurotransmitter serotonin. In PTSD and depression, one's awareness of self-worth, value, and sense of well-being are greatly altered — so much so in some cases that the victim cannot be convinced of objective reality or the importance of life. Most people who suffer from PTSD and/or depression are unable to accurately interpret the stimuli to which they are exposed, including normal sensory stimuli as well as extrasensory stimuli. This illustrates that the cognitive-emotional self must be healthy for one to adequately interpret — let alone excel at interpreting — psychic impressions.

The frontal association cortex is responsible for: (1) an awareness of "self" in relationship to past and current experiences as well as to current and prospective future environments, (2) decision-making, (3) self-control in overriding emotions, (4) ordered thinking, and (5) one's abilities to plan and execute appropriate actions and reactions. Overall, adaptive intellectual and behavioral decisions are made by the frontal association cortex not only in response to interpreting normal sensory sensations but also in response to interpreting extrasensory sensations.

The parietal association cortex is responsible for the integration of conscious and unconscious sensory input from all regions of the body, including (1) proprioceptive input mediated by the cerebellum and (2) visual input mediated by the occipital lobe and the lateral geniculate nucleus in the thalamus. (The adjective *proprioceptive* is from the noun *proprioception,* which is the central nervous system conscious and unconscious detection of body position, movement, velocity, and force.) The parietal association cortex is not only responsible for receiving somatic sensory input during arousal from sleep and wakefulness but also extrasensory out-of-body sensations and faux body movements experienced during psychic visions, daydreams, and REM sleep.

The temporal association cortex is responsible for: (1) object recognition and identification, (2) language labeling (i.e., naming), (3) processing and coordinating auditory information and sound discrimination, (4) acquisition of declarative memories vis-à-vis the hippocampus, and (5) cognitive mapping and movement detection in spatial frameworks vis-à-vis the parahippocampal gyrus. The temporal association cortex is responsible for interpreting words "heard," images "seen," and movements "witnessed" and experienced during extrasensory sensations.

In combination, occipital/parietal/temporal association cortices are responsible for the coordination of activities in the primary sensory and motor visual areas of the occipital lobe with the functions of the parietal and temporal association cortices noted previously. These association cortices are responsible for interpreting and acting on extrasensory sensations "seen" during psychic visions, daydreams, and REM sleep.


## The Role of Memory

The conscious and unconscious retrieval of memories from past experiences and learned information are very important to correctly interpret extrasensory sensations. Someone who is spiritually empathic may (1) "hear" extrasensory sensations as lone individual words, phrases, unrelated word strings, or sentences and/or (2) "see" extrasensory sensations as scenarios, scenes, or vignettes during psychic visions, daydreams, or REM sleep. Multiple scenarios, scenes, or vignettes may represent sequential events, simultaneous events, overlapping events, or disordered events. Disordered events need to be placed in proper order by the spiritually empathic recipient.

Much of the Book of Revelation recorded by John the Apostle is a saga of apocalyptic events. Typically, a saga is a detailed narrative of multiple scenarios, scenes, or vignettes — some of which are easily connected by the reader and some of which are not so easily connected by the reader. To be sure, some of the prophetic scenes that the Apostle John saw and recorded are sequential, some are simultaneous, some are overlapping, and some are disordered, needing to be placed in proper order by the student of the Book of Revelation — but only after the student has read the entire book many times to better discern and comprehend the interconnectivity of its elements.

As he retold the prophetic images and events that he saw, the Apostle John sometimes had to draw from his own past experiences and learned information in order for him to describe them metaphorically and/or metaphysically because he could not describe literally what he himself had never seen or experienced before. This is the nature of interpreting prophetic elements that are not familiar to the spiritually empathic recipient. To be sure, it is helpful to be highly verbal and articulate, but languaging skills alone will not encode — or, for that matter, decode — complex prophetic elements.

Information is acquired, stored (i.e., retained) as memory, and retrieved from memory. Categories of memory include: (1) immediate memory (retention measured in seconds), (2) short-term memory (retention measured in minutes), (3) long-term memory (retention measured in days, weeks, months, and years), and (4) far-memories (retention measured in multiple lifetimes).

Initially, declarative memories (i.e., memories expressible in language) are acquired by the temporal lobe, stored for the short-term in the hippocampus and related structures, and stored for the long-term at a variety of sites throughout the cerebral cortex.

Simultaneously, declarative memories are also impressed upon the mind of the electromagnetic body double and are either suppressed and inhibited or reactivated and retrieved in subsequent lifetimes.

Initially, nondeclarative memories (i.e., memories, *for example,* related to learned motor skills and geometric puzzle solving) are acquired in diverse regions of the brain working together — including the parietal lobe, frontal lobe, basal ganglia, amygdala, and cerebellum — and stored for the long-term in those same sites. Paradoxically, the temporal lobe is not involved in the acquisition, storage, or retrieval of nondeclarative memories. From this, it is clear that declarative and nondeclarative memories are dissociated in the brain because they are determined by systems that are virtually independent. Simultaneously, nondeclarative memories are also impressed upon the mind of the electromagnetic body double and are either suppressed and inhibited or reactivated and retrieved in subsequence lifetimes. The far-memory of nondeclarative skills accounts for some individuals at an early age (i.e., child prodigies) who demonstrate remarkable prowess of motor and engineering skills for which they have received little or no training.

Concerning consciousness related to general psychism (i.e., universal consciousness), the author of *The Biology of Psychism from a Christian Perspective* makes a distinction between (1) memory that is electromagnetic in nature (i.e., metaphysical memory) and (2) memory that is physical in nature (i.e., biological memory). Because everything everywhere is a function of consciousness, the two kinds of memories are not only related but interdigitated.

Memory that is electromagnetic in nature is encoded in universal consciousness on an etheric, or astral, plane. In order for the imagination of the Creator-God to be laid down in physicality, it is first laid down electromagnetically. (The imagination of the Creator-God is both a metaphysical and mathematical function of His timeless memory.) Only after the Creator-God's imagination has been laid down electromagnetically can it be expressed physically. For biological life, the Creator-God's electromagnetic templates are expressed physically in: (a) phylogenetic memory (from the encoding and decoding of species-specific genetic material); (b) ontogenetic memory (from experiences after conception until the time of physical death); and (c) biochemical memory from subatomic, atomic, molecular, and supramolecular chemical and physical properties and the interactions of those properties in protoplasm (especially in sarcoplasm and neuroplasm).

Innate, instinctive, and reflexive behaviors (including protoplasmic taxes) for human beings can be automatic behaviors or adaptive behaviors (or even maladaptive behaviors). For human beings, these behaviors reflect physical memory that is vertebrate-specific, mammalian-specific, primate-specific, species-specific, gender-specific, and cellular-specific. *For example,* motility within a cell, locomotion for an individual, skeleto-muscular gait, and sexual attraction all express a metaphysical principle that is encoded in biological life based on electromagnetic principles that are expressed sequentially and/or simultaneously: (a) phylogenetically, (b) ontogenetically, and (c) biochemically.

Human behaviors based on phylogenetic, ontogenetic, and biochemical memories include behaviors related to: feeding, drinking, reproduction, locomotion, foraging, hunting, predation, protection, fighting, shielding, escaping, facial expression, gesticulation, oral communication, fears, threats, carrying, holding, balancing, and responding to noxious odorants and potentially poisonous tastants.

Concerning memory in relationship to demonic influences and possession, unclean spirits are not omniscient. Therefore, unclean spirits are forced to depend on our retrievable memories in order to reconfigure and embed them into scenarios, scenes, and vignettes that are the most tempting to us personally. Unclean spirits desire for us to accept their unholy ideas, thoughts, imagery, and projected behaviors as if they were our own and act on them during our daydreams or REM sleep. It is most important to unclean spirits that, if we act on them subconsciously in our daydreams or REM sleep, it increases the probability we will enact the same behaviors consciously during wakefulness, thereby (1) widening their demonic sphere of influence and (2) allowing them to burrow more tightly (i.e., further entrench themselves) into our limbic systems — where, minimally, they can continue to influence us or, maximally, fully inhabit us for complete control — in which case we are either incapacitated ourselves or driven to commit acts of terror in order to help incapacitate and manipulate others.

## The Role of Language

Language plays an important role in general psychism, specific psychism, and the passing of information and skills from one generation of human beings to the next generation.

......

In general psychism and specific psychism, the language of the Creator-God subsumes: (1) speaking and declaring, (2) generating and composing, (3) hearing and listening, and (4) seeing and viewing.

(1) Speaking and declaring. For the God of the Holy Bible, the Creator-God's spoken Word is represented by Jesus Christ. Therefore, speaking and declaring include creating, healing, sacrificing, saving, reconciling, restoring, redeeming, ingathering, and ruling. When

seeking to understand the triune nature of the Creator-God, the following analogy can be helpful:

> When one is speaking about one of the lobes of the cerebrum, it is fully understood that one is also speaking about the cerebrum in general. Similarly, when one is speaking about the Son of God, it is fully understood that one is also speaking about the Creator-God in general.

(2) Generating and composing. For the Creator-God, the generated and composed Word is represented by the prophecies of the Old Testament, the entire canon of the Holy Bible, and the modern prophetic gifts of the Holy Spirit. It is through language that abstract truths and spiritual facts become concrete to human beings who believe in the God of the Holy Bible. In contrast, human beings who do not believe in the God of the Holy Bible have *spiritual receptive aphasia*. *Spiritual receptive aphasia* is the inability to understand the generated and composed Word of the Creator-God.

In Heaven, souls in Jesus Christ think empirically. There is no need in Heaven for us to think abstractly or even analytically: Everything we think in Heaven is based on empirical truths and facts of being that are seen spiritually. Therefore, we do not rationalize in Heaven; we do not induce or deduce what is true. In Heaven, we do not believe in what we do not see because we see spiritually what already exists.

(3) Hearing and listening. For the God of the Holy Bible, the heard Word is represented by the Holy Spirit. Therefore, hearing and listening include hearing the Holy Bible spoken aloud (remember, many people throughout the world are not literate), interpreting, teaching, counseling, advising, helping, comforting, and expressing the gifts of the Creator-God as they are operated by His Holy Spirit

(i.e., always in the right place and at the right time). When seeking to understand the triune nature of the Creator-God, the following analogy can be helpful:

> When one is speaking about one of the lobes of the cerebrum, it is fully understood that one is also speaking about the cerebrum in general. Similarly, when one is speaking about the Holy Spirit, it is fully understood that one is also speaking about the Creator-God in general.

(4) Seeing and viewing. For the Creator-God, the seen and viewed Word is represented by His creation and the truth of His Being. Human beings see His physical creation and come to understand His creative nature by recognizing the Creator-God's evolving design. As human beings see His physical creation, they also come to understand His spiritual creation metaphorically and metaphysically.

......

In passing information and skills from one generation of human beings to the next generation, the primary purpose of language subsumes: (1) understanding the gospel message, (2) confessing one's sins, (3) sharing the gospel message, and (4) praising the Creator-God for salvation. Although other biological organisms are able to communicate with each other, sins cannot be confessed and the message of salvation cannot be conveyed by the waggles of bees, the calls of songbirds, the vocal clicks of whales, or the screeches of monkeys.

One of the reasons that the Creator-God chose human beings to house the souls of the fallen Adamic race is because human beings have cerebral hemispheres sufficiently developed to transmit information and skills from one generation to the next through spoken as well as written language. Language provides the scaffolding for the construction of our thoughts.

Human beings have an innate capacity for language imitation that transmits complex conceptual information from one generation to the next. We use arbitrary and abstract written symbols to achieve this. Although other animals may convey information and skills, the information and skills are neither complex and conceptual nor codified in transferable written form.

Human beings have lateralization of brain activities relative to language. In other words, the right and left cerebral hemispheres demonstrate specializations. In 97% of human subjects tested, the left cerebral hemisphere is responsible for expressing speech sounds and using their lexical, grammatical, and syntactical meanings in language production and comprehension. In contrast, the right cerebral hemisphere grants *bounce* to words spoken and written. In this context, *bounce* is referring to the prosody of emotional meanings, which is the emotional coloring and tone given directly to spoken language through inflection and volume and indirectly to written language through phraseology and nuance.

Although there may be an oral tradition in the transmission of specific information and certain skills from one generation to the next, it is the written tradition that codifies information and skills not only to teach the information and skills to others but also to further expand and refine, polish, and perfect the information and skills being taught. *For example,* this book is but one step to further steps. (In other words, this book is not the final step. Like all other books, it is intended as a bridge to additional steps.)

# Chapter Two:

# Hindrances to Personal Psychism

# The Transduction of Electromagnetic Energy to Electrochemical Energy

Whatever else and wherever else in absolute space-time the Kingdom of God is or isn't, the Kingdom of God lies electromagnetically "within us"[11] and "at hand"[12] — which is to say, "right next to us" — as "hidden leaven"[13] and "hidden treasure."[14] However, unless we are reborn in Christ Jesus through the Creator-God's Holy Spirit, human beings cannot electromagnetically see, hear, experience, or enter[15] the hidden Kingdom of God or accurately understand its mysteries.[16]

The following paragraph describes the two primary mechanisms by which the Holy Spirit, the angels of the Creator-God, and the saints in Heaven impinge words, thoughts, ideas, concepts, images, visions, and feelings electromagnetically upon the nervous system of human beings who are either (1) somewhat sensitive to receiving psychic impressions or (2) highly susceptible to receiving psychic impressions:

(1) Externally-sourced pico bursts of electromagnetic psychic energy are responsible for the excitation of vibrational modes in molecules

---

[11]  Luke 17:21 KJV (Paraphrase)

[12]  KJV (Paraphrase) of Matthew 3:2, 4:17, 10:7; Mark 1:15, 12:34; Luke 10:9, and 21:31

[13]  Matthew 13:33 KJV (Paraphrase)

[14]  Matthew 13:44 KJV (Paraphrase)

[15]  John 3:3, 3:5 KJV (Paraphrase)

[16]  Matthew 13:11 KJV (Paraphrase)

---

associated with the plasma membranes of various neurons within the brain. (2) Additionally, the same pico bursts of electromagnetic psychic energy are absorbed by water in the neuroplasm (the cytosol or aqueous component of the neuron's protoplasm), contributing to increased voltage-gated nanoporation and action potential generation, which result in a nerve impulse that is propagated (i.e., conducted) along the nerve cell's plasma membrane in the direction of its axon terminals and continued by synaptic transmission to the next nerve cells in a sequence (i.e., second-order and third-order neurons).

In the two ways elaborated in the previous paragraph, electromagnetic psychic energy is transduced to biological electrochemical energy. This is how human beings receive psychic sensations. (The psychic sensations must be interpreted accurately if they are to be useful to the recipient and/or to others for whose purpose the recipient has received the sensations.)

During wakefulness, electromagnetic psychic energy is especially effective in regions and areas of the cerebrum that have been primed by the neurotransmitter serotonin. Here, *regions and areas of the cerebrum* specifically refer to those cortical locations in the cerebrum that receive second-order and third-order innervation from the serotonergic neurons of the raphe nuclei in the brainstem.

During wakefulness, REM sleep, and ecstasis,[17] one's (1) prayerful attitude (i.e., an abiding desire to please and commune with the

---

[17] *Ecstasis* comes from the Greek word ἔκστασις (ek´-sta-sis) [G1611] that refers to a trance-like state induced by the Holy Spirit. This Greek word is specifically translated as "trance" in the King James Version of the Holy Bible, denoting the state into which both the Apostle Peter and the Apostle Paul fell *(Acts 10:10; 11:5; 22:17)* when they each had visions induced by the Creator-God's Holy Spirit as they were praying.

Creator-God) and (2) self-sacrifice (e.g., through fasting, celibacy, and ministering to others) jointly heighten the sensitivity of the human nervous system's psychic apparatus to words, thoughts, ideas, concepts, images, feelings, and visions that hold transcendent, holy, and divine meanings.

In diametric opposition to the description in the previous paragraph, during wakefulness, REM sleep, and periods of demonic attack, one's (1) unholy attitude (i.e., an abiding desire to please one's carnal self) and (2) self-indulgence (e.g., by venting insatiable and unbridled sexual desires, rage, bloodlust, and addictions) jointly heighten the sensitivity of the human nervous system's psychic apparatus to words, thoughts, ideas, concepts, images, feelings, and imagined scenarios that hold unholy, hellish, and demonic meanings. All unholy, hellish, and demonic phenomena are hindrances to healthy personal psychism and individual spiritual growth. Therefore, it is important for us to understand such negative phenomena if we are to successfully treat and counter them prayerfully and metaphysically in ourselves and others.

# Human Flesh has a Mind of its Own

Human flesh has a mind of its own and that "fleshly mind" *(Colossians 2:18 KJV)* is also called *carnal mind* in the King James Version of the Holy Bible *(Romans 8:7)*. *Carnal mind* is opposite and opposing to the mind that is in Christ Jesus *(1 Corinthians 2:16 KJV; Philemon 2:5 KJV)*. *Mortal mind* is the other mind that is opposite and opposing to the mind that is in Christ Jesus. As explained previously, *mortal mind* is the vampiric semi-consciousness that indwells Satan, his fallen angels, and his unclean spirits, demons, or devils. *Mortal mind* is the evil collective force that motivates the personalities of all demonic beings; it joins them together. *Mortal mind* is in direct competition with the Supraconsciousness of the Creator-God's divine Mind. In comparison, *carnal mind* is the physiologic force that operates in individual human beings and motivates the personalities of all human beings to indulge lustful pleasures, avoid unpleasant circumstances, initiate confrontations, refrain from forgiveness, seek revenge and retaliation, and bully as well as terrorize. Because both *carnal mind* and *mortal mind* are opposite and opposing to the mind that is in Christ Jesus, they work in tandem during *the pre-Millennium*. And they will continue to work in tandem until the beginning of *the Millennium,* at which time *mortal mind* will be sequestered in the Pit of Hades for the full 1,000 years that Christ Jesus reigns on Earth *(Revelation 20:1-3 KJV)*. Carnal mind, however, will continue to operate in human flesh during *the Millennium.*

Because carnal mind is opposite and opposing to the mind that is in Christ Jesus, should human beings "mortify the deeds of their human body" *(Romans 8:13 KJV Paraphrase)* by committing suicide to unseat the power that carnal mind has over them? No. Christ Jesus wants us to overcome the power that carnal mind has over us, but he wants us to learn to be victorious over it by following his lead in exercising self-discipline and denying it control through prayer, resisting and rebuking temptation, and self-sacrifice while we are in corporeality. Christ Jesus does not want us to permit harm to ourselves except in the laying down of our lives to protect others or in divinely-appointed martyrdom.

Human flesh has always had, and will always have, a mind of its own. Throughout all of the millennia since the Adamic Fall until the future creation of "a new heaven and a new earth" *(Revelation 21:1 KJV)*, human flesh and the carnal mind that directs it have always been, and will continue to be, opposed to the Will of the Creator-God. Human flesh and carnal mind play a prominent role in the disobedience of human beings to the Will of the Creator-God — that is, from the Adamic Fall (but not as the cause for the Adamic Fall) until Christ Jesus returns to Earth at the end of *the Tribulation* — due to the yielding of human beings to the temptations of their own flesh *(James 1:14-15)*. But human flesh and the carnal mind that directs it jointly play their greatest seditious role during *the Millennium* that Christ Jesus reigns on Earth. Why "greatest seditious role"? During *the Millennium*, Satan and his demonic forces — including his fallen angels and unclean spirits (the latter of which are the discarnate souls of the evil dead) — are no longer able to influence human beings by: (1) inflaming their lusts, (2) implanting images in their sensitive and susceptible minds, or (3) inhabiting their souls and possessing their human bodies.

At the end of *the Tribulation*, when Christ Jesus returns to Earth, Satan and his demonic forces are altogether incapacitated because the director of their collective consciousness (i.e., Satan) as well as his minions are imprisoned for 1,000 years in the Pit of Hades. Thus, in addition to the activity of Satan, the activity of all fallen angels and all unclean spirits also ceases during *the Millennium:* The evil motives of all demonic forces are frozen in time and space. Human beings are inaccessible to demonic forces during that period of time.

As a reminder here, Good (i.e., Righteousness) and Evil (i.e., Unrighteousness) each have a collective consciousness based on their motives. The motive for all righteous created beings is to please the Lord God Almighty. The motive for all unrighteous fallen beings is to compete with and conquer the Lord God Almighty and His righteous created beings by separating and dividing them all from one another.

In other words, throughout *the Millennium* — which is to say, the 1,000 years of peace during that Christ Jesus reigns on Earth — there is no demonic activity in the earth plane of consciousness. Demonic activity does not resume until the end of *the Millennium,* which culminates in World War IV — referred to as the Battle of Gog and Magog in Revelation 20:8. There is no demonic activity throughout *the Millennium* for these two reasons: *First,* Christ Jesus is reigning on Earth, and the reign of Christ Jesus on Earth itself suppresses demonic activity because of the ubiquitous presence of the Holy Spirit, which is continually poured out on all humankind during that period of time *(Joel 2:28-29; Acts 2:17-18). Second,* Satan and his minions are bound, or imprisoned, in the Pit of Hades for the entire 1,000 years of *the Millennium (Revelation 20:2-3; Isaiah 22:17-25, 24:21-23, and 25:5).* That they are bound not only incapacitates Satan's evil influence on human beings but also incapacitates the evil influence on human beings by all of Satan's hordes. However, although humanity does not have to fight against Satan's mortal mind (the vampiric semi-consciousness of Satan), humanity does have to fight daily throughout *the Millennium* against its own flesh and the carnal mind that directs it.

During *the Millennium,* human beings cannot claim, or even think to claim, that Satan's mortal mind is leading them to commit sinful acts.

All wrongful acts committed by human beings during *the Millennium* are entirely of their own choosing and doing. Thus, there is an even greater responsibility, proportionately so, placed on human beings during *the Millennium* to override the desires of their own flesh, and the carnal mind that directs those desires, by "bringing into captivity every thought to the obedience of Christ" *(2 Corinthians 10:5 KJV)*. Why? The desires of carnal mind are incapable of reining themselves in. Carnal mind is forever separated from the mind that is in Christ Jesus.

During *the Millennium,* human beings are still subject to their own fears, lusts, selfishness, pretentiousness, ignorance, malice, and covetousness. During *the Millennium,* human beings still entertain unclean thoughts, feelings, ideas, associations, images, affiliations, and desires — specifically those of a sexual, earthy, worldly, egotistical, cunning, conniving, selfish, fearful, carnal, narcissistic, egocentric, exploitive, manipulative, condemning, judgmental, rude, crude, irreverent, vulgar, willful, wasteful, lustful, thieving, addicting, unforgiving, resentful, vengeful, retaliatory, prejudiced, impatient, jealous, envious, covetous, haughty, prideful, boastful, greedy, arrogant, selfish, snide, smug, sarcastic, slanderous, stingy, cruel, hateful, and immature nature. During *the Millennium,* the only difference is that Satan and his demonic forces and their evil collective consciousness (i.e., *Satan's mortal mind)* are no longer able to spark, ignite, inflame, or fan those unclean thoughts, feelings, ideas, associations, images, affiliations, and desires: During *the Millennium,* people on Earth do that entirely on their own without the aid of any unseen evil force. It is in this way that there is an even greater burden during *the Millennium* placed on control over one's own flesh and the carnal mind that directs it.

Here are some practical recommendations for people to remember during *the Millennium*. Throughout *the Millennium,* human beings should be ever vigilant:

> Because the carnal mind [i.e., the mind operating according to fleshly desires] is enmity against God [i.e., in direct opposition to God], it is not subject to the law of God — neither, indeed, can it be.
>
> *Romans 8:6-7 KJV Paraphrase*

> Human beings must always watch and pray that they do not enter into temptation. Although God's Holy Spirit in one's soul is ever willing to do the right thing, human flesh is ever weak to do the wrong thing.
>
> *Matthew 26:41 KJV Paraphrase*

> It is God's Holy Spirit that makes alive; human flesh, and the carnal mind that directs it, profit nothing.
>
> *John 6:63a KJV Paraphrase*

> If human beings live after the flesh, then they will die. But if they live through God's Holy Spirit, they mortify the deeds of the human body, and they will remain alive.
>
> *Romans 8:13 KJV Paraphrase*

> Those who belong to Christ Jesus crucify [in daily self-sacrifice] the human body with its lusts and desires.
>
> *Galatians 5:24 KJV Paraphrase*

Because the tendency to rationalize and justify sin remains with human beings during *the Millennium*, a solid understanding of abnormal psychology, psychoanalysis, and psychotherapy will be useful during that period of time for healthcare practitioners to knowledgeably inform themselves and others: (1) why we human beings do the things we do; (2) how to overcome what we do that is harmful to ourselves and our relationships; and (3) how to override and undo what we have a tendency to do because we are still in the flesh. However, studying and applying psychological principles during *the Millennium* does not mean that human beings should abandon studying and applying principles of the Supraconsciousness of the Creator-God's divine Mind in favor of behaviorism, family systems theory and therapy, or any other psychoanalytical system, methodology, or tool.

Although the Creator-God's Holy Spirit is freely poured out on all flesh throughout *the Millennium,* sins of the flesh will continue to attract souls that remain in a corporeal condition. That is why there is still a tendency during *the Millennium* to hide personal sin, especially through self-rationalization and self-justification. Just because the Lord Jesus is on Earth during *the Millennium,* and just because the Creator-God's Holy Spirit daily falls afresh on human beings throughout *the Millennium,* does not mean that the entire Earth turns into some giant commune with the exchanging of flowers and peace signs or other gratuitous, superficial expressions of love and optimism.

There are additional reasons that the knowledge of abnormal psychology, psychoanalysis, and psychotherapy remains useful to healing practices and personal psychism during *the Millennium:*

(1) During *the Millennium,* human beings will still have to contend with their limbic systems and paralimbic cerebral cortex (i.e., cortex adjacent to the limbic system), which includes phylogenetically ancient and primitive cerebral regions known as *paleocortex* and *archicortex. Paleocortex* ("ancient cortex") is found: (a) in the temporal lobe's parahippocampal gyrus, (b) at the junction of the temporal and frontal lobes in olfactory cortex known as the pyriform (piriform) cortex, and (c) in a few closely-related regions to (a) and

(b). *Archicortex* ("first cortex") is found in the temporal lobe's hippocampus. *Paleocortex* and *archicortex* are histologically simpler and, therefore, credibly thought to be: (a) older than the *neocortex* of the cerebrum from an evolutionary standpoint and (b) involved in some of the brain's most primitive functions. Many of these functions are hindrances to personal psychism because they vent the fleshly desires of one's carnal mind.

(2) During *the Millennium,* human beings will still possess their so-called "reptilian" and "rat" brain centers (more formally referred to as the brainstem and mesolimbic pathway, respectively). These centers are brain regions responsible for: (a) involuntary reflexes that control thoughts, emotions, and behaviors related to seeking comfort, avoiding discomfort, and surviving instinctively as well as (b) disordered thoughts, emotions, and learned behaviors related to addiction, compulsion, and inferior nurture, education, and training. These reflexes and disorders are also hindrances to personal psychism because they vent the fleshly desires of carnal mind. (Read the sections in this chapter entitled *Dopamine as a Hindrance to Personal Psychism* and *Chemical Dependence as a Hindrance to Personal Psychism.*)

(3) During *the Millennium,* human beings will still be subjected to: (a) their own inherited, idiosyncratic personalities, dispositions, and temperaments; (b) their own animal instincts — including brutality, rage, sexual lust, jealousy, and envy; and (b) tragic and traumatic accidents and severe physical, mental, and emotional injuries that happen to themselves as well as to their loved ones. During *the Millennium,* human beings will even continue to experience flesh-related insecurities and addictions. All of these attractions and events are hindrances to personal psychism because they, too, vent the fleshly desires of carnal mind.

To be sure, human flesh is a formidable foe to living according to the Will of the Creator-God. The carnal mind that directs human flesh forever stands opposed to the operation of the Creator-God's Holy Spirit in personal psychism. The Holy Spirit within men and women always stands ready to overcome, but the flesh remains prone to fail because it is weak, frail, and erring *(Matthew 26:41)*. That is why, during *the Millennium,* human beings must deal successfully with inner conflicts and imbalances physically and psychologically as well as metaphysically, spiritually, and supernaturally to have daily victory over their ongoing personality predispositions, animal instincts, and traumatic experiences.

During *the Millennium,* human flesh and the carnal mind that directs it prove that not all intrusive thoughts and emotions are or were (depending on when you are reading this) of demonic origin during *the pre-Millennium.* During *the Millennium,* the origin of unclean thoughts, feelings, and actions is from one's own flesh and the operation of carnal mind through the inherent, inherited vulnerability of flesh.

The actions of various neurotransmitters and hormones in the human body help students of the Holy Bible to understand that human beings have always wrestled against their own flesh and blood (i.e., their own physiologically-induced and physiologically-mediated inner conflicts) in addition to the spiritual enemies against which they also wrestled.

The Holy Bible is clear that, from the time of the Adamic Fall until the beginning of *the Millennium,* the most significant battlefield for human beings would be in the spiritual realm:

> For we wrestle not against flesh and blood but against principalities, against powers, against the rulers of the darkness of this world, and against spiritual wickedness in

high places.

*Ephesians 4:12 KJV*

The passage of Scripture just quoted refers to external evil forces and power struggles *before* the return of Christ Jesus to Earth, but the passage does not refer to inner conflicts induced or mediated by the body's own neurotransmitters and hormones. Indeed, human beings have always regularly fought the effects of neurotransmitters and hormones that: (1) heighten fear, rage, and aggression; (2) stimulate the libido as well as various associated immoral behaviors; and (3) heighten abilities during predatory activities (either when one is stalking or when one is being stalked). Abilities heightened during predatory activities include arousal, hyperarousal, vigilance, hypervigilance, strategizing, and resulting reflexive motor behaviors — all of which translate to a jungle or forest environment just as well as they translate to a school or office environment (although they may translate in subtler ways in a school or office environment).

All human beings during *the Millennium* will continue to wrestle with the urges of their own human flesh and the carnal mind that directs it. They will continue to wrestle with their own behaviors, attitudes, and activities that stem from the production of specific neurotransmitters and hormones. In other words, human beings will continue to wrestle with positive and negative feedback mechanisms that stimulate behaviors, attitudes, and activities that almost seem to be uncontrollable and, in some cases, are uncontrollable (i.e., compulsive). They will continue to wrestle with various addictions, including those promoted by biochemical rushes induced from drugs, spectator sports, sexual orgasms, predatory behaviors, and general risk-taking — such as from participatory sports, daredevil activities, illegal activities, and gambling. What plagued human beings who lived before *the Millennium* will also plague human beings who live during *the Millennium*. To be sure, human conflicts during *the Millennium* are not induced and mediated by external evil forces; they are induced and mediated by individual-specific physiological responses as well as by species-specific biology. In other words, human beings have wrestled with their own flesh and the carnal mind that directs it, and they will continue to wrestle with them during *the Millennium*.

Although human beings continue during *the Millennium* to wrestle with their own flesh and the carnal mind that directs it, they can still turn to the Creator-God for spiritual, emotional, mental, physical, and psychic help in combating and overturning their own animal instincts and biologically-driven predispositions. To be sure, such victories are never easy. One can sense Apostle Paul's frustration with his own flesh and blood in his statement: "I do not do the good that I want to do, but I do the evil that I do not want to do" *(Romans 7:19 KJV Paraphrase)*, which precipitated the following conclusion and accompanying question from him:

> *O wretched man that I am! Who will deliver me from this [fleshly] body of death?*
>
> Romans 7:24 KJV Paraphrase

The Apostle Paul knew that the only way for human beings to overcome physiologically-induced and physiologically-mediated temptations is through crucifying, or sacrificing, one's own flesh daily:

> Knowing this, that when our carnal self is crucified with Christ Jesus, the body of sin [i.e., the power of human flesh to tempt] is destroyed in order that we should not serve sin.
>
> *Romans 6:6 KJV Paraphrase*

It is difficult for many people to accept that their souls live in the bodies of animals. Regardless of what else we are or are not, human beings are animals. Often, we refuse to acknowledge that human beings are part of the Animal Kingdom. We would rather not concede that human beings are vertebrates, mammals, and primates. For people who have difficulty accepting this, they have misconcluded that the dichotomy between the spiritual and natural is contrived or insulting to the Creator-God as well as to humankind. They don't want to know that individual-specific physiology and group-specific biology shape instincts, habits, behaviors, personality, gender identity, and sexual orientation. They don't want to know that conditions like Tourette syndrome, schizophrenia, criminal insanity, and drug addictions are of genetic and/or biochemical origins and not of demonic origins.

# One Theorem and Its Corollaries Regarding Human Flesh

## Theorem

Because human flesh is inherently dishonest and predisposed to sin, all human beings lie to themselves, to others, and to the Creator-God.

## Corollaries

1. All human beings are inherently dishonest because they are in the flesh. Being in the flesh makes them inherently dishonest.

2. Trust no one except Jesus Christ because everyone in the flesh is inherently dishonest to themselves, to others, and to the Creator-God.

3. It is only when we admit that we are inherently dishonest that we are honest.

4. Trusting only in Jesus Christ enables people in the flesh to have meaningful relationships with one another.

5. If we trust solely in Jesus Christ, we can never be disappointed.

6. If we trust in ourselves or other people in the flesh, we will be disappointed.

7. Although some people are less dishonest than other people, they are still inherently dishonest because they are in human flesh.

8. Although some people are less sinful than other people, they are still predisposed to sin because they are in human flesh.

9. Encourage human beings to trust only in Jesus Christ instead of trusting in themselves or other people in the flesh.

10. Discourage people from trusting people in the flesh — including themselves individually as well as others in the flesh.

11. People in the flesh can only have meaningful relationships with others to the degree that they are honest with themselves.

12. To the same degree that we are dishonest with ourselves is the degree to which we are dishonest with others and with the Creator-God.


Christ Jesus instructs his disciples to "watch and pray that we not enter into temptation because, although our spirit is willing, our flesh is weak" *(Matthew 26:41 KJV Paraphrase).* Here, *spirit* (from the Greek *pneuma)* is referring to that part of ourselves that is rational, makes decisions, and is capable of acting. Thus, despite the saved soul's moral agency, which — in consort with the Creator-God's Holy Spirit — leads us on the path to Righteousness, the compulsivity of our flesh works against us and may override our decisions if we are not unceasingly mindful in prayer of what we want to do, need to do, and are doing. This same flesh will work against us during *the Millennium.* However, that the Creator-God's Holy Spirit will be poured out upon all mankind during *the Millennium* will help us to resist the compulsivity of our human flesh *(Joel 2:28-29; Acts 2:17-18).*

During *the Millennium,* human beings must think spiritually — that is, prayerfully and metaphysically — if they are to have victory over their own animal instincts and biologically-driven predispositions. In the following four sections are examples of flesh and blood conflicts over which human beings can have absolute victory during *the Millennium* through application of this truth.

# Dopamine as a Hindrance to Personal Psychism

Dopamine is a neurotransmitter produced by dopaminergic neurons in two distinct, adjacent areas of the midbrain (mesencephalon). The two areas are the *substantia nigra* and the *ventral tegmentum*. Dopamine is a neurotransmitter that is biochemically related to epinephrine and norepinephrine. All three of these substances (dopamine, norepinephrine, and epinephrine) are known as *catecholamines* because they each have: (1) a catechol moiety at one end of their molecules (catechol is a six-carbon ring structure with two hydroxyl groups [—OH groups] that forms the central core, or nucleus, of the catecholamine molecule) and (2) an amine group at the opposite end of their molecules (an amine group is a derivative of ammonia [$NH_3$] where one, two, or all three of the hydrogen atoms have been replaced by the atoms of other elements). (See Figure Eight for related catecholamine structures derived from the amino acid tyrosine.)

Dopaminergic neurons from the midbrain innervate the basal ganglia[18] in the cerebrum, which establish: (1) limbic (i.e., reward-seeking) and

---

[18] *Basal ganglia* are clusters of nerve cell bodies that lie deep within the cerebral hemispheres (in subcortical white matter deep to the neocortex). The *basal ganglia* contain histologically identifiable regions, including the corpus striatum (this *striatum* includes the nucleus accumbens as well as the caudate and putamen nuclei), globus pallidus, and ventral pallidum. (Some neuroscientists include the orbitofrontal cortex as part of the basal ganglia.) The reason that the regions of the basal ganglia are named here is to help the student who is seeking additional information about dopaminergic pathways in neuroscience textbooks because, although the names of the regions

motor (i.e., muscle control and coordination) loops with the thalamus that circuit back to the basal ganglia as well as (2) thalamocortical connections with neocortical divisions of the limbic system.

In popular culture and pseudoscience, the neurotransmitter dopamine is often presented as responsible for feelings of pleasure within the brain. That understanding is inaccurate. However, it is accurate to state that the neurotransmitter dopamine is responsible for activating feelings within the brain relative to (1) the anticipation and prediction of a reward, (2) reward-seeking behaviors, and (3) the reinforcement of addictive behaviors. I will use (I) baking bread, (II) riding a roller coaster, and (III) gambling on a slot machine to help explain what I mean:

(I) Wafting odorants from baking bread and stored memories of those odorants (and stored memories of related tastants) activate (a) certain areas of limbic-related cortex to perceive the wafting odorants as pleasant (vis-à-vis the orbitofrontal and cingulate cortex) and (b) certain areas of limbic-related cortex to perceive them as familiar (the orbitofrontal, pyriform, and amygdala cortex — the latter two of which are in the temporal lobe). Additionally, dopaminergic neurons from the midbrain release molecules of the neurotransmitter dopamine, which stimulate many cerebral areas to anticipate the actual eating of the bread. Anticipating the eating is different from the actual eating. (*Wanting* and *not wanting* are different from *liking* and *disliking*.)

---

may be given in such books, it might not be clear to the student that all identifiable areas belong to the *basal ganglia*. One final note is that the name *basal ganglia* is a misnomer because, technically, *ganglia* are collections, or clusters, of nerve cell bodies outside of the central nervous system. Because the *basal ganglia* are inside the central nervous system, they really could have been named *basal nuclei*.

COO⁻

CH₂−CH−NH₃⁺

HO

**Tyrosine**

COO⁻

CH₂−CH−NH₃⁺

HO

OH

**Dihydroxyphenylalanine**

CH₂−CH−NH₃⁺
     H

HO

OH

**Dopamine**

OH
CH−CH−NH₃⁺
     H

HO

OH

**Norepinephrine**

OH
CH−CH−NH₂⁺
     H
     CH₃

HO

OH

**Epinephrine**

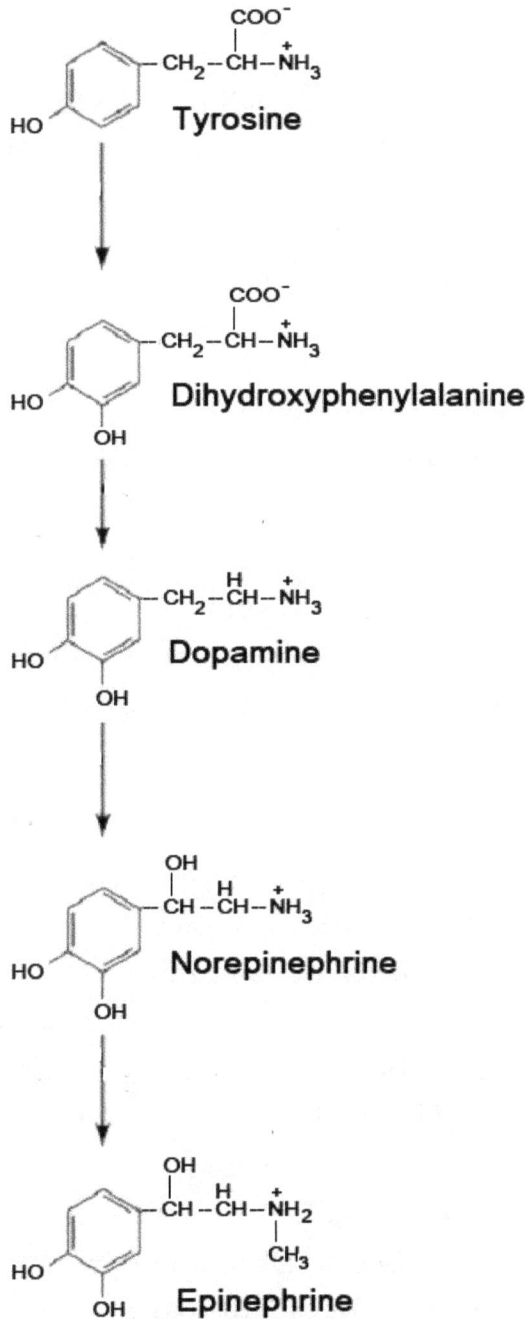

# Biosynthesis of Catecholamines
# from the Amino Acid Tyrosine
# Figure Eight

(I, continued)

Dopamine is responsible for the feelings of anticipation, but dopamine is not responsible for the actual sensation of pleasure (or disappointment) that one gets from the eating. Other neurotransmitters and hormones are responsible for those sensations during eating and digesting the bread.

(II) Waiting in a long line to ride a roller coaster and even going uphill on the roller coaster can be exhilarating for young children. Dopamine contributes to those feelings of exhilaration, but dopamine is not responsible for the sensations of pleasure (or displeasure) that the children get from going downhill on the roller coaster. Other neurotransmitters and hormones are responsible for those sensations (but not the exact same set of neurotransmitters and hormones responsible for such sensations from eating and digesting bread).

(III) After an adult deposits money in a slot machine whose wheels spin, the player pulls the lever (or presses a button) and the wheels begin to spin. As the wheels are spinning, the player experiences great excitement from anticipating and predicting a reward. That particular excitement ends when the wheels halt. Then, the player either likes or dislikes the result. The feelings of excitement as the wheels are spinning are different from the feelings of either liking or disliking the result. Dopamine is responsible for the excitement experienced during the spinning of the wheels. Dopamine is not responsible for the sensations of pleasure (or displeasure) from the result. Other neurotransmitters and hormones are responsible for those sensations (but not the exact same set of neurotransmitters and hormones responsible for such sensations in either (I) the bread or (II) the roller coaster examples given previously).

Dopamine is responsible for sensations from anticipating and predicting a reward, but dopamine is not responsible for sensations associated with receiving a reward. Although some dopaminergic neurons may be part of a neural pleasure pathway, dopamine itself is not directly responsible for sensations of pleasure; rather, dopamine is responsible for the anticipation of a pleasurable reward. Relative to a pleasurable reward, dopamine regulates drive (although not exclusively). Other substances — *for example,* circulating gastrointestinal tract hormones and the brain's endogenous opioid neurotransmitters (including dynorphins, endorphins, and enkephalons) — are responsible for such sensations as satiety, a positive mood, pleasure, and euphoria. (The proverbial pathway to a person's heart may be through his or her stomach but only if that pathway is reinforced by the person's dopamine-activated limbic system.)

The actual eating of baked bread, the actual downhill riding on a roller coaster, and the actual results from one bet on a slot machine can all be anticlimactic because their associated feelings may not compare with one's feelings from anticipation and prediction. The fun, excitement, and exhilaration from the anticipation and prediction of a pleasurable reward related to dopamine production might cause some individuals to habitually eat bread, ride roller coasters, or gamble. And their habitual behaviors might lead to compulsion because of the strong sensations experienced from sustained dopamine production and the inability to override such sensations by decision-making areas of the brain in the frontal cortex. Such compulsions are always maladaptive and harmful to one's personal psychism (among other things, of course). Additionally, higher than normal dopamine levels in the brain inhibit serotonin activity. You will recall from Chapter One of this book that serotonin helps prime the brain to receive psychic impressions during periods of wakefulness. Therefore, because of their inhibitory effects on serotonin, higher than normal dopamine levels in the brain are hindrances to personal psychism.

It should be noted that the Creator-God — *He-Who-Is-Righteousness-in-itself* — is more compassionate than self-righteous people toward those who have mental disorders or addictions with associated compulsions. The Creator-God is more compassionate because He understands that the disorders, addictions, and related compulsive behaviors are solely initiated and sustained by human flesh and the carnal mind that directs it. Of course, the Creator-God wants us to learn how to control our reward-seeking behaviors and our appetites for anticipating and predicting rewards, but He does not condemn individuals who are unable to do so. Why? The Creator-God understands that some disorders, addictions, and compulsive behaviors (especially those related to long-term mental disorders and chemical addictions) override and overtake limbic system- and frontal lobe-related decision-making, volitional control, and free will. Because some maladaptive behaviors are uncontrollable and, therefore, forced upon us, the Creator-God understands that spiritual intercessions as well as behavioral, cognitive, and emotional therapies in combination with drug therapies may all be required (sequentially or in tandem) to help some victims overcome behavioral problems that are spiritual, psychological, psychiatric, genetic, and/or physiologic in nature.

Although some neuroscientists might argue that so-called free will is only the conscious awareness of what someone subconsciously intends to do, saved people know that free will is a gift to us from the Creator-God and that our free will is tested, tempted, and tried in terms of our actions while we are in corporeality. Eventually, the desires of the flesh disappear when flesh disappears at the time of its death, but our resolve to do the right thing or the wrong thing does not disappear. Resolve is a metaphysical tangible in psychism. Our resolve does not disappear in eternity. Indeed, we know that we have free will because, although our flesh (especially our insular cortex) refuses to relinquish control to the Creator-God's Holy Spirit, we can override that refusal through our resolve to do the right thing in seeking to please the Creator-God. When a soul is finally unencumbered by its flesh, its resolve to please the Creator-God is freed to fully reflect the Creator-God's Glory (i.e., the brightness of His Being).

(1) Activating dopamine release from presynaptic dopaminergic neurons, (2) suppressing the reuptake of dopamine by the same neurons, (3) prolonging the presence of dopamine in receptors on postsynaptic neurons, and/or (4) an unusually high number or concentration of dopamine receptors on postsynaptic neurons can lead some people into irreversible chemical addictions and related compulsive behaviors. The best thing to do is to not abuse addictive substances to begin with. And the next best thing to do is to seek therapeutic help, prayerful intercession, and practitioner-prescribed medication to help control one's desires for addictive substances (in addition to gradually having the addictive substance titrated down to zero in one's daily regimen).

Regardless of cause, all dopamine imbalances within the brain hinder personal psychism. Dopamine imbalances play a primary or secondary role in at least some forms of the following mental disorders: psychosis, schizophrenia, endogenous depression, attention-deficit/hyperactivity disorder (ADHD), flat affect, obsessive-compulsive disorder (OCD), hypoactive sexual arousal disorder, sexual aversion disorder, and substance abuse disorder. Relative to substance abuse, (1) the following drugs have *direct* effects on increased dopamine presence: cocaine, amphetamines, caffeine, and nicotine; and (2) the following drugs have *indirect* effects on increased dopamine presence: ethyl alcohol (ETOH), tetrahydrocannabinol (THC), and opioids.

If you have an inherited or a developmental mental disorder, seek professional help. If you have a predilection for substance abuse, seek professional help. Even if you are a long-term substance abuser, seek professional help. Although others might, no one who belongs to the Creator-God will judge or condemn you. Why? We are all sinners who have fallen far short of the glory of the Creator-God. Your personal psychism will bloom as you respond favorably to the help you receive. Regardless, your ultimate goal should not be enhanced personal psychism. Your ultimate goal should be to please the Creator-God commensurate with His Will for us to live a healthy life — spiritually, emotionally, mentally, physically, and psychically. To live up to your personal psychism potential, you must become and remain anchored in Christ Jesus.

# Chemical Dependence as a Hindrance to Personal Psychism

## Reward, Pain, and Addiction

As explained in the previous section, the neurotransmitter dopamine drives sensations associated with the anticipation and prediction of pleasurable rewards (i.e., reward-seeking). Biblically speaking, such dopamine-driven anticipation helps to explain the physiological basis for our indulging "lusts of the flesh," "lusts of the eyes," "lusts of uncleanness," "lusts of what is forbidden," and "lusts of evil things." Human beings lust after, desire, or yearn for pleasurable rewards — many of which can be harmful to their personal psychism and intimate relationship with the Lord God Almighty. Generally speaking, these modalities, as component parts of the natural man, war against the unified spiritual man in an effort to destroy by tearing apart and separating· the person from others who belong to Christ Jesus. (Derived from the Bible, the phrases "natural man" and "spiritual man" are non-gender-specific.)

In our efforts to enhance personal psychism and telepathic communion with the Creator-God, we should always seek to replace desires for temporal rewards with desires for eternal rewards. *For example,* insight on one eternal reward that we should continually seek comes to us in the following commentary on our human life by Christ Jesus at the end of that life: "Well done, my good and faithful servant" *(Matthew 25:21, 23 KJV Paraphrase).* In other words, we should seek approval from the Creator-God as an eternal reward. Indeed, a desire for eternal rewards is the basis for this command of Christ Jesus: "Seek first the Kingdom of God and His Righteousness, and all of your needs will be met" *(Matthew 6:33 KJV Paraphrase).* Obeying this command is evidentiary of our trusting in the Lord

Jesus Christ with certitude. (To be sure, the ultimate eternal reward for a human being is the salvation of his or her soul.)

When you hit your head on a sharp object, crack your elbow against a hard surface, bump your shin on a metal bed frame, or stub your toe on a rock, you instantly try to mitigate the sensation of pain by patting, rubbing, or massaging the injured area. The physiological basis for your reflexive response is the stimulation in the injured area of mechanoreceptors (i.e., a variety of receptors related to touch, stretch, microvibrations, and pressure). Mechanoreceptors have dendritic terminals, generally encapsulated, that have lower thresholds for nerve impulse generation and conduction than the unencapsulated dendritic terminals of nociceptors (i.e., pain receptors that have free or naked nerve endings). Although mechanoreceptors are not receptive to pain, they are more sensitive to sensory stimuli than the nerve endings of pain receptors. The axon diameters of mechanoreceptors are larger than the axon diameters of pain receptors; the axons of mechanoreceptors are generally myelinated and the axons of pain receptors are generally unmyelinated; and, as a result, the conduction velocities for mechanoreceptors are faster than those for pain receptors. In addition, the ascending sensory pathways for touch and pain are parallel in the dorsal horn (i.e., posterior or sensory horn) of the spinal cord, allowing for neural interactions between the two kinds of receptors (i.e., mechanoreceptors and nociceptors). As a result, when stimulated by a pat, a rub, vibration, or a massage, mechanoreceptors help to modulate (dampen) the intensity of pain felt from nociceptors. That is why you pat, rub, or massage an injured area. (Specific descending neural pathways help modulate ascending pain pathways, too.)

(1) Just as finger pats on the surface of the skin help to modulate sensations of itching from stimulated free nerve endings (i.e., naked nerve endings or unencapsulated dendrites) in the epidermis and dermis, and (2) just as friction and pressure from finger pats and palm rubs on the surface of the skin as well as whole-hand deep joint and muscle massages help to modulate sensations of pain from free nerve endings (i.e., naked nerve endings or unencapsulated dendrites) in the skin, subcutaneous layer, and soft tissues (fascia) of joints and muscles, so does our unceasing desire to please the Creator-God, when coupled with an unending gratitude to Him for salvation, help to modulate both physical and emotional pain in the human being. An unceasing desire to please the Creator-God and an unending gratitude to Him for salvation are the two major components of the "unceasing prayer" recommended to us by the Holy Spirit through Apostle Paul in 1 Thessalonians 5:17 KJV. These two components are also prerequisite for us to experience spiritual ecstasy (review Footnote 17 on page 114), which is sometimes visited upon us by the Creator-God's Holy Spirit in response to such prayerful attitudes. (To reiterate, desire and gratitude are the two major components of unceasing prayer.) These descriptions help to explain a few ways in which the Creator-God can be our reward while we are still on Earth.

Pleasurable sensations from rewards and analgesic (pain-relieving) effects are primarily experienced in the following opioid-sensitive pleasure centers (i.e., reward hotspots) of the brain: specific nuclei in the basal ganglia, the orbitofrontal cortex, the hypothalamus, the insular cortex, the midbrain (in periaqueductal locations), the pons (in rostral locations), and the medulla (in rostral ventral locations). (All of the regions just listed are either parts of the limbic system or significantly allied to the limbic system.) Opioid-sensitive neurons are also found in the dorsal horn (i.e., posterior or sensory horn) of the spinal cord. Pleasurable sensations and analgesic effects from opioids include: a sense of satisfaction; good mood; emotional warmth; amusement; inspiration; joy; euphoria; ecstasy; orgasmic release; mitigation, modulation, and inhibition of pain; and heightened feelings of self-worth. It is no wonder why exogenously administered opioids are used to mitigate physical and emotional pain. Also, it is no wonder why they are addictive (i.e., habit-forming).

## Depressants

In general, depressants slow the activity of the central nervous system by reducing stress, pain, anxiety, and guarded inhibitory behaviors. They also interfere with decision-making, motor activity, and concentration. Exogenously administered depressants include (1) opioids, (2) ethyl alcohol, (3) sedative-hypnotic drugs, and (4) $\Delta^9$-tetrahydrocannabinol (THC) from *Cannabis* (marijuana). (THC has some hallucinogenic and stimulant properties as well.)

Susceptible channels (psychically-gifted people) who become chemically dependent on exogenously administered depressants have a greater risk of experiencing hellish and demonic hallucinations during wakefulness, daydreams, and nightmares as well as being subjected to demonic influences, demonic attacks, and demonic possessions. To be sure, chemical dependencies impede the accurate interpretation of psychic impressions by people who are sensitives or susceptible channels. Because the purity of the channel depends on the channel's purity, the impressions themselves — as well as their interpretations — become confused, murky, and jumbled. At the same time that they impede psychic impressions and accurate interpretations, these intoxicants open neural gateways to demonic influences.

## Opioids

The pleasurable sensations and analgesic effects that accompany rewards are often activated by the release of the body's own natural opioids (i.e., endogenous opioids), such as those neuropeptide transmitters that belong to the categories of: (1) enkephalins (concentrated in the thalamus and hypothalamus), (2) endorphins (concentrated in the pituitary gland), and (3) dynorphins (concentrated in the posterior pituitary gland, hypothalamus, and small intestine). There are more than twenty endogenous opioids that are widely distributed throughout the brain and generally co-localized with serotonin. Endogenous opioids are also found in spinal cord interneurons. Endogenous opioids play important roles in reward- and addiction-reinforcement. Exogenously administered opioids play similar roles.

*Endogenous* opioids are named *opioids* because they bind to the same postsynaptic plasma membrane receptors as exogenously administered opium and its derivatives — *for example,* morphine, heroin, and codeine. (Etymologically, the category name *endorphin* is derived from the words *endogenous* and *morphine*.) For many people, exogenously administered opioids have become the drugs of choice to activate their pleasure centers, alleviate stress, reduce pain, and help them feel good about themselves. Unfortunately, chronic exposure to such addictive drugs: (1) changes neural circuitry in the brain, (2) eliminates healthy psychic abilities in favor of unhealthy psychic abilities from carnal and demonic influences, and (3) destroys telepathic communication with the Creator-God. Exogenously administered opioid drugs are responsible for decreased abilities in memory and learning, chemical addictions, substance abuse, and recurring compulsive behaviors. Synthetic opioid drugs are significantly more potent and much more addicting than natural opioids that are exogenously administered.

Following is a practical conversion table for the morphine equivalencies of some common exogenously administered opioids:

| Opioid | mg per day | Morphine Equivalent (Daily) |
|---|---|---|
| Codeine | 10 | 1.5 |
| Hydrocodone | 10 | 10 |
| Hydromorphone | 4 | 16 |
| Morphine | 10 | 10 |
| Oxycodone | 10 | 15 |
| Oxymorphone | 9 | 27 |
| Fentanyl | 25 μcg/hour | 60 |

### Opioid Conversion
### Table One

### Depressants other than Opioids

Ethyl alcohol (ETOH) interferes with normal neurotransmission within the central nervous system. Alcoholism is not only responsible for physical and psychological damage, it inhibits the development of one's personal psychism as well as opens one up to psychic attacks from other people and demonic entities. Demonic attacks are poignantly demonstrated in delirium tremens (DTs) during ETOH-withdrawal, which delirium is especially demonstrated by tormenting visual and auditory hallucinations.

Sedative-hypnotic drugs include barbiturates and benzodiazepines. These categories of drugs are anti-anxiety and anti-panic intoxicants that relax the body and induce sleep as well as diminish pain by enhancing the inhibitory effects of the neurotransmitter gamma-aminobutyric acid (GABA). Anxiety is associated with increased neural activity in the prefrontal cortex, amygdala, and anterior cingulate gyrus. Panic is associated with increased neural activity in the amygdala, ventromedial nucleus of the hypothalamus, and the locus coeruleus. The hypnotic effects of these intoxicants especially permit the physical takeover of susceptible channels by demons.

The psychoactive component of marijuana, THC, mimics the effects of the body's own endogenous cannabinoids (endocannabinoids), which are unconventional neurotransmitters. They are unconventional because (1) they are not released by exocytosis and (2) they have a retrograde impact on presynaptic neurons. Both endocannabinoids and exogenously administered cannabinoids are responsible for psychomotor relaxation by altering the neurodynamics of the basal ganglia and cerebellum; they also mitigate and inhibit pain by altering the neurodynamics of the neocortex, hypothalamus, hippocampus, caudate putamen,[19] and substantia nigra in the midbrain. When taken to excess by susceptible channels, exogenously administered cannabinoids open neural gateways to increased carnal lusts and demonically-engendered hallucinations. Unless one is taking THC as an analgesic, abstinence is advised.

------

[19]   Together, the caudate and putamen nuclei of the basal ganglia are known as the *caudate putamen.*

# Stimulants

In general, stimulants are responsible for increased and sustained activity of the central nervous system. They include cocaine and its derivatives, various drugs in the category of amphetamines, and caffeine. These stimulants primarily have their impact on neural activity by increasing the availability of dopamine at the synaptic level. (To a lesser extent, these stimulants increase the availability of norepinephrine and serotonin as well.) They increase and sustain neurotransmission (1) by inhibiting the uptake of dopamine (a) at presynaptic terminals and (b) by adjacent support cells and (2) by inhibiting the primary enzymes that catabolize (degrade) dopamine. For these two reasons, stimulants are responsible for an increased, sustained availability of dopamine within the brain.

Because cocaine, amphetamines, and caffeine increase the availability of dopamine at synapses in the brain, depending on the level of stimulant intoxication, these stimulants are responsible for increased: wakefulness, attention, arousal, euphoria, anxiety, panic, temporary psychosis, grandiosity, anger, aggression, confusion, and repetitive compulsive behaviors. It should be emphasized that the euphoria included here is drug-induced and carnal and, therefore, is not to be confused with the joy induced by the Creator-God's Holy Spirit.

Although nicotine is a stimulant, it operates through different receptors than cocaine, amphetamines, and caffeine. It operates through nicotinic acetylcholine receptors (nAChR). Regardless, addiction to any stimulant lowers the ability of the prefrontal cortex to execute decisions that override compulsions habituated especially in the insular cortex.

......

Prayer and gratitude as well as contentment are prerequisite for dynamic, healthy personal psychism. All drug addiction is responsible for the discontentment that impairs and eventually erases healthy psychic abilities. The Apostle Paul testified that he had learned to be content no matter the circumstance *(Philippians 4:12 KJV)*. If we are to tap into and exercise our natural psychic gifts and talents, we must learn to be content through unceasing prayer and gratitude. If we become addicted to drugs, we will suffer psychologically, physically, and psychically from confusion, depression, anxiety, paranoia, diminished cognitive abilities, and dissociative disorders — all of which invite demonic forces to overtake and eventually control us.

# Involuntary Physiologic Responses to Horribly-Stressful Incidents, Accidents, and Emergencies

## Introduction

1. *Trusting in the God of the Holy Bible with certitude* does not prevent all horribly-stressful incidents, accidents, or emergencies with their unexpected or unintended physiologic outcomes.

2. *Believing in the Lord Jesus Christ as personal Savior* does not prevent all horribly-stressful incidents, accidents, or emergencies with their unexpected or unintended physiologic outcomes.

3. *Laboriously memorizing the entire Bible and claiming victory through the restatement of its truths* does not prevent all horribly-stressful incidents, accidents, or emergencies with their unexpected or unintended physiologic outcomes.

4. *Experiencing signs and wonders from the one true Creator-God* does not prevent all horribly-stressful incidents, accidents, or emergencies with their unexpected or unintended physiologic outcomes.

5. *Rigorously practicing positive thinking and optimism daily* does not prevent all horribly-stressful incidents, accidents, or emergencies with their unexpected or unintended physiologic outcomes.

6. *Successfully learning biofeedback techniques and yogic traditions* does not prevent all horribly-stressful incidents, accidents, or emergencies with their unexpected or unintended physiologic outcomes.

7. *Prepping for an apocalyptic future by purchasing firearms and building a family bunker with enough food and medicine for seven*

*years* does not prevent all horribly-stressful incidents, accidents, or emergencies with their unexpected or unintended physiologic outcomes.

8. *Wisely investing in the stock market and annuity programs* does not prevent all horribly-stressful incidents, accidents, or emergencies with their unexpected or unintended physiologic outcomes.

9. *Physically exercising daily and eating sensibly* does not prevent all horribly-stressful incidents, accidents, or emergencies with their unexpected or unintended physiologic outcomes.

10. *Expecting the unexpected* does not prevent all horribly-stressful incidents, accidents, or emergencies with their unexpected or unintended physiologic outcomes.

11. *Accurately predicting the future for yourself and others* does not prevent all horribly-stressful incidents, accidents, or emergencies with their unexpected or unintended physiologic outcomes.

12. *Living your life in altruistic benevolence with a pleasant personality* does not prevent all horribly-stressful incidents, accidents, or emergencies with their unexpected or unintended physiologic outcomes.

13. *Fully understanding your purpose in life* does not prevent all horribly-stressful incidents, accidents, or emergencies with their unexpected or unintended physiologic outcomes.

14. *Receiving the healthiest nurture possible, receiving superior moral training, and receiving superior cognitive, emotional, physical, spiritual, and psychic skills* do not prevent all horribly-stressful incidents, accidents, or emergencies with their unexpected or unintended physiologic outcomes.

15. *Being financially secure within a climate-controlled home and having healthy food to eat* does not prevent all horribly-stressful incidents, accidents, or emergencies with their unexpected or unintended physiologic outcomes.

16. *Praying without ceasing* does not prevent all horribly-stressful incidents, accidents, or emergencies with their unexpected or unintended physiologic outcomes.

17. *Accurately claiming your immortality* does not prevent all horribly-stressful incidents, accidents, or emergencies with their unexpected or unintended physiologic outcomes.

18. *Being called and chosen by the Creator-God* does not prevent all horribly-stressful incidents, accidents, or emergencies with their unexpected or unintended physiologic outcomes.

19. *Believing that there is a Creator-God and that He rewards those who diligently seek Him* does not prevent all horribly-stressful incidents, accidents, or emergencies with their unexpected or unintended physiologic outcomes.

20. *Making exhaustive lists about the uncertainties of human life* does not prevent all horribly-stressful incidents, accidents, or emergencies with their unexpected or unintended physiologic outcomes.


Even if all of the previous twenty circumstances given in italics are a reality for you today:

1. You can still die from chronic kidney failure.

2. You can still take a bullet to your temple.

3. You can still have one of your hands or feet chopped off.

4. You can still be a victim of adultery and family drug abuse.

5. You can still be raped and murdered.

6. You can still be a victim of a mall shooting or wilding attack.

7. You can still watch your child, spouse, or parent die.

8. You can still be imprisoned with people who are evil, uncultured, and grossly stupid with a medieval mindset.

9. You can still fall down a flight of stairs and injure yourself critically.


The one truth that puts all of the twenty circumstances in proper perspective is that, if we believe the Creator-God exists, we will seek to please Him and be rewarded spiritually with eternal life and eternal blessings *(Hebrews 11:6 KJV)*. The Creator-God Himself is our life, our reward, and our blessing regardless of whatever else we have or do not have and regardless of whatever else we receive or do not receive.

For as long as human beings exist, there will be horribly-stressful incidents, accidents, and emergencies on Earth. Horribly-stressful incidents, accidents, and emergencies will even exist throughout *the Millennium* that Christ Jesus reigns on Earth. Just because he will be reigning on Earth throughout *the Millennium* does not mean that we will be able to float down a flight of stairs. Because we will still need to walk down a flight of stairs, some of us will fall down those stairs. Accidents and emergencies will continue to happen during *the Millennium*. Aortic aneurysms will burst. Bones will be broken. Children will injure themselves on playgrounds. Heimlich maneuvers will still be performed. And mechanical parts on physical conveyances will wear down and break while we are traveling in them.

In other words, although *the Millennium* will be a time of unparalleled and unprecedented peace, kindness to one another, good health, prosperity, devotion to the Savior, and cognitive and emotional inspiration through the outpouring of the Creator-God's Holy Spirit, horribly-stressful incidents, accidents, and emergencies will still occur. This section is written to help its readers understand that it will still be necessary for them to prepare for horribly-stressful incidents, accidents and emergencies during *the Millennium* through medical and psychological education, risk management, and the establishment of (1) rules for safety and (2) policies and procedures for responding to unusual events. This section is intended to confirm that flesh and the carnal mind that directs it will still exercise involuntary physiologic control over human beings during *the Millennium*.

It is metaphysically true that *there are no accidents in God,* but it is patently false that horribly-stressful incidents, accidents, and emergencies — and involuntary physiologic responses to them — will not exist on Earth during *the Millennium*.


## Taxes

Taxes (pronounced *taks'-eez*) are involuntary physiologic responses to external stimuli by animals. (Tropisms are involuntary physiologic responses to external stimuli by plants.) Examples of taxes include barotaxes, chemotaxes, hydrotaxes, phototaxes, thermotaxes, and electromagnetotaxes.[20] A taxis (singular of *taxes*) is considered: (1) a *positive* taxis if an organism moves or reorients itself *toward* the environmental stimulus or (2) a *negative* taxis if an organism moves or

---

[20] The word *electromagnetotaxes* has been coined by the author of *The Biology of Psychism from a Christian Perspective* to represent the orientation or reorientation of an organism's body, body part, cell, or cellular structure to an electromagnetic force field that has its origin in general and/or specific psychism (i.e., in universal and/or individual consciousness).

reorients itself *away from* the environmental stimulus. Responses to taxes are considered innate behaviors because they are fixed and unchanging for a species. *Examples* of taxes for the human body include most nonspecific defense mechanisms as well as some specific defense mechanisms related to immunity.

Other innate behaviors for the human body include physiologically-induced and physiologically-mediated responses such as: (1) involuntary, uncontrolled, and unlearned reflexes (i.e., autonomic responses); (2) instincts; (3) hyperarousal; (4) clitoral and penile engorgement with blood; and (5) libido-related *presenting* and *mounting*. (*Presenting and mounting* are obvious in most primates other than human beings. These and other innate sexual behaviors will be covered in the following section entitled *Sex Steroid Hindrances to Personal Psychism.*)

The subsections entitled *Taxes* and *The Autonomic Nervous System* are presented here to help readers understand specific ways in which human beings will continue to be controlled by their own flesh and the carnal mind that directs it even during *the Millennium.*

## The Autonomic Nervous System

The ulterior motives of flesh and the carnal mind that directs it are in operation for as long as we remain in corporeality as human beings. The autonomic nervous system and the tissue and organ functions it controls (i.e., effectors or targets) constitute one major way in which we have no conscious control over certain physiologic activities. Simply stated, autonomic nerves are not under conscious control.

Although some spiritually-minded individuals might argue that we can control involuntary responses and reactions by learning to utilize biofeedback mechanisms, yogic traditions, positive thinking, optimism, and declaring biblical truths, all of that so-called control goes out the window during horribly-stressful incidents, accidents, and emergencies that trigger spontaneous responses mediated and modulated by one's autonomic nervous system. Indeed, the activities of the autonomic nervous system can change at a moment's notice from excitation to inhibition or from inhibition to excitation depending on rapid variances in the body's internal and external environments. *For example,* that is why human beings lose control of various sphincter muscles associated with urination and defecation when they experience certain forms of fear as they are confronted by predators or find themselves in horribly-stressful situations. Such loss of control has nothing to do with their individual spiritual maturity or personal evolution.

The endocrine system is the glandular system responsible for producing hormones. Hormones are secreted directly into the bloodstream for their distribution to target tissues and organs. Together, the autonomic nervous system and the endocrine system regulate and coordinate various innate and uncontrollable activities of the human body. In many instances, the autonomic nervous system and endocrine system overlap in regulating and coordinating physiologic processes. *For example,* some substances are produced that function as both hormones and neurotransmitters. Such substances are often referred to as "neurohormones." In general, neurohormones belong either to the category of *biogenic amines* or the category of *neuropeptides*. Examples of prominent biogenic amines that function as neurohormones include the catecholamines (1) epinephrine (adrenalin) and (2) norepinephrine (noradrenaline). Both epinephrine (E) and norepinephrine (NE) are synthesized in the adrenal medulla; norepinephrine is also synthesized in: (1) the *locus coeruleus* of the pons in the brainstem (described in an earlier section and shown in Figure Three) and (2) the sympathetic nervous system (described in paragraphs that follow). Epinephrine and norepinephrine are examples of substances that will continue during *the Millennium* to contribute to physiologically-induced and physiologically-mediated inner conflicts that are uncontrollably innate to human behavior.

Originally, the autonomic nervous system was called *autonomic* because it was thought to operate independently of the central nervous system. Of course, that supposition is not true because its activities are regulated by the hypothalamus and medulla oblongata with inputs from the cerebrum and limbic system, but the autonomic nervous system *is* responsible for unconscious, involuntary, and automatic reflexive control of (1) cardiac muscle, (2) smooth muscle in the walls of arteries, respiratory passages, and the gastrointestinal tract, and (3) various glands.

Following are important generalities about the autonomic nervous system:

(1) The autonomic nervous system has both a sympathetic division and a parasympathetic division.

(2) In human beings, the sympathetic division is also known as the thoracolumbar division because its motor nerves exit from the spinal cord at the levels of the thoracic and lumbar vertebrae.

(3) In human beings, the parasympathetic division is also known as the craniosacral division because its motor nerves exit the central nervous system either through various cranial nerves (III, VII, IX, and X) or from the spinal cord at the level of the sacral vertebrae.

(4) Most tissues and organs that are innervated by the autonomic nervous system receive motor nerves from both its parasympathetic and sympathetic divisions. In other words, they receive *dual innervation* from the two major divisions of the autonomic nervous system.

(5) For those tissues and organs that have *dual innervation,* if the effects from one motor division are excitatory, then the effects from the other motor division are inhibitory.

(6) The sympathetic division contributes to "fight-or-flight" responses and the parasympathetic division contributes to "rest-and-digest" responses. "Fight-or-flight" responses increase the body's basal metabolic rate by utilizing the body's stored energy *(for example,* through glycogenolysis and lipolysis), and "rest-and-digest" responses decrease the body's basal metabolic rate by conserving, storing, and replenishing the body's supplies of energy *(for example,* through glycogenesis and lipogenesis).

(7) The motor neurons of the autonomic nervous system release either the neurotransmitter acetylcholine (ACh) or the neurotransmitter norepinephrine (NE) at their junctions (i.e., axon terminals) with effector tissues and organs.


The sympathetic division of the autonomic nervous system enables the body to respond to stressful incidents, accidents, and emergencies. During a stressful incident, accident, or emergency — or even the threat of one — the sympathetic division overrides the parasympathetic division by increasing: (1) cardiac rate, (2) strength of cardiac muscle contractions, (3) blood pressure, (4) dilation of blood vessels feeding skeletal muscles and various glands (vasodilation), (5) rate and depth of breathing, (6) dilation of respiratory passages (bronchodilation), (7) blood glucose levels, and (8) production and secretion of epinephrine and norepinephrine by the adrenal medulla.

(1) Although the adrenal medulla is found inside of the adrenal cortex, and (2) although some cortical cells are found within the medulla, and (3) although cortisol produced by specialized cortical cells induces the conversion of epinephrine from norepinephrine in cells of the medulla

(see Figure Eight for its biosynthesis pathway), the adrenal medulla is essentially a different organ from the adrenal cortex due to differences in microscopic anatomy (histology) as well as embryologic origin.

The adrenal medulla originates from embryonic neural tissue and is a sympathetic ganglion whose nerve cell bodies have no axons and secrete their neurotransmitters/neurohormones/hormones directly into the bloodstream. (A *ganglion* is a cluster of nerve cell bodies outside the central nervous system. A *nucleus* is a cluster of nerve cell bodies inside the central nervous system.) When sympathetic motor neurons of the spinal cord excite the nerve cell bodies in the medulla, increased levels of norepinephrine and epinephrine are produced and secreted by exocytosis into the bloodstream. Both norepinephrine (15-20% of the adrenal medullary output of catecholamines) and epinephrine (80-85% of the adrenal medullary output of catecholamines) intensify and prolong "fight-or-flight" effects from the sympathetic division of the autonomic nervous system. Because its increased levels also contribute to nervousness and feelings of doom, epinephrine and its "fight-or-flight" effects repress and suppress receiving extrasensory sensations in all sensitives and susceptible channels, even the most gifted. (The only exceptions occur when the Creator-God's Holy Spirit directly intervenes or intercedes on our behalf.)

During *the Millennium*, human beings must think spiritually and strategically — that is, prayerfully and metaphysically — if they are to have victory over their animal instincts and biologically-driven predispositions. Following are two examples of flesh and blood conflicts over which human beings can have victory during *the Millennium* through the Creator-God's absolute truth:

First, as already noted, epinephrine is responsible for physiologic responses to stress caused by real as well as perceived threats from environmental stimuli. Produced in response to such threats, epinephrine enables human beings to have enough energy, oxygen, and blood flow: (1) to stay and defend themselves or (2) to turn and flee. That is why epinephrine is partly responsible for the "fight-or-flight" response. However, spiritually-minded people know that there is a third option other than fleeing or fighting: We can remain exactly where we are despite the involuntary physiologic effects we are experiencing — not to stay and fight but to love and forgive and trust in the Creator-God. In other words, we *can muster the necessary courage to* transcend and override natural responses to our individual physiology and biochemistry. This broadens possible responses from just "fight-or-flight" to "fight-or-flight-or-freeze." Human beings can have the presence of mind in Christ Jesus to stand by faith (i.e., *freeze)* without yielding to their fears and epinephrine's physiologic imperatives for their physical actions and reactions. Here, it is not that we are pretending that we are not experiencing physiologic imperatives; rather, we are overriding them even as we are experiencing them. This is part of real victory in Christ Jesus.

Second, sometimes the combined effects of epinephrine and the brain's enkephalins, endorphins, and dynorphins (i.e., the brain's so-called *natural opioids* discussed in the previous section) trigger an addictive pleasurable "rush" from extreme sports, daredevil activities, and other forms of risk-taking like gambling or participating in illicit or immoral activities. However, through Christ Jesus, spiritually-minded individuals can transcend and override their desires to experience this rush: (1) by refusing in Christ Jesus to put themselves in potentially harmful, dangerous, or unhealthy situations that are addictive in nature, tempting, and unwise; and (2) by praying to the Creator-God to not be led into temptation. Through Christ Jesus, we can even fight memories from our past that have been indelibly encoded in our brains through various combinations of neuro-transmitters, neurohormones, and hormones.

In summary, neurotransmitters, neurohormones, and hormones often make human beings victims of their own animal instincts, biological predispositions, and indelible painful or addiction-related memories. The only way that human beings can become victors over their own physiology is for them to understand who they are as animals at the same time that they understand who they are supposed to be as spiritual beings in Christ Jesus. Refocusing our attention away from biological imperatives and thoughts associated with addictive behaviors to absolute spiritual truth by meditating on the Creator-God's written Word and by praying to Him is requisite during *the Millennium* if we are to overcome temptations and physiologic imperatives from our own flesh and the carnal mind that directs it. Physical inaction does not preclude spiritual action. Indeed, physical inaction often requires spiritual action.

# Sex Steroid Hindrances to Personal Psychism

Sex steroid hormones — including progesterone as well as various estrogens and androgens (*estrogens* and *androgens* are categories of sex steroids) — are not considered neurotransmitters or neurohormones. However, sex steroid hormones may be thought of as neuromodulators because of their major feedback and regulatory impacts on brain physiology that influence mood, affect (i.e., observable manifestations of emotion), arousal, satiety, pleasure, anxiety, depression, rage, aggression, libido (sex drive), and specific behaviors related to gender and sexual affinity (i.e., identification, attraction, and orientation). Sex steroid hormones are included in *The Biology of Psychism from a Christian Perspective* because they are additional examples of endogenous substances that will continue during *the Millennium* to contribute to physiologically-induced and physiologically-mediated inner conflicts that are innate to human behavior.

The actions of sex steroid hormones, along with those of epinephrine and norepinephrine, also help students of the Holy Bible to understand that human beings have always wrestled with their own flesh and blood (i.e., their own physiologically-induced and physiologically-mediated inner conflicts) in addition to whatever spiritual enemies with which they have also wrestled.

Although individual human females raised in violent families, crime-ridden environments, and territories with civil wars or prolonged social unrest can themselves become violent, physically aggressive, predatory, and barbaric (brutal) in their actions, the preponderance of evidence points to human males as the primary source of murders, rapes, physically-violent crimes, and wars throughout the Earth.

One of the reasons for the inequality of males and females relative to murders, rapes, crimes, and wars is provided by higher concentrations of circulating dihydrotestosterone (dihydroxytestosterone) in the blood plasma of males. (1) Dihydrotestosterone (DHT) is the most active of all endogenous androgens — six times more active than testosterone (the principal androgen and immediate precursor to dihydrotestosterone), thirty times more active than androstenedione, and sixty times more active than dehydroepiandrosterone (DHEA) and dehydroepiandrosterone sulfate (DHEAS). (2) Although measurable amounts of the three androgens androstenedione, dehydroepiandrosterone sulfate, and testosterone are found in the circulating blood plasma of human females, there is only a negligible amount of dihydrotestosterone present in their blood plasma. (3) Measurable levels of circulating androgens in reproductive age females are primarily produced and secreted by the innermost layer of the adrenal cortex, the ovaries,[21] and adipocytes (fat cells); and most dihydrotestosterone in reproductive age females is produced in their skin from circulating precursors. (4) In reproductive age human females, the adrenal cortices are responsible for the majority of circulating dehydroepiandrosterone sulfate, and the ovaries are responsible for the majority of circulating testosterone. After menopause, most androgens continue to be produced by the adrenal cortices although the ovaries may continue to produce androgens for a limited time.

In both males and females, androgens contribute to libido, sexual fantasies, sexual arousal, erections (penile as well as clitoral), sexual addictions, and mating behaviors like *presenting* and *mounting*.

---

[21] In human females of reproductive age, ovaries primarily use these androgens: (1) androstenedione and (2) testosterone as precursors for these estrogens: (1) estrone and (2) estradiol.

Female dogs that have had a bilateral oophorectomy (both ovaries removed) will sometimes mount the extended legs of their owners' houseguests because such mating behavior is induced by circulating androgens from hyperactive adrenal cortices. Although *presenting* and *mounting* are less obvious mating behaviors in human beings than in other mammals, subtle exaggerations of the lumbar curvature and reflexive pelvic thrusts occur in both human females and males during sexual arousal as well as intercourse.

Generally, libido and sexual self-discipline in human males are more problematic than libido and sexual self-discipline in human females because of the high levels of circulating dihydrotestosterone in males. This is further compounded by sociocultural factors that permit — and even encourage — sexual promiscuity, polyamory, aggression, and risk-taking in males at the same time that they encourage sexual abstinence, monogamy, and submissiveness — as well as discourage sexual fantasies, sexual arousal, and sexuality — in females.

Dihydrotestosterone (DHT) is more potent than its immediate precursor, testosterone, because DHT binds with greater affinity to androgen receptors in target cells (all endogenous androgens bind to the same kind of androgen receptor in target cells). Unlike the receptors of neurotransmitters, which reside in the plasma membranes of nerve cells, androgen receptors reside in the cytoplasm of target cells and translocate to the cellular nucleus after androgens attach to them (provided, of course, that a few additional factors are functioning normally).

Because of the effects of circulating dihydrotestosterone on developing brain architecture and diurnal rhythms in brain physiology (especially in the limbic system and closely related cerebral regions and areas), personal psychism is negatively impacted by dihydrotestosterone (as well as its synthetic, exogenous analogs). For this reason: (1) *as a group,* human females of all ages are more spiritually intuitive and sensitive or susceptible to psychic impressions than human males; (2) *as a group,* prepubescent males are more spiritually intuitive and sensitive or susceptible to psychic impressions than pubescent or postpubescent males;[22] (3) *as a group,* males at any age with hypogonadotropism,[23] hypogonadism, and/or gonadal (testicular) failure are more spiritually intuitive and sensitive or susceptible to psychic impressions than males with average or above average levels of circulating dihydrotestosterone. (This does not mean that there are no exceptions to these three generalizations.)

The previous paragraph is the most important paragraph in this titled section because its three generalizations help to explain: (1) differences in psychic abilities based on levels of circulating dihydrotestosterone; and (2) the intense hatred that Satan has for (a) females; (b) homosexual males (depending on their levels of

---

[22] Credible research using functional imaging techniques has shown that there are similarities between heterosexual women and homosexual men regarding the activation of the anterior hypothalamus by androgens. The same research has shown that there are similarities between homosexual women and heterosexual men regarding the activation of the anterior hypothalamus by estrogens.

[23] *Gonadotropins* are hormones produced and secreted by the anterior pituitary gland (adenohypophysis) that stimulate the gonads (testes and ovaries) to produce their spermatozoa or ova as well as sex steroid hormones. The release of *gonadotropins* is stimulated by specific *releasing hormones* (once referred to as *releasing factors)* produced by the hypothalamus.

circulating dihydrotestosterone); and (c) transgender(ed) males[24] (depending on their levels and kinds of hormone therapies).

Make no mistake, Satan hates all human beings, but he especially hates human females because, *as a group,* they are less prone to physical violence, aggression, predation, sexual addiction, and brutality (barbarism). Satan also hates human females because, *as a group,* they are more intuitive, psychic, and nurturing at the same time that they are less prone to control by demonic forces. To be sure, Satan also hates human females because his enemy and conqueror, Christ Jesus, was born of a woman, as prophesied in Genesis 3:15:

> "And I [the Lord God Almighty] will put enmity [hostility] between you [Satan] and the woman, and between your offspring and her offspring; her offspring [specifically, Christ

---

[24] In the early 21st century, *transgender* and *transgendered* are words whose meanings are still in flux and currently used as umbrella terms applied to a variety of individuals, behaviors, and groups involving tendencies to vary from traditional and customary gender roles or cultural norms. Because some people prefer the use of the word *transgender* and others prefer the use of the word *transgendered,* the present author uses the following form in this book: *transgender(ed).*

For the sake of clarity, *transgender(ed)* refers to someone whose sense of personal gender does not correspond with their birth sex. *Transgender(ed) male (trans male)* refers to someone who self-identifies as male although born biologically as female. In contrast, *intersexual* refers to someone who has been born with physical sexual ambiguity in one or more of the following categories: genetic, chromosomal, biochemical, histological, internal anatomic, and/or external anatomic.

Jesus] shall bruise your head, and you shall bruise his heel."

This also helps to explain why Satan's preferred tool for inducing fear and creating terror throughout the world is the human male. *As a group,* human males are more easily controlled by demonic ideations related to rage, aggression, territorialism, predation, brutalism, entitled sexual promiscuity, and sexual addiction. However, in stark contrast, it should also be remembered that courage and bravery in defending the weak, submissive, and vulnerable are also exemplified by human males with high levels of dihydrotestosterone.

The effects of dihydrotestosterone on psychic abilities are insidious. They are especially insidious when they are combined with a lack of healthy nurture, including discipline during childhood and active sexual addictions post-puberty. Altogether, (1) dihydrotestosterone, (2) an emotionally-impoverished childhood with few behavioral guidelines, (3) active sexual addiction, and (4) indelible personal memories of sexual immorality can (a) create challenges that are almost insurmountable for some human males to overcome as well as (b) open doors in them for demonic influences and even demonic possession. (It is important to remember that indelible personal memories do not die until the flesh that owns them dies.)

*Question: What confirms that Satan finds human females more loathsome than human males?*

It is no accident that, before *the Millennium,* the final, end-time Antichrist — and the one-world government he promulgates — will continue to endorse the subjugation of women. The following prophetic verse in the Book of Daniel confirms this:

Neither shall the Antichrist regard the God of his fathers nor the desires[25] of women, nor shall he regard any god: for he shall magnify himself above all.

*Daniel 11:37 KJV Paraphrase*


To date, Islam and its Qur'an, Hadith, and Sharia constitute the most cleverly organized and greatest systematic ideology that Satan has ever orchestrated for his followers. This ideology will serve as the basis for transnational government during *the Tribulation*. Through the Qur'an, Hadith, and Sharia, Islam seeks to control women by keeping them prisoners in their own homes, beating them, raping them, enslaving them, claiming their inferiority to males, stoning them, berating them, murdering them in honor-killings, forcing female pre-teens to have sexual intercourse, amputating their clitorides (plural for *clitoris*) in female genital mutilation (FGM), requiring them to obey dress codes that are medieval, and disfiguring them by throwing acid at them or cutting off their lips, noses, or ears in order to punish, shame, and silence them. In contrast, Islam permits human males absolute rights above females in all matters. There is a permanent, inherent inequality of men and women in Islam. Males are considered forever superior to females; females are considered forever inferior to males. All of this exists because Satan finds females more loathsome than males, and he knows that the egos of most men are more fragile and need to be

---

[25] *Desires* is used in its plural form in the Hebrew Masoretic Text of the Jewish Bible. When the Hebrew word is translated into English in the King James Version of the Holy Bible as *desire* (i.e., in its singular form), it is being used as a collective noun that refers to wishes, wants, approbations, and aspirations.

pandered to in order for them to be more easily controlled by him.[26]

*Question: Why does Satan find human females more loathsome than human males?*

Satan hates women more than he hates men because he is unable to control human females as easily as he can control human males. Satan controls men by fanning the flames of: (1) their sexual passion and libido; (2) their predatory, aggressive, and violent tendencies; and (3) the need of their fragile egos to feel superior as well as exercise territorial dominance over others. *As a general rule,* women do not start wars or battles; they do not rape and pillage; and they are more sensitive to the needs of others. *As a group,* human females are more emotional, nurturing, and intuitive than human males. Although adult women produce androgens in their ovaries and adrenal cortices, they produce only a negligible amount of circulating dihydrotestosterone. For all of these reasons, *as a group,* human females are less brutish and more insightful — and they possess greater psychic abilities than human males. For these reasons, human females constitute a major threat to Satan.

Satan hates women more than men because, if any group of people is going to identify his motives, actions, and involvement in evil activities, women will. Human females possess the insights necessary to identify Satan as the primal source of disharmony and hatred. For these reasons, Satan wants to keep human females under lock and key. Satan knows that, *as a group,* women are more intelligent in some

---

[26] For additional insights on the insidious nature of Islam and its role in end-time events, read *Revelation of Antichrist* by Rev. Joseph Adam Pearson, Ph.D., Christ Evangelical Bible Institute, Copyright 2021. ISBN 978-0996222488.

forms, domains, and modalities than men — which is not to say that women make better governmental leaders than men. *For example,* in efforts to do away with patriarchal hegemony and nationalism, some male and female feminist-minded politicians in the early 21st century: (1) have helped to create gender confusion in the raising of *theybies* rather than *male and female babies* (in principle if not in terminology); and (2) have ignorantly given their countries over to migrants who will never support democracy let alone their ill-conceived notions of multiculturalism. They are short-sighted because they have embraced popular philosophies and abandoned Christ Jesus as well as solid biblical teaching and understanding.

During *the Millennium,* human beings must think holistically, strategically, and spiritually — that is, prayerfully, biblically, metaphysically, and psychically — if they are to have victory over their own animal instincts and biologically-driven predispositions.

# Chapter Three:

# Psychism through the Lens of the Holy Bible

Chapter Three has been written in response to the unfortunate demonization of anything and everything related to psychism by some students and teachers of the Holy Bible. This chapter is intended to shed enough light on psychism so that students and teachers of the Bible might: (1) learn not to fear psychism or misinterpret the Bible based on their fears of it as well as (2) learn to understand and embrace everything that the Creator-God has in store for humankind.

# The Isaiah Touch

In the Holy Bible, the following was recorded by the Prophet Isaiah:

In the year that the King of Judah, Uzziah, died, I saw the Lord God Almighty sitting upon a throne, high and lifted up, and His train of glory filled the temple. Above His throne stood six seraphs: each one had six wings. With two wings, each covered his face, and with two wings each covered his feet, and with two wings each flew. And one cried to another, and said: "Holy, Holy, Holy is the Lord of Hosts: the whole Earth is full of His glory." And the posts of the door moved at the sound of the one who cried, and the whole house was filled with smoke.

Then I said: "Woe is me! I am undone because I am a man of unclean lips who dwells in the midst of a people of unclean lips. I am undone because I have seen the King, the Lord of Hosts."

Then, one of the seraphs flew to me, having a live coal in his hand that he had taken with tongs from the altar: And he laid the live coal upon my mouth, and said: "Behold, this has touched your lips, and your iniquity is taken away, and your sins are purged."

I also heard the voice of the Lord, saying: "Whom shall I send? Who will go for us?" Then I said: "Here I am. Send me." And He said: "Go, and tell this people 'You indeed hear, but you do not understand; and you indeed see, but you do not perceive.' Make the heart of this people fat [arrogant and self-entitled], and make their ears heavy, and shut their eyes so that they do not perceive with their eyes or understand with their ears and in their hearts — in order that they not repent and receive salvation."

Then, I said: "Lord, how long?" And He answered: "Until the cities are wasted without inhabitant and the houses without man, and the land is utterly desolate. Until the Lord has scattered people far away and there is a great forsaking throughout the land. However, yet will there remain one tenth of the people, and the tenth will return and be eaten as a teil tree and an oak tree, whose substance is in them as they cast their leaves. (Their holy seed is their true substance.)"

*Isaiah 6:1-13 KJV Paraphrase*

Relative to psychism, the following metaphysical inferences can be drawn concerning iniquity and sin: (1) *iniquity* is one's turning away from the Creator-God by refusing to do His Will; (2) sin is action based on that turning; (3) corporeality is the visible sign of iniquity; (4) no one in corporeality can see the Creator-God face-to-face without annihilation of one's physical being (not annihilation of one's soul); (5) iniquity is only expunged and sins are only purged (remitted or paid for) by the shed blood of Christ Jesus and the personal acceptance of that blood as the sole sacrifice acceptable to the Creator-God in atonement for our iniquity and sins; (6) spiritual understanding is psychic hearing (hearing psychically); (7) spiritual perception is psychic seeing (seeing psychically or psychic sight); (8) the salvation or redemption of one's soul is personal repentance raised exponentially to the power of eternity by the blood of Christ Jesus shed for all errant souls; and (8) the Lord God Almighty has reserved a tithe of the people of Israel (ten per cent of the Jewish people) as a tribute to Himself.

# On Psychic Reasoning

When Prophet Isaiah was in the Spirit, he was woebegone because he stood before the Lord God Almighty. Isaiah knew that he was "a man of unclean lips who dwelt in the midst of a people of unclean lips." In other words, Isaiah was aware of his unholy, fleshly nature; he was intimately aware of his own iniquity. As a student of Torah, perhaps he remembered that the Lord had said to Moses: "You cannot see My face (i.e., the fullness of My presence) because no human being shall see its fullness and live" *(Deuteronomy 33:20 KJV Paraphrase).*

Isaiah knew that only purified and purged souls can see the Creator-God's Fiery Presence. Purified from what? Iniquity. Purged of what? Sin. It must have been terrifying for Isaiah, knowing that he was seeing the holiness of the Creator-God. Yet, despite his being in the Creator-God's Fiery Presence, Isaiah was not "undone" — which is to say, he was not annihilated. No, to the contrary, he was made fit for a purpose of the Creator-God: (1) First, Isaiah was cleansed of his unholy nature. A seraph had flown to him and touched his lips with a live coal from the altar of the living Creator-God. (2) Then, hearing and answering the Creator-God's call, Isaiah was commissioned to carry this divine judgment to his fellow human beings from the Lord: "You indeed hear, but you do not understand; and you indeed see, but you do not perceive." To be sure, this judgment is a prophecy fulfilled whenever entities shut themselves off from the Creator-God. However, unlike those about him, Isaiah had *the touch* — which is to say, because he had been touched by the Lord, he had been given the moral sensitivity and mental capacity to see and hear the things of Spirit. In short, Prophet Isaiah was capable of *psychic reasoning*.

What is *psychic reasoning?*

Generally speaking, *reasoning* is the process whereby human beings use ideas, facts, and truths to make conclusions. *For example,* human reasoning includes both inductive and deductive mental powers. In contrast, *psychic reasoning* includes perception and discernment — that is, the ability to see through and hear beyond the thoughts and things of this world to the thoughts and things of the world of Spirit.

Metaphysically speaking, *consciousness* is the state wherein souls are aware of the thoughts that pass through them and of the source for those thoughts. *Unconsciousness* is death — the state wherein souls are totally unaware of the spiritual warfare that is going on within them and around them. *Subconsciousness* is slumber — the state wherein souls are only slightly aware. And *supraconsciousness* is true wakefulness, reflection, and enlightenment — the state wherein souls experience the Creator-God and all that He is — and the state wherein souls are not only aware psychically of the thoughts that pass through them but also of the thoughts that pass through others. To be sure, *psychic reasoning* and individual *consciousness,* as well as *supraconsciousness,* are positively correlated. *Psychic reasoning* enables an individual to know the truth without having to depend on mere speculation, hypothesis, or opinion. *Psychic reasoning* permits individuals to know divine ideas, spiritual facts, and truths of being from within themselves.

People who daily focus on, consider, and inquire as to their divine nature are privy to information that disinterested and unconcerned people are not. The former eventually come to ascertain, discern, and determine what the Utmost is. Spiritual truth becomes resolved to them. And they are sure of the truth of what they see and hear because they know that they have yielded their eyes and ears to the Lord God

Almighty. They acknowledge that the Creator-God is the Sovereign not only of their souls but of the entire universe.

*Psychic reasoning* is a process of the heart and not the head. When the caul of darkness has been removed from off the heart, — when the heart has been circumcised of selfishness, — when the commandments of the Creator-God have been inscribed upon the fleshly tablets of the heart, and — when a soul seeks out ways for the Creator-God's love to be expressed through its heart, only then is an entity ready to apprehend divine ideas, spiritual facts, and truths of being. Until that time, an entity is either dead or asleep to the true purpose and real meaning of life.

How does one get *psychic reasoning?*

It begins with a softening of the heart, such softening occurring in mortals whenever they come to believe in the Creator-God as both Father and Son. In other words, the Isaiah touch requires mortals to become open to the world of Spirit before that world's metaphysical elements can be both seen and heard. Where does this touch begin? It begins and ends with our love for the Creator-God and our concern for others.

## The Seed of Concern

*Personal psychism* is the capacity to receive and interpret psychic impressions, thoughts, feelings, and ideas. *Personal psychism* is a quality that the Creator-God shares with those who are like Him — which is to say, who are made in His complete image and perfect likeness. In varying degrees, many in the earth plane of consciousness are psychic. But, whether their sensitivity is finely attuned to the thoughts, feelings, and ideas of the Creator-God, and relatively free from the static of a carnal mind, or coarsely focused and subject to the interference of that fleshly mind's noisome pestilence, depends on the objects of their concern. Thus, what happens to the spiritual gift of psychic sensitivity — this gift of the Creator-God's Holy Spirit — depends on the individual. Concern for others refines it. Concern for one's carnal self and human identity, however, inverts sensitivity to touchiness, defensiveness, and vulnerability.

If souls are to labor productively in this field of earth (i.e., corporeality), they need to: (1) have a fuller sense of what concern for others is as well as (2) grow spiritually and mature through cultivating that concern within themselves. To be sure, such growth can occur independently of the written or spoken word, but it cannot occur without the earnest pursuit of understanding that thoughts and ideas originate either from the mind of the Creator-God (an immortal and divine Mind) or from the mind that is opposite, opposing, contrary, and contradictory to it (the vampiric semi-consciousness of Satan's mortal mind), such mind no real mind at all.

Although most people in the earth plane of consciousness would claim that they are the originators of the thoughts and ideas that pass through them or the feelings they experience, they are, in fact, transponders (i.e., receivers and retrievers) of them. And which ones they receive and which ones they retrieve depend greatly on the objects of their concern and the degree to which they are concerned about them. Souls who feel a wide open concern for others through their love for them freely receive the thoughts, feelings, and ideas of the Creator-God. However, souls who feel a huge concern for the false image they have of themselves, or the image they would like others to have of them, close themselves off from those thoughts, feelings, and ideas, thereby opening themselves up to psychic attack from below. The dichotomy is just that sharp and distinct. Two different and separate worlds are present side-by-side: the perfect world of the

Creator-God and the nether-world of self-will. The two worlds represent two different states of mind. From which world we in the earth plane of consciousness (itself an in-between world) receive thoughts, feelings, and ideas depends on which world we are more open to through our concern.

In the truest metaphysical and highest spiritual sense, the heart of an entity is its concern. If an entity is mostly concerned with the false image it has of itself, then its heart can be described as *foolish, proud, hardened, stubborn,* or *uncircumcised.* If an entity is only concerned with the mortal, or dead, self it has in front of it, then its heart can be described as *evil* or as *having been turned to stone.* The heart of our dear Lord Jesus Christ can be referred to as *bleeding* because of his total concern for the well-being and salvation of others; also, it can be referred to as *sacred* because of the love of the Creator-God that tabernacles in it. Those in the earth plane of consciousness who strive to become *pure in heart (Matthew 5:8)* — that is, unconcerned with matters of self-will — receive the thoughts, feelings, and ideas of the Creator-God in proportion to their concern for the things of God. According to their degree of selflessness, hearts can be described as *melting, contrite, understanding,* or *soft.*

Although souls in dust travail to be delivered from their iniquity and sin *(souls in dust* is the present author's phrase for *human beings),* they should not be of *heavy* heart. Rather, their hearts should be *glad* that the substantive nature of the Creator-God will be revealed to them through hearts *broken* of self-will. (Remember, the consciousness of general psychism constitutes the one true and only real universal substance.) In the reality of the Creator-God, His children have one heart, *whole* and *circumcised* in its dedication to good. Thus, at the heart of the children of God is their concern for the Creator-God and for one another. When that concern is lost, children of God turn themselves into something that cannot exist in the reality of the

Creator-God. And they lose the integrity of their personal psychism as well.

Selfless love, the highest degree of concern that we can have for others, is indicated by humility, which is an expression of our gratitude for the opportunity we have to be returned to the Creator-God. Though it may sound abhorrent to those who employ only a corporeal sense of reality, humility should be an obsession to those who seek to please the Creator-God. Why? No one can do greater in the earth plane of consciousness than walk with an inner, quiet love of the Creator-God and outwardly express concern for others by serving as a channel for Him to meet the needs of others. No one on Earth can hope to achieve a higher status than putting others before himself or herself.

It is noteworthy to add that humility never draws attention to itself. If entities feel the need to inform others of their humility, then they have fallen to the cunningness of self-will. That one can be humble at the same time he or she is telling others of his or her own personal humility is a self-evident absurdity. However, the meekness of humility should never be confused with weakness, just as submission to the Creator-God's Will should never be confused with subjugation to evil. Though perfectly meek and completely submissive to the Father's Will, Christ Jesus never indulged evil. He openly rebuked it despite consequences to his human frame. Though humble, our Lord Jesus remained unafraid of evil throughout his sojourn here in flesh.

Most men and women who would say that they are spiritually-minded do not see eye-to-eye with one another because they really do not have the same concern for others that they have for themselves individually. If any of us are ever to be healed of divisiveness or reconcile any of our differences, we must see eye-to-eye on the weightier matter of concern for others. It is through this concern that souls are known in Heaven as children of God and members of the body of His Christ.

Just how important to psychic reasoning is concern for others? The heart is the observatory of the soul. The larger the heart, the bigger the space in which an entity dwells and the more of the Creator-God's perfect world the soul can see and hear. Remember, the Creator-God's heart is so large that it spans eternity. Let us, then, strive to be like Jesus Christ and love others as he loves us, that we might hear and see the Creator-God and help others to do the same. (Selflessly loving others does not mean that we indulge their parasitic natures.)

## Psychic Hearing

The author of *The Biology of Psychism from a Christian Perspective* makes a distinction between (1) psychic hearing (hearing psychically) and (2) far-hearing (clairaudience). (1) Psychic hearing (hearing psychically) is one's ability to understand metaphysical meanings embedded in spoken and written words. (2) Far-hearing (clairaudience) includes the inaudible hearing of: (a) specifics about possible, probable, or inevitable future events; (b) messages from entities who live in incorporeal states of being and transmit their thoughts and words telepathically; and (c) words of instruction and/or comfort spoken by the Creator-God's Holy Spirit. Because far-hearing is only heard inwardly, the present author also refers to it as *faux hearing* because it does not involve the outer ear, middle ear, or inner ear. (Here, the word *faux* is not meant to imply that messages from far-hearing are inherently false, deceptive, or fake.)

*Psychic hearing* is spiritual understanding. It is the capacity to comprehend the things of the Creator-God's Holy Spirit. It is the mental and metaphysical grasp of heavenly concepts. It includes the ability to interpret, or hear beyond, mere human words. Like *psychic seeing,* or *seeing psychically, psychic hearing* is representative of elevated personal consciousness that permits us to understand the mysteries of the Creator-God and the secrets of the human heart.

Jesus Christ often punctuated his parables with the statement: "Whoever has ears to hear, let that person hear" *(Matthew 11:15, 13:9, 13:43; Mark 4:9, 4:23, 7:16, 8:18; Luke 8:8, 14:35).* What did he mean? He simply meant: "Whoever has the capacity to understand, let that person understand."

*Psychic hearing* is a gift from the Creator-God — which gift always keeps on giving because it enables those who have it to understand more and more of the things of the Creator-God's Holy Spirit. What is the gift given in response to? It is given in response to a "broken and contrite heart" *(Psalm 51:6 KJV),* which is the only offering acceptable to our Creator-God, and the only offering that permits our individual wills to bend to His Will.

The word of the Lord God Almighty came to Prophet Ezekiel, saying: "Son of man (i.e., *human being*), you dwell in the middle of a rebellious house, the inhabitants of which have eyes to see yet see not and have ears to hear yet hear not because they are a rebellious people" *(Ezekiel 12:1-2 KJV Paraphrase).* Because rebelliousness is the same as lawlessness (i.e., going against the Will of the Creator-God), souls who transgress God's laws turn themselves away from Him and prevent themselves from hearing Him and His truth. They harden their hearts to the truth of His perfect world. But broken and contrite hearts open themselves up to that world, even though they are still in this mortal coil, so they can catch a glimpse of His truth here and there and, also, hear His still, small voice within their souls.

To hear and understand a little of the Creator-God's spiritual universe makes one long to be completely returned to it. That is why there is such an ache in the hearts of those who know where they presently are (i.e., in a fallen state of being) and where they would like to be (i.e., in a glorified state of being). They long to be restored to the state of consciousness they were in before the beginning of this world as the pure white, whole-souled, and holy beings they once were, shining forth as stars in the Creator-God's spiritual heavens. They long to return to the time when, and place where, they were clad in the Creator-God — when the Creator-God dwelt within them without measure and where they were in their one true and only real glory, *His* glory — the brightness of His Being.

*Psychic hearing* is different from listening. Listening is simply paying attention. Although attentiveness is necessary to understand a psychically-received word, listening alone will not allow people to *hear* (i.e., understand) what is being said. *For example,* many have listened to the good news that Heaven is just within their reach, but few have actually *heard* it. How do we know this to be true? When one understands such good news, one's actions reflect it. Today, few people reflect the Creator-God's truth.

Have you ever wondered why our Lord Jesus often used parables? First, parables are excellent teaching devices. Second, knowledge that is hidden from the worldly man or woman is conveyed to the spiritual self through parables. Third, although parables permit listeners to understand to the degree that they can *hear,* parables also present challenges for souls to exercise more of their sense of hearing (souls who accept that challenge always want to grasp just a little bit more of what is intended). And, fourth, the spiritual images intended in parables, once understood, impinge hard upon the consciousness of real hearers, leaving a lasting impression within their souls and minds. Thus, Christ Jesus taught the multitudes in parables so each person could hear according to his or her own capacity and, also, so each who could hear insightfully might be challenged to work toward an ever greater understanding, regardless of his or her current level of comprehension. When our Master said: "unto you that hear shall more be given" *(Mark 4:24 KJV Paraphrase)*, his intended meaning included "to those who understand shall be given the opportunity to understand even more."

Once, after having delivered a parable to a crowd, Christ Jesus was approached by his disciples and asked: "Why do you speak to them in parables?" *(Matthew 13:10 KJV)* The Messiah responded:

> "It is given to you to know the mysteries of the kingdom of heaven, but to them it is not given. Whoever possesses the capacity to understand shall be given abundantly more understanding, but whoever does not possess the capacity to understand shall have even that which he understands taken away. For this reason I speak to them in parables. Although they see with their eyes, they do not perceive; and although they hear with their ears, they do not understand. In them is fulfilled the prophecy given to Prophet Isaiah, which states: 'Although hearing, you shall hear but shall not understand; and, although seeing, you shall see but shall not perceive. For your heart is waxed gross, and your ears are dull of hearing, and you have closed your eyes; in case you should see with your eyes and hear with your ears and understand with your hearts and should be converted, and I should save you.' But blessed are your eyes (i.e., the eyes of his disciples) because they see, and blessed are your ears for they hear. Truly, I say to you that many prophets and righteous people have desired to see the things that you see but have not seen them and to hear the things that you hear but have not heard them."
>
> *Matthew 13:11-17 KJV Paraphrase*

In other words, failing to understand is often a self-appointed curse that prevents people from understanding the thoughts and things that belong to the Creator-God. Christ Jesus asked obdurate and obstinate people the following question and provided the answer as well: "Why do you not understand my speech? Because you cannot hear my word" *(John 8:43 KJV Paraphrase)*. He provided this further explanation: "The person who belongs to God hears God's words; therefore, you do not hear them because you are not of God" *(John 8:47 KJV)*.

One parable told by Jesus — the parable of the sower — divides hearers into classes. Following is a version of that parable compiled from elements of the slightly different versions found in Chapter Thirteen of Matthew, Chapter Four of Mark, and Chapter Eight of Luke:

> "A sower went out to sow his seed. And, as he sowed, some seed fell by the wayside and was trodden down and devoured by the birds of the air. Some of the seed fell on stony ground, where there was not much dirt; immediately, it sprang up but became quickly scorched by the sun and withered because it had no established roots. And some seed fell among thorny weeds, but the thorny weeds grew along with the seed and choked it, causing it to be fruitless. Yet other seed fell on good soil and grew and yielded fruit in different proportions. Whoever has ears to hear, let that person hear."

Here is the interpretation that Jesus gave for the parable of the sower (again, as a compilation from the same three Gospels):

> "Hear (i.e., understand) the parable of the sower: 'The sower sows the word of God. Those by the wayside are they who hear, but, after they have heard, Satan comes immediately and takes away the word that was sown in their hearts so they do not believe and, therefore, cannot be saved. And those that are sown on stony ground are those who hear the word and

receive it with a glad heart but have no root in themselves and, therefore, only endure for a short time (later, when affliction or persecution comes for the word of God's sake, they are immediately offended). And those that fell among thorny weeds are they, who, when they have heard, go forth and are choked with the pressures and pleasures of this life and, therefore, bring no fruit to perfection. However, the seed that fall on good soil are the individuals, who — with an honest and good heart — having heard the word, treasure it and bring forth fruit in varying proportions.'"

After having read the parable of the sower and its interpretation, three things should be obvious to those who hear psychically. First, something is necessary for us to receive and understand the spoken or written word of the Creator-God: an open heart. Second, something in addition to psychic hearing is necessary for us to keep that word within our hearts: a deepened faith, the root of which enables souls to hold on to their faith during the times they are tempted, tested, and tried. And, third, for souls to inherit the Kingdom of Heaven, they must be willing to patiently keep the word of the Creator-God — which is to say, daily perform His Will — so they might bring forth fruit. What is the word of the Creator-God? And what is His Will? That we love Him with all our heart, and all our soul, and all our mind, and that we love our neighbors as constituent parts of our one true and only real self *(Matthew 22:37-40)*. Such all-encompassing love is not only necessary if we are to psychically hear His word and do His Will, but also if we are to keep His commandments through both the best and worst of times.

Although Prophet Daniel was praying to the Lord God Almighty when he said: "hear me and do, refrain not" *(Daniel 9:19 KJV Paraphrase)*, those words can also be applied to the children of men *(children of men* is the biblical equivalent of *human beings)* concerning the inclination of their own ears and their own *refraining not.* Children of men should not only come to spiritual understanding but also not refrain from good works. In other words, if seeing is believing, then psychic hearing should include putting love into action. St. James stated it this way:

> Be doers of the word and not hearers only, deceiving yourselves. If anyone is a hearer of the word and not a doer, that person is like someone seeing his face in a mirror: The person sees but forgets what was seen when he is no longer in front of the mirror. Whoever looks into the perfect law of liberty, and continues in it, being not a forgetful hearer but a doer of the word, this person shall be blessed in his doing.
>
> *James 1:22-25 KJV Paraphrase*

Using another phrase from the Bible, it can be said that many today are "dull of hearing" *(Matthew 13:15 KJV; Acts 28:27 KJV; Hebrews 5:11 KJV)* — that is, they are incapable of psychically understanding the spoken or written word of the Creator-God. However, despite this fact and the unpleasant circumstances that surround the dull of hearing because of it, those who hear psychically should be joyful, remembering these words of the Master:

> "Truly, I say to you, the person who hears my word, and believes on Him who sent me, has everlasting life and shall not come into condemnation; rather, that person has been passed (i.e., phased) from death to life."
>
> *John 5:25 KJV Paraphrase*

The author of *The Biology of Psychism from a Christian Perspective* has dissected enough sheep brains and human brains to know that the temporal lobe of the sheep brain is proportionately larger in the cerebrum than the temporal lobe of the human brain. This is significant because Wernicke's area, the auditory cortex, is the primary area of the cerebrum responsible for the comprehension of spoken language. In 97% of all human beings, Wernicke's area is in the posterior superior portion of the left temporal lobe. It is because their temporal lobes are so well-developed that sheep have an auditory recognition sense that is acute enough to recognize the subtle differences in voices between and among various human beings. That is why sheep are able to auditorily recognize the voice of the shepherd who leads them, cares for them, and calls them. Christ Jesus said:

> The barn doorkeeper opens the door to the shepherd, and the sheep recognize the shepherd's voice. The shepherd calls the sheep by name and leads them out of the barn. Then, once they are out, the shepherd goes in front of the sheep and the sheep follow him because they know his voice.
>
> *John 10:3-4 KJV Paraphrase*

Unless souls in dust can hear psychically, truths will not ring true to them nor will they know whom to follow or whom to believe. Christ Jesus also said: "My sheep hear my voice, and I know them, and they follow me" *(John 10:27 KJV)*. It is hearing psychically what the Creator-God says that leads the flock back home to the kingdom within. In contrast, those who cannot hear psychically remain lost in the darkness of selfishness and sin. And, for those who already believe, without a more finely-attuned sense of hearing there will be no additional room within them for the continued building of their faith. As the Apostle Paul stated: "faith comes by specifically hearing the word of God" *(Romans 10:17 KJV Paraphrase)*. Souls in dust will not have their faith deepen unless they continue to hear the word of the Creator-God in psychic understanding. This means that we, who are still in flesh bodies, should never assume that we are done growing or that we understand all that there is to understand. We need to remind ourselves that no matter how much our knowledge increases, it will always remain fragmentary as long as we are on Earth.

We need to be reminded that the Apostle Paul also said:

> We know in part and we prophesy in part. But when that which is perfect comes, that which is in part shall be done away with.
>
> *1 Corinthians 13:9 KJV Paraphrase*

Because prophecy is mentioned in the previously-cited passage, it is appropriate to reiterate that human intelligence alone is insufficient for the accurate interpretation of prophetic utterances or psychic sensations. Hearing psychically, or understanding spiritually, is necessary — unless "the words are closed up and sealed" *(Daniel 12:9 KJV)* — in which case, their meaning can neither be opened nor revealed until it is permitted and enabled by the Creator-God. In "the Revelation of Jesus Christ" *(Revelation 1:1 KJV)*, the Apostle John wrote: "Blessed is the person who reads, and they that hear the words of this prophecy, and keep those things which are written therein because the time is at hand" *(Revelation 1:3)*. John was not referring to those who read or hear using their earthly senses but to those who read and hear psychically — which is to say, *perceive* and *understand* using their psychic senses. Except for the utterances of "the seven thunders," which John had been instructed to "seal up" *(Revelation 10:4 KJV)*, that beloved Apostle had been told "to not seal the statements of the prophecy of the Book of Revelation because the time is at hand" *(Revelation 22:10 KJV Paraphrase)*. Thus, the Book of Revelation is now open to those whose belief in the Creator-God rests on the Lord Jesus Christ, such belief counted as foolishness by the worldly-wise. In other words, souls entrenched in corporeality cannot psychically hear the testimony of Jesus — which testimony is "the spirit of prophecy" *(Revelation 19:10 KJV)* — unless they first believe in him as the chief witness of the Creator-God's love for them. Why is it desirable to understand the testimony of Jesus? "The person who has received his testimony has set to his seal that God is true" *(John 3:33 KJV Paraphrase)*. In other words, those who understand his prophecies concerning what is to happen in the not-too-distant future will never doubt in the God of the Holy Bible and, hence, will not lose faith even during their fiercest trials and tribulations.

Authentic Christians should understand why some people will never share their beliefs, their faith, their joy, or their understanding. They cannot control others nor should they want to. As Christ Jesus said: (1) "Everyone that is of the truth hears my voice" *(John 18:37 KJV Paraphrase)*. And (2) "The person that hears you hears me, and the person who despises you despises me, and the person that despises me despises the One who sent me" *(Luke 10:19 KJV Paraphrase)*. The Apostle John added: "We are of God; they who know God hear us; those who are not of God do not hear us. It is in this way that we know the spirit of truth and the spirit of error" *(1 John 4:6)*. Simply stated, if souls love the Creator-God, they will hear all they will ever need to know. Truth need not be sought if one is open to it. The Creator-God reveals truth psychically to His *begotten-again* — which is to say, those born of Him through their belief in Jesus Christ as their personal Savior.

What is revealed truth? Revealed truth is the inner knowledge that teaches men and women about their divine and immortal nature as the sons and daughters of the Creator-God. How do people come to know just who and what they are in the Creator-God? They learn through revealed truth — the truth that is unveiled to the heart of the inner self (the so-called *hidden* man and *hidden* woman).

Truth is revealed to those who desire to understand life spiritually, such desire not common within the earth plane of consciousness. Revealed truth begins in the recognition that life is spiritual and divine; and, if the soul is sufficiently yielded to good, revealed truth expands into a sustained apperception of the reality of the Creator-God. Thus, an entity to whom truth is revealed becomes increasingly aware of the consciousness in which it can "live and move and have its being" *(Acts 17:28 KJV),* which is not in dust (i.e., corporeality).

This statement: "The answers to all questions can be found within" is not a statement applicable only to those who live within the confines of a monastery or convent. No, the true contemplative life can be experienced by us all because it is a *way* and not a *where* of living. The true contemplative life is one that seeks to recognize the Creator-God throughout its every moment and movement. Is it possible for one to achieve such a state of awareness in this busy world of appearances? Yes, but it calls for the perpetual inner desire to be *of God.* Those who wish to "know as they are known" *(1 Corinthians 13:12 KJV)* must be willing to pay the price required. They must be willing to decrease in pride so that the family borne of the Creator-God's love might demonstrate true increase.

It is recorded in Genesis 11:1 that, after the flood, "the whole Earth was of one language and speech." It is also recorded in the same chapter that it wasn't until the descendants of Noah decided to make a name for themselves — a name apart from the name, or identity, they had in the Lord God Almighty — that their language became confounded and they became separated from one another. In addition to the literal meaning in the biblical story of the tower of Babel, there are both metaphorical and metaphysical meanings — meanings that speak of the time when incorporeal beings fell to a lower state of consciousness because of the false pride that had developed in their hearts.

In Hebrew, *Babel* means "confusion." Dissecting that word into its primitive particles *(ba* and *bel),* we find that *Babel* also means "in destruction." That *confusion* manifests itself *in destruction* should be obvious to everyone who can hear psychically. Perhaps you have heard that "a lie has a thousand faces." Well, when considering all human beings, that saying could be amended to "a lie has a billion faces." Why? There is, and can be, only one face of the Creator-God and only one genuine appearance of His complete image and perfect likeness. (Whoever can hear, let them hear.)

It is prophesied in *The Book of the Prophet Zephaniah* that, at the time of the end, the Creator-God will return to His people "a pure language in order that all may call upon the Name of the Lord and serve Him with one consent" *(Zephaniah 3:9 KJV Paraphrase).* Such a time has already arrived for those who have passed through Christ Jesus to the *other side,* and such a time will exist for all who are eventually raised to life again through "the blood of the Lamb" *(Revelation 5:14; 12:11 KJV).*

Spiritual concepts are the real words and language of revealed truth and psychic hearing. When you come down to it, the spoken and written language of human beings is actually quite crude. Earthly language is a limited vehicle for spiritual meaning, just as the physical body is a limited vehicle for the soul. However, such language can be used to convey messages to those who hear psychically, the highest meaning of which is above and beyond that given by mere dictionary definitions. The messages are conveyed to the higher self — the inner man and woman — if, and only if, Jesus Christ sits enthroned within their souls. Because the heart is the core of the soul, without Jesus Christ within our hearts, no one can really hear anything of value.

# Psychic Seeing

The author of *The Biology of Psychism from a Christian Perspective* makes a distinction between (1) *psychic seeing (seeing psychically or psychic sight)* and (2) *far-seeing (clairvoyance)*: (1) *Psychic seeing* is one's ability to understand metaphysical meanings behind common or uncommon physical objects and corporeal events and experiences. (2) *Far-seeing (clairvoyance)* includes psychic visions, psychic daydreams, and psychic REM sleep dreams of: (a) specifics about current events or possible, probable, or inevitable future events; (b) visitations from entities who live in incorporeal states of being (i.e., angels of God or redeemed souls in Heaven); and (c) views of reality or future events presented by the Creator-God's Holy Spirit.

*Psychic seeing* is spiritual and metaphysical insight. As indicated in the previous paragraph, it is the mental capacity to sense and perceive spiritual and metaphysical meanings behind common or uncommon physical objects and corporeal events and experiences. It also includes the ability to (1) *glimpse* the reality of the Creator-God and (2) *detect* objects that exist in eternity as well as events that occur there. (*Glimpse* and *detect* are the operative words here.) In other words, *psychic seeing* provides the inner view that resolves things into thoughts and thoughts into things. And it includes the ability to see beyond the things of this world into spiritual matters and things divine. Like *psychic hearing*, or *hearing psychically, psychic seeing* is representative of elevated personal consciousness that permits us to understand the mysteries of the Creator-God and the secrets of the human heart.

The Holy Bible teaches that the Creator-God is visibly hidden from *mortal man* (i.e., *mortal man* represents human beings collectively). Job said: "Behold, I go forward but He is not there; and backward, but I cannot perceive Him. I go on the left hand, where He works, but I cannot behold Him. He hides Himself on the right hand so that I cannot see Him" *(Job 23:8-9 KJV Paraphrase)*. Elihu, Job's friend, later added: "With clouds He covers the light, and commands it not to shine by the cloud that comes in between" *(Job 36:32 KJV Paraphrase)*. In desperation, King David asked: "How long, Lord? Will You hide Yourself forever?" *(Psalm 89:46 KJV Paraphrase)* Prophet Isaiah exclaimed: "I will wait upon the Lord, who hides His face from the house of Jacob, and I will look for Him" *(Isaiah 8:17 KJV Paraphrase);* and "Truly, You are a God who hides Yourself, O God of Israel" *(Isaiah 45:15 KJV Paraphrase)*. Speaking to all *children of men* (the biblical phrase for human beings), these words came through Prophet Isaiah: "Your iniquities have separated you from your God, and your sins have hidden His face from you" *(Isaiah 59:2)*. Isaiah also declared this truth: "Since the beginning of the world, human beings have not heard nor perceived by the ear, neither has the eye seen, O God, beside You, what You have prepared for the person who waits for You" *(Isaiah 64:4 KJV Paraphrase)*.

Expanding on the idea that the Creator-God and the things of the Creator-God are hidden from mortal man, the Apostle Paul wrote:

By His Holy Spirit, God has revealed to His elect the things He has prepared for those who love Him. His Holy Spirit searches all things, even the deep things of God. What man knows the things of a man except the one who has the spirit of man within him? Likewise, no man knows the things of God except those to whom the Holy Spirit has revealed them. We have not received the spirit of this world but, instead, the Holy Spirit, which is of God, that we might know the things that are freely given to us of God — and of which we speak, not in the words that the wisdom of man uses, but in the words that the Holy Spirit teaches, comparing spiritual things with spiritual things. But the natural man does not receive the things of the Spirit of God because they are foolish to him; neither does he understand them because they are spiritually discerned.

*1 Corinthians 2:10-14 KJV Paraphrase*

It is impossible for the natural man (i.e., the human being) to comprehend the things of the Holy Spirit because such things are not only foreign to him but permanently separated from him as well. Only the *inner self,* the *holy self,* the *glorified self,* the *hidden self,* the *spiritualized self,* the *higher self,* the *supraself,* or the *renewed self* can see the things of the Creator-God. At the time of the fall of spiritual beings — when selfish pride originally entered our souls and hardened our hearts — a shadow fell from the never-before-hewn wall between us and the Creator-God and its shadow was immediately cast over the land that He had made. In this way were spiritual beings expelled from the Creator-God's Paradise. Thus did God, and the things of God, become hidden from the fallen Adamic Race. And thus did mortality and the shadow of death (i.e., corporeality) become our self-imposed curse. Hence, any souls in dust who have the desire to see the Creator-God and the things He created must be willing to see beyond the chimera of corporeality (i.e., its illusion).

As the heart of an entity is its concern and the ear of an entity is its understanding, so is the eye of an entity its view. Whether an entity's view is of (1) the nether-world of self-will or (2) the world of the Creator-God depends on the object of its desire. If a soul sees from a world of self-will (i.e., that is its standpoint), then it sees through a glass darkly and fulfills the prophecy of Prophet Isaiah, reiterated by Christ Jesus and Apostle Paul, that "seeing you shall see but not perceive" *(Isaiah 6:9 KJV; Matthew 13:14 KJV; and Acts 28:16 KJV).*

*Psychic seeing* is a facet of the gift of spiritual sensitivity. It is the precious inner sight that allows the disciples of spiritual truth (i.e., the followers of Christ Jesus) to view the perfect world of the Creator-God while they are still on Earth. To be sure, those who are already completely immersed within the world of the Creator-God (i.e., the saints already returned to Heaven) are closer to Him than we are (the word *we* referring to those of us still enmeshed in the fabric of corporeality), but that does not preclude our seeing the saints in Heaven, nor does it prevent us from glimpsing Him, His world, and His truth.

Our spiritual vision widens as our concern for others intensifies. It enlarges as we grow toward the Creator-God. Today, different degrees of spiritual sight are found among souls in dust proportionate to the desire they have to help others. To be sure, there are those whose concern for others has opened their inner eye — their true *third eye* — to the bright world beyond and the so-called other side of life. However, the vast majority of souls in dust are blinded by their own iniquity and sin.

......

## The Third Eye and the Pineal Gland

Biologically speaking, there are precedents for referring to the pineal gland as the *third eye.* You will recall from Chapter One of this book that the pineal gland is part of the epithalamus in the diencephalon (see Figure Three for the location of the pineal gland). You will also recall that the pineal gland is indirectly influenced by sunlight through the release of norepinephrine by noradrenergic neurons from the locus coeruleus (see Figure Three for the location of the locus coeruleus). The neurons of the locus coeruleus are stimulated to produce norepinephrine during periods of sunlight and, thereby, inhibit the production of the sleep-inducing hormone melatonin. That fact alone helps to substantiate the *third eye* status of the pineal gland. However, that status is further substantiated phylogenetically by the intracranial pineal glands of many non-mammalian vertebrates, including some fish, amphibians, reptiles and avians, where photoreceptor cells are evident when their pineal glands are viewed histologically (i.e., microscopically). These non-mammalian pineal gland photoreceptors have histologic similarities to retinal photoreceptors, and they play important roles in daily and seasonal activities especially related to (1) diurnal periods of wakefulness and sleep and (2) annual reproductive cycles. Although mammalian pineal glands (human beings are mammals) lack photoreceptors, their pinealocytes (i.e., the major cell type in mammalian pineal glands) are indirectly regulated by periods of light and darkness as already indicated.

Although Rene Descartes was inaccurate in his conclusion about the pineal gland being the seat of man's soul, through histologic and comparative anatomic observations of the pineal gland, it is accurate to conclude that the pineal gland metaphysically represents the *third eye* by which a spiritually-enlightened human being peers into the world of the invisible when that world is opened to him or her by the Holy Spirit of the Creator-God. It is important to emphasize here that human beings do not open the door to the world of the invisible because that would be unseemly. *For example,* human beings *never* initiate or control contact with departed souls in Heaven. Those who say they do are *always* perpetrating a hoax.

In certain non-mammalian vertebrates *(for example,* in specific amphibians and reptiles), an extracranial pineal gland is in the center of the forehead; in other non-mammalian vertebrates, an intracranial pineal gland is located directly under the cranium as an evagination of the epithalamus and not centrally located in the brain as is the case in most mammals (including human beings). Since the external dot, mark, or jewel on the forehead worn by some Jains, Buddhists, Hindus, and Jews *(Ezekiel 16:12)* represents the energy center of inner sight that aligns with the pineal gland, it is also understandable why this area on the forehead is sometimes referred to as the *third eye* — as is the case relative to the Ajna chakra (i.e., energy vortex) of Hindu tradition.

Should we attribute the initial association of the human pineal gland with the *third eye* to accident, coincidence, anatomic study, or psychic seeing? *Psychic seeing* — specifically, metaphysical insight concerning the electromagnetic body double — is the correct answer.

It is important to emphasize to the readers of this book that modern human anatomic structures are themselves no longer what they represent metaphysically. *For example,* the pineal gland itself is *no longer* the *third eye* and spiritual vision no longer takes place there. All human structures simply represent a supernatural reality that existed within original Man (capitalized here to distinguish from human beings) and still exists within the electromagnetic body double of every restored soul (i.e., each saved human being).

The invisible and electromagnetic body double for each saved person is a shadow or type of etheric impression — more specifically, a spiritual *alto relief* (or high definition image) — of immortal man's original somatic identity. (This is in contrast to the spiritual *bas relief* — or low definition image — found in unsaved persons.) Just as the photograph of a person only *represents* the person, so too do the anatomic structures of human beings merely represent higher spiritual verities. Just as the photograph of a person is not the actual person, so too are modern human anatomic structures *not* verities-in-themselves. They are merely the vestiges of verities.

......

In his sermon on the mount, Christ Jesus stated that "the light of the body is the eye. Therefore, if your eye is single, your whole body shall be full of light" *(Matthew 6:22 KJV Paraphrase)*. At one level of spiritual understanding, that message could be rendered: "If we look only toward the Creator-God, we shall be filled with His light." In other words, it means that what we are filled with depends on what we are looking at (i.e., what is of interest to us).

Perhaps it will help you to understand the truth of the last statement if you recognize how that truth is parodied here on Earth. Sometimes, when our attention is caught by something pleasing to the eye, we become so enraptured by it (i.e., enamored of it) that we forget ourselves and almost believe that we are one with what we are seeing. Of course, that is an inaccurate perception and not a physical reality because it is impossible for corporeal beings to become one with objects they are looking at. However, in the realm of Spirit, such unions do exist.

To *see* in the Spirit requires one to *be* in the Spirit. However uncommon it is for souls in dust, such an inclusion does not require us to have already made a final transition to Heaven from corporeality. From studying the Bible, we can conclude that the Prophets Moses, Isaiah, and Ezekiel and the Apostles Paul and John saw what they saw by being in the Spirit at different times during their lives. But seeing spiritually like prophets or apostles requires that we die to the nether-world of self-will in order to be alive in the Creator-God through Christ Jesus. Why? It is only in direct proportion to our emergence in the Creator-God's perfect world through selfless efforts and reliance on Christ Jesus that we are permitted to catch glimpses of His world.

Souls in dust who have little love in them for the Creator-God and little love in them for others are limited to a physical view of the universe and confined by earthly reasoning to only deduce the meaning of activities in this earthly sphere of activities. However, that is not the case for those who are being raised to life through Christ Jesus. No, they receive the balm of Gilead and the salve of salvation that they might see and know who the Creator-God is and who they are in Him. Mortal senses, which include human analytics and emotions as well as the physical senses, can only hinder us as much as we permit them. In the final analysis, we are the ones who impose restrictions on — as well as set boundaries to — what we individually see.

There are three primary possessions with which each soul enters and leaves this world: resolve, motive, and view. Our view is one of our primary possessions. We own nothing else other than our resolve, motive, and view. (1) We cannot own the spiritual gifts we receive. Such spiritual bounties not only have their origin but also their operation in the Creator-God; in fact, they must be continually dedicated to Him if they are to be continually received. (2) We cannot own the events we experience; at best, they can only be taken with us as memories, themselves views of the past that help us plan for the future. (3) We cannot own our spiritual strengths; they merely reflect the attributes that belong to the Creator-God. (4) We cannot own our weaknesses: either they are dissolved through correction or they take possession of us (in which case, our weaknesses end up owning us). (5) We cannot own our faith; not only is Christ Jesus the "author and finisher" of our faith *(Hebrews 12:2 KJV),* faith must be shared with others if it is to be maintained and grow. And (6) we cannot own the love of the Creator-God because it is to be reflected back to Him and manifested through us toward others. In metaphysical sum, we do not possess anything except our resolve, motive, and view.

Christ Jesus said that he had come into the world "for judgment that they who do not see might see and that they who see might be made blind" *(John 9:39 KJV Paraphrase).* Jesus was referring to: (1) the lifting of the veil from the eyes of those who previously did not have the opportunity to understand him as the Word of God and (2) the concomitant concealing of himself as the fulfillment of Messianic prophecy from those who would be exposed to the gospel of salvation yet refuse to believe on him as the promised Christ.

Later, nearer to the hour of his crucifixion, Jesus Christ also said:

> "Yet a little while and the world will see me no more; but you shall see me. Because I live, you also shall live. At that day, you shall know that I am in my Father and that you are in me and that I am in you. Whoever has my commandments and keeps them, that is the person who loves me. And the person who loves me shall be loved of my Father, and I will love him and I will manifest myself to him."
>
> *John 14:19-21 KJV Paraphrase*

One of his followers asked Christ Jesus: "Lord, how is it that you will manifest yourself to us and not to the world?" In response, he answered:

> "If a person loves me, he will keep my words, and my Father will love him, and we will come to him and reside in him."
>
> *John 14:23 KJV Paraphrase*

How we act or react to the various circumstances in which we find ourselves depends on how we view ourselves. If we view ourselves as the sons and daughters of the Creator-God (i.e., the children of light), then we act accordingly. In contrast, if we view ourselves as the sons and daughters of lawlessness and rebellion (i.e., the children of darkness), then we act in keeping with that frame of reference. We reveal who we are by what we do, which is just another way of saying that "every tree is known by the fruit it produces" *(Luke 6:44 KJV Paraphrase).*

To which standard an entity subscribes determines what it sees. If an entity views things from a world of self-will, then its vision is obscured by the mist of darkness that surrounds it. On the other hand, if an entity looks inwardly-out from a world of increasing selflessness (such world a place where we find our one true and only real self), then it perceives the spiritual universe, at first dimly but then more clearly, as the spiritual light at the end of the tunnel.

If an entity sees its human self as all-important, it falls easy prey to selfish and sinful thoughts and feelings. It is easily fooled by demonic forces into protecting, promoting, and pleasing the false image it has of itself. To such an individual, the Creator-God does not exist. Why? Its spiritual vision is clouded by the shadows of mortal mind and carnal sense. Hence, those who live in their own selfish world move about in the blackness of darkness committing acts whose origin is demonic. Such people would laugh scornfully at you if you told them that the erring thoughts, feelings, ideas, and images that come to them are not their own (which is not to say that they don't eventually assume ownership of them after they have willingly entertained, accepted, indulged, and acted on them).

Our Master said:

> "If your eye is evil, then your whole body is full of darkness. If, therefore, the light that is in you is dark, how great is its darkness!"
>
> *Matthew 6:24 KJV Paraphrase*

In other words:

> If what we are turned toward (i.e., facing) is not of the Creator-God, then we are not reflecting the light that is in Him and of Him. And, without His light, we are subject to delusions and confusions from the spirit of darkness.

It is when entities reflect more and more of the Creator-God's light that they come to know the substantive nature of the Holy Spirit and the emptiness of the spirit of darkness — until, finally, "having no part dark" *(Luke 11:36 KJV)*, they are fully found in the body of Christ. Those thus reborn understand that physical matter in and of itself, despite its crudeness, can be neither good nor evil. They understand that it is merely evidence of the limitations imposed on mortals by their own iniquity, which is coincidental to their original fall from the Creator-God's true creation. Here, we should be reminded that it was not matter that tempted us to fall from our seat within the Supraconsciousness of the Creator-God's divine Mind. It was the thought entertained and acted upon that we could live apart from the Creator-God's Will and be as immortals — that is, "be as gods" *(Genesis 3:5 KJV)* — which banished us from His Paradise.

An entity's view of corporeality indicates the level of its spiritual maturity. Most often, that view is demonstrated by the importance he or she places on material possessions and earthly standing rather than by their written or spoken words. To those intent on satisfying the false image they have of themselves, matter becomes merely a device — a medium, as it were, for both mortal mind and carnal sense — through which they heap their own grief and fall to an even lower vibrational level, stepping further away from the crown of life that the Creator-God has in store for them (i.e., His glory). Although it would seem that we should strive for a better life by questing for more possessions and a higher social standing, entities who hope to reenter the Kingdom of God must come to see earthly achievements — as well as this entire world of appearances — for what they are. To glimpse the truths of a universal Mind (the mind that was, and still is, in Christ Jesus), we must be willing to relinquish selfish, material views of life and replace them with selfless, spiritual ones.

When souls in dust are open to the truth of the Creator-God, an insightful understanding of the world beyond grows within. As entities conduct themselves in a manner befitting children of God, they come to perceive that the real world of truth is eternal space filled by the Creator-God's love and that the seeming expanse of the material universe (an infinite vacuum containing matter) is, at worst, a parody and, at best, a metaphysical allegory of His spiritual universe. Gradually, those who continue to progress spiritually come to live completely in the world of Spirit, at which time — albeit they may be cognizant of other worlds — they *know* no other.

When those who are passing through the earth plane of consciousness understand that the Creator-God's created beings are not really *of* dust, they gradually come to view an earthly terrain, all of its inhabitants, and their own human forms as just holographic shadows that obscure the Creator-God's perfect world. And, as they look over the expanse of this physical world toward that greater reality, structures built by human hands lose their extrinsic meaning and, finally, earth and sea and wind vanish in a flame of truth. Then, a whole new world is opened to them through their psychic sight.

In reality, the earth plane of consciousness is between two worlds. Upon it are shadows cast from the nether-world of self-will. Yet within it, through humility and selflessness, one can catch glimpses of light from the Creator-God's perfect world. The importance of that truth cannot be overemphasized because it provides the basis for a spiritual perspective in this earthly sphere of activities and, also, because it encourages entities to question the origin of the thoughts, feelings, ideas, and mental images they have rather than just passively accept them as their own.

Perhaps the view elaborated here provides too simplistic an answer to life's problems for those who are weighed down by earthly knowledge. But, for those who are simple at heart, it provides a release from the things that would tempt or torment them. Though it is unpleasant, entities in the earth plane must recognize that there is such a thing as evil if they are to close the gates of their own individual consciousness to it. Those who would be more like Christ Jesus must learn the difference between good and evil if they are to cling to the one and reject the other. To understand that evil thoughts, carnal feelings, foolish ideas, and vulgar mental images have their origin in the "father of lies" *(John 8:44 KJV)* allows one to effectively cast them out through the authority that the Creator-God has given to us in Christ Jesus and immediately begin working on the weaknesses that allowed them entrance in the first place.

Christ Jesus came to grant salvation and give psychic sight to souls in dust that they might see the realities of the Creator-God. If we follow in his footsteps, the love of the Creator-God that we permit to indwell us lights our way so that we can perceive the origin and meaning of the things we encounter and experience here. Additionally, by following in his footsteps, we see the purpose — as well as purposelessness — of the individual and collective movements of souls in dust. When we love as the Creator-God would have us love, we begin to approach the Kingdom of God. And, as we approach it, we begin to understand where we are, why we are, and what we should learn on our journey back to the "Godhead" *(Acts 17:29 KJV; Romans 1:20 KJV; Colossians 2:9 KJV)*. However, our inner sight can only be reopened for us through our intent to fulfill the commandments of

Christ Jesus because such fulfillment provides the key to the door of the Creator-God's perfect world. It is impossible for us to enter by any other means or through any other way. As Ralph Waldo Emerson so eloquently wrote: "What lies behind us and what lies before us are tiny matters compared to what lies within us."

......

While we are on Earth, it is through psychic hearing and psychic seeing that we enter Heaven (that is, experience the Kingdom of God). Come now, and let us reason *psychically* together (adapted from *Isaiah 1:18 KJV*).

# Telepathy and Spirit Communication

Spirit communication, the communication between discarnates and incarnates, occurs. I know. I have been communicated to. Unfortunately, however, most people in the earth plane of consciousness have great difficulty in accepting the plausibility, veracity, and validity of spirit communication, generally for one or more of the following three reasons: (1) Admitting that there are levels of existence beyond this world would disturb most people because they have come to accept corporeality as the only reality. Such an admission would throttle their belief in mortal man as the center of the Creator-God's universe and, thus, make them extremely uncomfortable. (2) Forgetting that there are children of light as well as children of darkness, many — especially many who call themselves Christian — have erroneously equated all spirit communication with biblical necromancy, the conjuring of familiar spirits, and demon-possession. And, (3) although they have the capacity for receiving and understanding ideas from the Creator-God's sphere of activities, some remain ignorant of spirit communication either (a) because they have not been challenged to examine the issue or (b) because they have not accepted the challenge. Realizing that people in the first two categories cannot be made to change their views, it is for those who belong to the third category that I write about spirit communication. It is my hope that more people will gain a better understanding of what spirit communication is as well as what it is not.

Is spirit communication biblical? Is there some biblical basis upon which Christian believers can work to understand and accept certain forms of spirit communication as Christ-minded?

To answer the two questions just posed, let me first answer the question "Is telepathy biblical?" Telepathy, the inaudible and unwritten communication of mind to mind, is certainly biblical. When the king of Syria queried his most intimate subjects concerning which one of them was telling the king of Israel his attack plans, they responded: "None of us, my lord, O king, but Elisha, the prophet that is now in Israel, tells the king of Israel the words that you speak in your bedchamber" *(2 Kings 6:12 KJV Paraphrase)*. That idea is developed further in the Old Testament when Solomon admonishes: "Curse not the king, no not even in your bedchamber, because a bird of the air shall carry the voice, and that which has wings shall tell the matter" *(Ecclesiastes 10:20 KJV Paraphrase)*.

In the New Testament, it is recorded that when "certain of the scribes said within themselves: 'This man, Jesus, blasphemes,'" Christ Jesus, "knowing their thoughts, said: 'Why do you think evil in your hearts?'" *(Matthew 8:4-5 KJV Paraphrase)* And, "when the scribes and Pharisees watched him to find out if he would heal on the Sabbath (that they might find an accusation against him)," it is again recorded that Christ Jesus "knew their thoughts" *(Luke 6:7-8 KJV Paraphrase)*. How was Christ Jesus able to read the thoughts of others? Simply stated, he "perceived their thoughts in his spirit" *(Mark 2:8 KJV Paraphrase)*. In other words, consistent with the verbiage in *The Biology of Psychism from a Christian Perspective*, Christ Jesus electromagnetically received psychic sensations of thoughts and feelings from others through his *psychic apparatus* (see Chapter One).

Telepathy involves the electromagnetic sending and receiving of thoughts from one person to another. (Spiritual empathy involves psychically sensing the emotions of others.) Metaphysically speaking, fully-formed thoughts are winged objects that fly through the air, which is why they are sometimes figured in the Bible as birds. In flight, thoughts are identifiable by those who see electromagnetically with their psychic sight, which is sometimes given by the Creator-God as a heritable talent (although not always used by its recipients for His glory). And the particular ideas that thoughts carry and express (the *songs* of these so-called birds) are made known to those who, attuned to their higher self, hear electromagnetically with their psychic ears.

Why is it important to understand telepathy in order to understand spirit communication? If thoughts can be communicated from mind to mind on Earth, then they can be communicated from mind to mind between Heaven and Earth. "There is a veil that separates this world from the next" you say? In response, I say: "Not since that veil was torn in two by the crucifixion of Christ Jesus." The Bible teaches that the curtain that separated us from the Holy of Holies and from direct communion with the Creator-God — which formed an invisible barrier between this world and the next — was "rent in two from top to bottom" when Christ Jesus took upon himself the sins of the world at the time of his crucifixion *(Mark 15:37-38 KJV Paraphrase)*. What significance does such tearing hold concerning spirit communication? It means that, when the veil of self-ignorance and self-pride that enshrouds a person's heart is pierced by personal contrition and acceptance of the sacrifice of Christ Jesus for sins, communication from the spirit world becomes possible. That is not to say that it is common or that it will happen. That is to say it becomes *possible*.

The Apostle Paul wrote:

> It is not expedient for me to boast, but I will boast about visions and revelations from the Lord to a man I knew in Christ more that fourteen years ago. Whether he was in or out of his physical body, I do not know; only God knows. Regardless, this man had been caught up to the third heaven. And I knew such a man (again, whether he was in or out of his physical body, I do not know, but God knows), who shared how he was caught up into paradise and heard unspeakable words. They were *unspeakable* because it is not

lawful or seemly for anyone to repeat them. About this, I will boast, but I will not boast about myself except about my own weaknesses.

*2 Corinthians 12:1-5 KJV Paraphrase*

Some translators of the Greek New Testament are unsure if the previous Scripture describes Paul's own vision when he was caught up to the third heaven (i.e., a first person account) or if it describes the experiences of a man whom Paul knew (i.e., a third person account). Regardless, the focal point for us here is the statement: "Whether he was in or out of his physical body, I do not know; only God knows." If the account is first person, it indicates that Paul was unsure if he was in or out of his own physical body when he had the experience. If the account is third person, it indicates that Paul was unsure if the spirit of the man whom he knew was in or out of his physical body when that man had the experience. Whichever is the case, the serious student of the Bible must conclude that Paul recognized and accepted the possibility of separation of the soul from the physical body and the reality of an "out-of-the-body" experience (i.e., astral projection or soul travel) — just as the Apostle John must have accepted such a possibility and reality when he experienced and wrote: "I was in the Spirit on the Lord's day (Sunday), and I heard behind me a great voice similar to a trumpet" *(Revelation 1:11 KJV Paraphrase)*. Like the Apostles Paul and John, we need to acknowledge that "there is both a natural, or physical, body as well as a spiritual body" *(1 Corinthians 15:44 KJV Paraphrase)*.

There is a biblical basis for accepting the legitimacy of spirit communication in the transfiguration of Christ Jesus on the mount (probably Mount Hermon), when he spoke with both Moses and Elijah *(Matthew 17:1–8; Mark 9:2–8; Luke 9:28–36; 2 Peter 1:16–18)*. If this biblical basis exists, then why do most authentic Christians have such a negative attitude toward spirit communication? The answer is that, in the Old Testament, there are strong invectives against people who have "familiar spirits" and definite directives against consulting with them. The following three quotes in the Bible are from the Lord God Almighty Himself:

Do not pay attention to people who have familiar spirits (spirit guides). Neither should you seek after soothsayers (clairvoyants) to be defiled by them. I am the Lord your God!

*Leviticus 19:31 KJV Paraphrase*

A man or woman who has a familiar spirit (spirit guide) or who is a wizard (clairvoyant) shall surely be put to death: they shall stone them with stones: their blood (i.e., their sin) shall be upon them.

*Leviticus 20:27 KJV Paraphrase*

When you arrive in the land that the Lord your God gives you, you shall not follow the idolatrous practices of those nations. There shall not be found among you anyone who makes his son or daughter pass through the fire or who uses divination, or is an observer of times, or a fortune teller, or a witch (spell caster), or a charmer of magic, or a consulter with familiar spirits (spirit guides), or a necromancer (one who speaks with the dead). All who do these things are practitioners of idolatry. Because of their idolatries, the Lord your God will drive them out from before you. You shall be perfect with the Lord your God. For these nations, whose lands you shall possess, follow observers of times and diviners. But, as for you, the Lord your God has not permitted you to do so.

*Deuteronomy 18:9-14 KJV Paraphrase*

The English verb *to divine* simply means: (1) "to guess or deduce from what one already knows" or (2) "to ascertain on the basis of what information is available to one." In context, the Old Testament noun *divination* is translated from the Hebrew word קֶסֶם (keh'sem) [H7081], which has both a negative sense and a positive sense. The negative sense is related to idolatrous practices by false prophets, and the positive sense is related to practices by true prophets, or oracles, of the God of the Holy Bible. (Through his minions, Satan always tries to ape or mimic what the Creator-God does.)

Comments on these idolatrous practices are also found in the Second Book of Kings:

> And King Manasseh made his son pass through the fire, and observed times, and used enchantments, and dealt with familiar spirits (spirit guides) and wizards (clairvoyants): he employed much wickedness in the sight of the Lord to provoke Him to anger.
>
> *2 Kings 21:6 KJV Paraphrase*

> Moreover, those who worked with familiar spirits (spirit guides), and the wizards (clairvoyants), and the idols, and all of the idolatrous practices that were spied in the land of Judah and in Jerusalem were done away with by Josiah, that he might obey the laws that were written in the book of the law that Hilkiah the priest found in the house of the Lord.
>
> *2 Kings 23:24 KJV Paraphrase*

When King Saul was disturbed over the Philistine armies gathering at Shunem, it is recorded that he consulted with a woman who had a familiar spirit (spirit guide) that he might communicate with the dead prophet Samuel, but Prophet Samuel responded in the following way to Saul: "Why have you troubled me by conjuring me" *(1 Samuel*

*28:15),* indicating his displeasure at having been disturbed in this way. Later, after King Saul's death, it was chronicled:

> Thus Saul died for the transgression that he committed against the Lord, in particular against the law of the Lord, which he did not keep, and also for asking counsel of one who had a familiar spirit (spirit guide) in order to enquire of it instead of enquiring of the Lord. Therefore, the Lord slew him and turned the kingdom over to David, the son of Jesse.
>
> *1 Chronicles 10:13 KJV Paraphrase*

Author's Notes: In today's world of psychic fakery and self-deception, anyone who claims to be led by spirit guides is either confabulating in the unwitting personification of their own psychic abilities (if they have them) or outright lying in an effort to deceive others. Yes, saved human beings are led by the Creator-God's Holy Spirit, ministered to by angels in Heaven, and counseled by saved souls who have already returned to Heaven, but we are not led by spirit guides unless we permit the demons that surround us to influence our thoughts and feelings and control our actions. Simply stated, saved souls on Earth do not have familiar spirits (spirit guides). Relative to receiving counsel from saved souls already in Heaven, fewer than 60,000 souls on Earth are receiving such counsel at any given time — and only for a prescribed period of time so that saved souls on Earth not shift their dependence to saved souls in Heaven (away from their sole dependence on the Creator-God). During *the Millennium,* however, communication between souls on Earth and souls in Heaven will be commonplace.

It makes good sense why the people of Israel were not to consort with susceptible channels who had familiar spirits. They were not to seek after any spirit except that of the Lord God Almighty, whose spirit is the Holy Spirit. They were to enquire of Him and Him alone. He and no one else was to be their "Wonderful Counselor" *(Isaiah 9:6 KJV)*. He was, and is, to be the sole source of our supply.

The Holy Spirit spoke the following through Prophet Isaiah:

> And, when they shall say unto you: "Seek unto those who have familiar spirits (spirit guides), and unto wizards (clairvoyants) that peep and mutter," say to them: "should not people seek unto their God rather than for the living to the dead?"
>
> *Isaiah 8:19 KJV Paraphrase*

There is no philosophical debate here concerning who is living and who is dead, only the solid advice from the Holy Spirit that the people who belong to the Creator-God should seek His counsel directly. If we are to progress spiritually, it should crystallize to us that we must learn to not depend on anything other than the Lord God Almighty Himself. Otherwise, we could be deceived into thinking that something else can take His place. Nothing must come between us and our Lord. Hence, rather than depending on others for our knowledge of the Creator-God and His Will, we must learn for ourselves to commune on our own with Him in order to learn who He is and what His Will is for us daily. When we first learned how to swim, it was helpful to have someone teach us and stand by us in the water to prevent accidents, but, eventually, we all had to learn to swim alone (i.e., without physical support). In the same way, it is good to have spiritual mentors and Bible teachers who look out for our best interests, but, one day, we all must learn to immerse ourselves fully in the Creator-God's Holy Spirit.

The following is recorded in the New Testament:

And it came to pass that as we — Paul, Silas, Timothy, Luke, and others — were going to prayer, a certain young woman possessed with a spirit of divination met us. (She brought her slave holders much gain by prophesying.) She followed us and cried out: "These men are the servants of the Most High God; they show us the way of salvation." She did this over many days. But Paul, being grieved, turned to her and said to the familiar spirit: "I command you in the name of Jesus Christ to come out of her." And the familiar spirit came out of her that same hour.

*Acts 16:16-18 KJV Paraphrase*

*Divination* in the preceding passage has been translated from the Greek word πύθων (pu´thon) [G4436] — which is derived from *Putho,* the older name for the region in which Delphi, the seat of the famous oracle, was located. Thus, the spirit of divination in operation here is one like that used by the oracle of Apollo at Delphi in ancient Greece. That the young woman was truly possessed — that is, cohabited by another entity against her will — is not only indicated by the use of the Greek word for *possessed* but also by the report: (1) that the Apostle Paul recognized the condition as possession; (2) that he commanded the familiar spirit to leave her; and (3) that there was a definite change in the girl from that time forward *(Acts 16:19).*

All things told, authentic Christians should not seek advice from so-called spiritists, animists, shamans, or mediums because, to do so, is to rob the Creator-God of His proper place in their lives as well as to cheat themselves out of His direct counsel. That is not to say that the Creator-God, His angels, or saved souls in Heaven cannot speak to us directly through clairaudience or indirectly through the psychomotor apparatus of another saved person, but, rather, that mortal man does not determine when, where, and through whom such communication occurs. If an angel of the Lord God Almighty can speak through a donkey *(Numbers 22:28)*, then surely the Lord can use a human being as well. Concerning these matters, I was given the following guidelines by a mentor from Heaven:

> An induction into what you refer to as a trance-like state — which I would much prefer that you call a state of susceptibility — the suggestion that brings about that state never originates from your plane. It would be unseemly. Keep this in mind: when you meet a person or persons who induce themselves or others into a state of susceptibility, you have confronted a hoax.

Souls in dust who involve themselves in invoking, conjuring, enticing, or divining discarnates are spiritually sick, biblically unsound, morally ill, and need to be healed.

Although most people in the earth plane of consciousness would say that communication with discarnates was never possible or that it is not now possible — and although most who would claim to have had such communications are self-deluded, outright charlatans, emotionally-unbalanced, or directed by evil — not one of them can take away from the fact that Christ-minded spirit communication has occurred. Concerning such communication, it is recorded in the Bible: (1) that Peter, James, and John saw Moses and Elijah talking with Jesus *(Matthew 17:3; Mark 9:4; and Luke 9:30-31)*; (2) that, after the crucifixion, Jesus appeared to (a) the women at his tomb *(Matthew 28:9; Mark 16:9; John 20:11-16)*, (b) to Cleopas and his traveling companion *(Mark 16:12; Luke 24:13-31)*, (c) to James *(1 Corinthians 15:7)*, (d) to the eleven Apostles three times *(Matthew 28:16-17; Mark 16:14; Luke 24:36; John 20:19 and 20:26)*, (d) to seven people at the sea of Tiberius *(John 21:1 and 21:14)*, (e) to over five hundred people at the same time *(1 Corinthians 15:6)*, (f) to Stephen at the time of his death *(Acts 7:56)*, (g) to Paul twice *(Acts 9:4-16; 18:9-10; 23:11)*, and (h) to John *(throughout the Book of Revelation)*; and (3) that, after the resurrection of Christ Jesus, "many bodies of the saints that slept (i.e., the saved who had died) arose and went into the holy city, and appeared unto many" *(Matthew 27:52-53 KJV Paraphrase)*.

# The Role of Uncertainty

Throughout the ages, the uncertainty of their futures has caused many people to turn their attention, time, and energy toward *soothsaying* (defined as "true or false prophecy, depending on context") through: astrology, fortune-telling, crystal-gazing, card-reading, palm-reading, tea-leaf reading, throwing-the-bones, Ouija boards, séances, spiritualism, and other pretentious means. Thus, many have turned away from entrusting their care to the Creator-God through a simple dependence on the One who is the real All-knower and Caretaker of their futures.

The real issue here is not if there are authentic psychics who can make accurate predictions. Nor is it if an astrologer's natal chart can accurately forecast sets of circumstances, opportunities, inclinations, and predispositions. Nor is it if someone has ever broken through to *the other side.* The real issue is if people are willing to become, and remain, the children of the Creator-God by entrusting themselves to His care while stepping out into the darkness of uncertainty that is set before them — such uncertainty their unknown futures.

It is easy to understand why many people are so willing to sell themselves to a false prophet, evil ideologue, neighborhood fortune-teller, itinerant mentalist, national cult leader, or even a domineering family member. They look for someone who has immediate answers and directions as well as the foreknowledge of what they must do to: (1) make their futures better and brighter, (2) relieve them of the responsibilities and burdens of free will, and (3) protect them from — and excuse them of — *failure.*

The single greatest challenge within the earth plane of consciousness is the uncertainty that faces everyone every day. Even Christians, who are *the saved* and saints of God... although they may have no doubts that the Lord God Almighty is who He said He is in the Holy Bible or that Christ Jesus is His Son... even they are tempted by the uncertainty that comes from living within this natural world. They know of others who have lost jobs, loved ones, lives, and limbs and they naturally wonder: "Am I next? Will that happen to me, too?" They know that accidents happen. Metaphysically, there are no accidents in God, but accidents do happen on Earth. Even the Creator-God acknowledged and provided for accidental death, *for example,* "when a man goes into the woods with his neighbor to chop wood and he lifts his axe to cut down a tree and the head of the axe slips off the handle and hits his neighbor and kills him" *(Deuteronomy 19:4-5 KJV Paraphrase).*

In his sermon on the mount, Christ Jesus addressed the uncertainty of our daily lives. He exhorted:

> Take no thought of your life, concerning what you shall eat or drink, nor even for your body, concerning what you shall wear, because your heavenly Father knows what you need.
> *Matthew 6:25 & 32 KJV Paraphrase*

Instead of our worrying about the uncertainties of tomorrow's food, drink, and clothing (where they will come from and how they will get to us), Christ Jesus instructed us to:

> "Seek first the Kingdom of God and His righteousness and all of these things shall be added unto you. Therefore, take no thought for tomorrow because tomorrow shall take thought for the things of itself. Sufficient unto today is the evil thereof."
> *Matthew 6:33-34 KJV Paraphrase*

To be sure, when we worry about the things of tomorrow, we find ourselves becoming increasingly weary of living today. Our physical bodies become heavier. Our minds become (1) duller concerning the things of the Spirit and (2) hypervigilant concerning the things of this world. Our hearts ache more. Our joys remain hidden. And our collective goal becomes the grave.

Should we hope to escape from grief while in this earthly plane? Should we hope to escape from sorrow or death? The following wisdom from Ecclesiastes helps to answer the preceding questions:

> To everything there is a season and a time for every purpose under heaven: A time to be born and a time to die; a time to plant and a time to harvest; a time to kill and a time to heal; a time to break down and a time to build up; a time to weep and a time to laugh; a time to mourn and a time to dance; a time to cast away stones and a time to gather stones together; a time to embrace and a time to refrain from embracing; a time to get and a time to lose; a time to keep and a time to cast away; a time to tear and a time to sew; a time to be silent and a time to speak; a time to love and a time to hate; a time of war and a time of peace.
>
> *Ecclesiastes 3:1-8 KJV Paraphrase*

Nothing is permanent except the love of our Creator-God. Uncertainty of tomorrow's earthly circumstances surrounds us, but we should look beyond such uncertainty to the certainty of our salvation and redemption in Christ Jesus. By entrusting our lives to the Lord, here and now, while attending daily to our earthly duties, responsibilities, and obligations, the "peace of God that passes all understanding" *(Philippians 4:7 KJV Paraphrase)* will overtake us and keep us less burdened — which is to say, burdened only by that which is within our Lord's Will for us. In Revelation, it is recorded that our resurrected Savior said to the church in Thyatira:

> "I will place upon you no other burden except what you already have. Remain steadfast until I return."
>
> *Revelation 2:24-25 KJV Paraphrase*

Yes, uncertainty of what tomorrow will bring is a definite burden. But Christians should neither slumber nor sleep because of the heaviness of that burden. Uncertainty is also a blessing in disguise. How is uncertainty a blessing? Uncertainty keeps us married to Christ Jesus. In vulnerability and weakness, our eyes must remain fixed on him as our Rock lest we fall into the surrounding pit of which we are in the midst.

It is a blessing as well that our Creator-God has kept secret the exact day and hour of our Savior's return. If we were to learn of the exact day and hour, many would slumber and sleep by adopting a fatalistic attitude. They would consider themselves relieved of the responsibilities of performing even the little bit of good that they do now. They would try to see to it that they got a head start on their promised rest. The Lord God Almighty knows us all too well. He knows that we are too vulnerable to learn specifics about our futures. In His infinite wisdom, He has kept our earthly futures hidden from our daily view. He keeps us in this uncertainty because He loves us. He hopes to foster our dependence on Him — a dependence that will glorify and honor His Holy Name at the same time that it returns us to Him.

It is against spiritual growth for mortal man to know the intimate details of everything that will happen tomorrow. Although the Creator-God is an open book on the topic of salvation, He is not an open book on all other topics. That is not to say that the Creator-God's angels have not been given charge over us so that we not dash our foot against a stone, stumble, and fall *(Psalm 91:11-12; Matthew 4:6; and Luke 4:10-11)*. And that is also not to say that we cannot receive a "word of knowledge" from His Holy Spirit *(1 Corinthians 12:8 KJV)*. Responsible adulthood — or, rather, the Spirit of God that dwells within us — enables us to accept the challenge to prepare for tomorrow by taking into consideration today as many things as possible (as far as we can ascertain) that could, can, might, and/or will happen in the future. Although we should never feel as if we have tomorrow within our back pockets, such preparation at least helps us to feel that we have done our part in preparing for our uncertain earthly futures.

It is uncertainty that has caused many of us to fear tomorrow. And such fear has caused many of us to turn toward greed, crime, bitterness, and/or addictive behaviors. It is only through the grace of our Creator-God that any of us have been, or are being, saved.

The conclusion to the matter of uncertainty is this: Although we cannot know or understand all of what will happen tomorrow, it should be sufficient for souls in dust to know and understand the most important things, including: (1) that we were created by the Lord God Almighty; (2) that we fell to an iniquitous state of being (i.e., mortality) by transgressing His laws; (3) that our salvation has been provided for us (a) in our acceptance of Christ Jesus as the promised Jewish Messiah and Savior of the world and (b) in our acceptance of his death on the cross as the only atonement acceptable to the Creator-God for the remission of our sins; and (4) that, if we so believe, we will one day see the Creator-God face-to-face and be with Him and His, forevermore. Of these truths, we can be certain.

# The Messengers of God

Throughout the Bible, there are many references to angels communicating with souls in dust:

(1) Hagar was twice directed by an angel *(Genesis 16:7-14; 21:14-19)*.

(2) Angels visited Abraham and Sarah to announce the birth of Isaac *(Genesis 18:1-5)*.

(3) Angels visited Lot and his family to warn them of the impending doom to Sodom *(Genesis 19:1-29)*.

(4) An angel intercepted Abraham's slaying of Isaac and prophesied that Abraham would be "the father of many nations" *(Genesis 22:1-24 KJV)*.

(5) Angels met with Jacob at different times during his life *(Genesis 31:13; 32:1)*.

(6) An angel appeared to Moses in a flame of fire from the midst of a thorn bush *(Exodus 3:4)*.

(7) An angel led and protected the children of Israel during their exodus from Egypt *(Exodus 14:19-24; 23:21)*.

(8) An angel gave instruction to the prophet Balaam concerning what he should say to Balak *(Numbers 22:22-35)*.

(9) An angel appeared to Joshua and spoke to him concerning what should be done regarding Jericho *(Joshua 5:13-15; 6:1-5)*.

(10) The angel of the Lord chastised the sons of Israel for not having obeyed him concerning what was to be done to the inhabitants of the

newly-taken Promised Land and the altars to their false gods *(Judges 2:1-7)*.

(11) An angel of the Lord visited Gideon *(Judges 6:11-14)*.

(12) An angel of the Lord appeared to Manoah and his wife to prophesy the birth of their son, Samson *(Judges 15:22)*.

(13) When the Creator-God sent a pestilence upon Israel for David's sin of taking a census, he did so by way of an angel *(2 Samuel 24:15-17)*.

(14) An angel brought enough food and water to Elijah to sustain him for forty days and nights *(1 Kings 19:1-8)*.

(15) An angel gave Elijah a message for King Ahaziah and directed him to meet with the third delegation that Ahaziah sent *(2 Kings 1:3-15)*.

(16) An angel of the Lord "killed in the camp of the Assyrians one hundred and eighty-five thousand" *(2 Kings 19:35; Isaiah 37:36; 2 Chronicles 32:21)*.

(17) The same angel that killed the Assyrians commissioned King David through the prophet Gad to purchase Ornan's (Araunah's) threshing floor as an altar to the Lord *(1 Chronicles 21:18-27)*.

(18) An angel delivered Shadrach, Meschach, and Abednego from the flames of the fiery furnace *(Daniel 3:28)*.

(19) An angel protected Daniel by shutting the lions' mouths *(Daniel 6:22)*.

(20) Angels helped bring the word of the Lord to Zechariah *(Zechariah, Chapters One through Six)*.

(21) An angel of the Lord appeared in dreams three separate times to Joseph *(Matthew 1:20-21; 2:13; 2:19)*.

(22) The angel Gabriel appeared to Zacharias to announce the birth of his son, the prophet John *(Luke 1:11-20)*.

(23) The angel Gabriel appeared to Mary to prophesy the births of Jesus and John *(Luke 1:26-37)*.

(24) Angels appeared to shepherds outside of Bethlehem to herald the birth of Jesus *(Luke 2:9-15)*.

(25) Angels ministered to Jesus after he was tempted by Satan *(Matthew 4:11)*.

(26) An angel strengthened Jesus during his trial at Gethsemane *(Luke 22:43)*.

(27) Angels greeted the women at the tomb of Jesus *(Matthew 28:2-7; John 20:12)*.

(28) The angel of the Lord opened the prison gates in order to release the Apostles *(Acts 5:19)*.

(29) An angel of the Lord directed Philip to the Ethiopian eunuch *(Acts 8:26)*.

(30) An angel told Cornelius to send for Simon Peter *(Acts 10:3-6)*.

(31) The angel of the Lord enabled Peter to escape from prison *(Acts 12:7-9)*.

(32) The angel of the Lord struck Herod dead *(Acts 12:21-23)*.

(33) The angel of God stood by Paul to strengthen him during the storm at sea *(Acts 27:23-26)*.

(34) An angel helped bring the revelation of Christ Jesus to the Apostle John *(Revelation 1:1)*.

Just who and what are angels?

Angels are created, spirit beings. Before the beginning of relative space-time (i.e., corporeality), all of them belonged to the Creator-God. At the time of the Luciferian Fall, some of the angels fell with Satan. Thus, now, angels are either of the Creator-God or they are of the Devil. If they are of the Devil *(2 Peter 2:4; Jude 6)*, they are called "fallen angels" and "messengers of Satan." If they are of the Creator-God, they are called "angels of the Lord," "heavenly messengers," "celestial bodies," and "the stars in His heavens." The angels of the Creator-God live, move, and have their being in eternity. They are created manifestations of the Creator-God. They are images in white — which is to say, *glorified beings.* They are not only His messengers but also His deputies, His ambassadors, His reapers, and the dispensers of His Wrath. To be sure, there is a hierarchy within the Creator-God's Heaven that includes angels, archangels, and the King of Kings, Christ Jesus, but there are also spiritually-enlightened souls who are within the body of Christ — a multi-membered, spiritual network — that can function as messengers for the Creator-God as well. Thus, the messengers of the Creator-God include unfallen created beings (angels) as well as redeemed souls who have already been returned to eternity (the heavenly saints). Altogether, all unfallen and redeemed spiritual beings constitute the multitude of the Lord God Almighty's Host, His army, and His chariots. Why army? Because they fight for Him. Why chariots? Because they all carry Him within their very being.

Angels of God are filled with and by the Creator-God's Holy Spirit. They have their identity in Him and He has His identity in them.

They are so much a part of the Creator-God's creation that they speak for Him and He speaks through them. *For example:* (1) Speaking for the Creator-God, the angel told Hagar: "I will make Ishmael a great nation" *(Genesis 21:8)*. (2) In similar manner, the angel who intercepted Abraham's sacrificing Isaac, said: "Lay not your hand upon the lad, neither do anything to him; for now I know that you fear the Lord God Almighty, seeing how you have not withheld your son, your only son, from Me" *(Genesis 22:12 KJV Paraphrase)*. (3) The angel said to Jacob: "I am the God of Bethel" *(Genesis 31:13 KJV)*. (4) Relative to the angel who led the children of Israel, the Lord God Almighty declared: "Beware of him and obey his voice. Do not provoke him because he will not pardon your transgressions since My Name is within him" *(Exodus 23:31 KJV Paraphrase)*. (5) Hagar called the name of the angel who spoke to her "Thou-God-who-sees-me" *(Genesis 16:13 KJV Paraphrase)*. (6) Abraham conversed with the Lord who visited him in the form of an angel" *(Genesis 18:1-33 KJV)*. (7) Before the Lord God Almighty spoke to Abraham about the destruction of Sodom and Gomorrah, he visited those cities in the form of an angel *(Genesis 18:20-33)*. (8) After Jacob had wrestled with an angel, he exclaimed that he had "seen God face-to-face" *(Genesis 32:30 KJV)*. (9) It is recorded that, at the same time an angel was appearing to Moses in the burning bush: "God called to Moses out of the midst of the bush" *(Exodus 3:4 KJV Paraphrase)*. (10) The Creator-God looked through the angel which protected the children of Israel *(Exodus 14:19-24)*. (11) It is recorded that when an angel of the Lord visited Gideon, it was the Lord God Almighty Himself who turned to talk with Gideon *(Judges 6:11-14)*. (12) And, after the angel stopped speaking with Manoah, Manoah said to his wife: "we shall surely die because we have seen God" *(Judges 5:22 KJV)*. In view of the twelve examples just cited, it should be obvious that any confusion between the Creator and His created angels comes from the fact that He cannot really be separated from those whom He entrusts to fully and completely perform His Will.

When Jacob was met by "the angels of God" *(Genesis 32:1 KJV)*, he said: "This is God's Host" *(Genesis 32:2 KJV)*, the Hebrew word from which *host* has been translated also meaning "army" and "dwelling." The Psalmist wrote: "The chariots of God are twenty thousand, even thousands of angels; the Lord is among them, as in Sinai, in the holy place" *(Psalm 68:17 KJV Paraphrase)*. When Elisha prayed that his young servant would see the reality of the Creator-God, it is recorded that "the Lord opened the eyes of the young man; and he saw: and behold, the mountain was full of horses and chariots of fire around Elisha" *(2 Kings 6:17 KJV Paraphrase)*. What are we to conclude? The angels of the Lord are His carriages and throne. The Lord God Himself indwells them, and they convey Him.

Why include the redeemed in Heaven as part of the host of God's created who serve as His messengers? Simply because they are spiritual beings remade anew. A biblical passage that might be used to argue against including the redeemed in Heaven as the messengers of the Creator-God is: "What is man that You are mindful of him? And the son of man that You visit him? For You have made him a little lower than the angels, and have crowned him with glory and honor" *(Psalm 8:4-5 KJV Paraphrase)*. That passage has been interpreted by some to mean that mankind is forever separate from His angelic host (in that human beings were made "a little lower than the angels"). However, that is not the significance that the author of Hebrews attaches to the passage. Quoting Psalm 8:4-5 almost word for word, the author of Hebrews wrote: "But we see Jesus, who was made a little lower than the angels for the suffering of death, crowned with glory and honor, that he by the grace of God should taste death for every man" *(Hebrews 2:9 KJV Paraphrase)*. It should be clear that: (1) when the Psalmist referred to "man," he was referring to mortal man; (2)

when the Psalmist referred to "the Son of Man," he was referring to Christ Jesus; and (3) that it was not mortal man who is crowned with glory and honor but the crucified Christ. Interestingly, in the King James Version of Psalm 8:5, the Hebrew word from which *angels* has been translated is the Hebrew word *Elohim,* the same plural word from which the words "God" and "gods" have been translated in the Old Testament and from which the word "immortals" can also be translated. Like angels, the redeemed in Heaven are *immortals:*

> I have said, "You are *gods* (i.e., immortals)*;* and all of you are children of the most High."
>
> *Psalm 82:6 KJV Paraphrase*

> Jesus replied: "Is it not written in your law: 'I have said, "You are gods?"' If he called them *gods* (i.e., immortals), unto whom the word of God came, and the scripture cannot be broken; do you say to him, whom the Father has sanctified, and sent into the world: 'You blaspheme,' because I said: 'I am the Son of God?'"
>
> *John 10:34 KJV Paraphrase*

Yes, when our lives revolve about Christ Jesus, like the angels in Heaven we also are immortals, the stars in God's universe, and the messengers of His goodness.

# Reincarnation and the Holy Bible

## I.

Reincarnation is the reentrance of unsaved fallen souls into corporeality as human beings. Although concepts of reincarnation are elaborated in at least some forms of Zoroastrianism, Hinduism, Buddhism, and Judaism, there is a dearth of systematic theology in Christianity associated with reincarnation. The major objections to reincarnation by Christian theologians include, but are not limited to, the ideas that: (1) reincarnation seems to negate the need for salvation through Jesus Christ alone; and (2) reincarnation seems to confuse the biblical notion of the resurrection of the human body. Although other objections exist, the two just mentioned are the most substantive.

In response to the two objections just posed: (1) Reincarnation does not negate the need for Christian salvation if one simply views reincarnation as the multiple opportunities for salvation that the Creator-God gives errant souls — which opportunities provide additional evidence of His unparalleled grace, mercy, and justice. (2) Reincarnation does not confuse the biblical notion of the resurrection of the human body if one understands that, at the time of Jesus Christ's return, the somatic identity (i.e., body) of the Christian believer is: either (a) reconstituted from the dust of a decomposed physical body into an *astral gelatinous*™ form (i.e., a spiritual body) in the case of a saint who is already with Christ Jesus in Paradise (i.e., already redeemed in Heaven) at the time of Christ Jesus' return to Earth; or (b) translated from a living physical body into an *astral gelatinous*™ form (i.e., a spiritual body) in the case of a saint who is still in corporeality (i.e., still in a human body) at the time of Christ Jesus' return.

## Astral Gelatinous™

At this juncture, it is important to explain *astral gelatinous*™. *Astral gelatinous*™ is a phrase that the author of *The Biology of Psychism from a Christian Perspective* first coined in the writing of his book entitled *Divine Metaphysics of Human Anatomy* (Copyright 2011, United States Copyright Office TXU-001-788-674, ISBN 978-0985772826).

The phrase *astral gelatinous*™ describes a substance that predominantly has spiritual qualities somewhat similar to the created substance of unfallen angels. This substance may also take on physical qualities depending on the dimensionality in which it is found. *For example,* when some angels enter the physical realm (i.e., insert themselves into relative space-time), they may voluntarily take on human form and appear to be human even though they did not originate from, or in, a biological life form. This is exemplified by the two angels who first visited Abraham and, later, Lot in the city of Sodom — which visitations are recorded in Chapters Eighteen and Nineteen of the Book of Genesis in the Holy Bible. At one time, certain angels even stepped into physicality in order to mate with human beings. This interaction is recorded in Genesis 6:1-4 as having taken place between "the sons of God" and "the daughters of men" *(KJV).* The giant *nephilim* (or "fallen ones") mentioned in the Holy Bible were the offspring of these unnatural sexual liaisons. (The sexual liaisons were *unnatural* because they took place between immortals and mortals.) The Holy Bible is clear that the angels who mated with human beings were relegated to the *bottomless pit of the Abyss in Hades* to await the Creator-God's Just Punishment for their transgressions (see verse 6 in the Epistle of Jude).

The unfallen creation that originally reflected God's complete image and perfect likeness was *astral gelatinous*™ in nature (i.e., *in essence*).

As a result of the Adamic Fall, the *astral gelatinous*™ substance of immortal beings, originally created in the complete image and perfect likeness of God, manifested as living physical substance (i.e., protoplasm). Consequently, the various cells, tissues, organs, and organ systems of the modern human being appeared, becoming mere representations, vestiges, remnants, and "fossilized impressions" of what they used to be. This *shattering*, or fracturing, of a portion of the Creator-God's original creation also produced *astral gelatinous*™ shards — or metaphysical monads, dyads, and triads — that joined in varying combinations and permutations to become all other biological organisms. From the standpoint of eternity, all of this occurred instantly. From the standpoint of the Genesis account in the Bible, all of this occurred in six days. From the standpoint of temporality, all of this occurred over eons of chronological time.

As indicated previously, at the return of Christ Jesus to Earth, all joint heirs with him receive their new somatic identities. These new somatic identities not only resemble the body of the ascended Christ Jesus but are also composed of the original *astral gelatinous*™ form and substance immortal beings had in the Creator-God before the Adamic Fall.

For the sake of clarity, gender and sexual identity do not exist in an *astral gelatinous*™ condition of being. Beneficial mental and emotional characteristics often associated with each gender and sexual identity on Earth are fused together for each individual being in Heaven. (There are no males, females, hermaphrodites, or intersexuals in Heaven.)

# II.

Most biblical Christians flatly reject reincarnation because the Holy Bible does not introduce it as a construct for a Judeo-Christian systematic theology. Perhaps the most damning Bible passage used against reincarnation is found in the Bible's Epistle to the Hebrews:

> {27} As it is appointed unto men once to die, and after this the judgment, {28} so also was Christ offered once to bear the sins of many; and to those who look for him shall he appear the second time without sin unto salvation.
>
> *Hebrews 9:27-28 KJV Paraphrase*

Biblical Christians fail to recognize the possibility that Hebrews 9:27 is referring to all souls collectively suffering *spiritual death* (i.e., spiritual mortality) at the same time in their original separation from the Creator-God due to their iniquity and sin that resulted in the Adamic Fall. (*Adam* is not only the name of an individual who lived approximately 4,000 years before Christ Jesus but also a plural Hebrew noun that represents created Adamic beings in the collective sense.) The point here is that one could read Hebrews 9:27 as follows: "it is appointed to all souls collectively to die once *[be separated from the Creator-God once]*" and not "it is appointed to each soul to experience only one human death."

To be sure, it is not appointed to all souls collectively to *die twice* in the biblical sense because only those souls who have irrefutably rejected Jesus Christ as their personal Savior are *twice dead (Jude 1:12 KJV)* from their being thrown into *the Lake of Fire* at the end of *the Millennium*. (The Lake of Fire is also known as *the second death*.) In other words, from the present author's perspective, the collective fall of all souls at the same time may be referred to as *the first death*, and *the first death* is not referring to the death of an individual human being.

Seen in this light, *the first death* (i.e., spiritual mortality, or our original separation from the Creator-God) was appointed to all souls at the same time ("once") because of their collective iniquity and sin in the Adamic Fall.

Again, for the sake of clarity, *the first death* is entirely different from *the second death:* (1) *The second death* is not referring to reincarnation. And (2) *the second death* is not appointed to all souls but, rather, only to those souls who have irrefutably rejected Jesus Christ as: (1) the *only-begotten* Son of the Creator-God; (2) God Incarnate (the Creator-God, or Word of God, in flesh); (3) the promised Messiah of Israel; (4) the one true Savior of the world; and (5) one's only personal Savior.

References to *the second death* are found in the Book of Revelation in the following verses:

> Those who have an ear, let them hear what the Spirit says to the churches: the person who overcomes [through faith in Christ Jesus] shall not be hurt of *the second death*.
> *Revelation 2:11 KJV Paraphrase*

> [Speaking of those who receive their new bodies at the time of Christ Jesus' return:] Blessed and holy is the person who has part in the first resurrection: on such *the second death* has no power, but they shall be priests of the Creator-God and of Christ, and shall reign with him a thousand years.
> *Revelation 20:6 KJV Paraphrase*

> {14} And death and hell were cast into *the Lake of Fire*. This is *the second death*. {15} And whoever was not found written in the Book of Life was cast into *the Lake of Fire*.
> *Revelation 20:14-15 KJV Paraphrase*

But the fearful, and unbelieving, and abominable, and murderers, and whoremongers, and sorcerers [false prophets], and idolaters, and all liars [apostates and heretics], shall have their part in the lake that burns with fire and brimstone, which is *the second death*.

*Revelation 21:8 KJV Paraphrase*

To summarize at this juncture: this short discussion of *the first death* and *the second death* is intended to clarify their meaning in order to help the reader understand that the two phrases are not referring to the reincarnation of individuals but, instead, to the collective separation of individuals from the Creator-God — temporary separation in the case of *the first death* and permanent separation in the case of *the second death*.

# III.

Reincarnation cultists are often self-driven to prove that reincarnation is mentioned in the Holy Bible. Unfortunately, their so-called proof is speculative, revisionist, and specious. Because they neither understand nor respect the authority of the Holy Bible, reincarnation cultists often invent places in Scripture that supposedly refer to reincarnation. *For example,* they might incorrectly use specific Bible verses like Matthew 11:13-14, Matthew 17:10-13, and Mark 9:11-13 to "prove" that John the Baptist was a reincarnation of the Old Testament Prophet Elijah.

Reincarnation cultists also try to revise history to help support their position that the earliest Christian Church embraced reincarnation. To be sure, one notable figure in the early Christian Church, Origen Adamantius (182 - 254 AD), believed in reincarnation, but his views on this topic were considered heretical by his contemporaries.

The Holy Bible does not refer to reincarnation. However, just because the Holy Bible does not refer to reincarnation does not mean that reincarnation does not exist. Similarly, just because the Holy Bible does not refer to electricity does not mean that electricity does not exist. There are those students and teachers of the Holy Bible who will say that statements supportive of reincarnation cannot be true because (1) such statements would be contradictory to the Holy Bible and (2) the Creator-God does not contradict Himself. To be sure, the Creator-God does not contradict Himself. However, as presented here, reincarnation is not really contradictory to any truth in the Holy Bible. Rather, an intelligent understanding of reincarnation helps to fill in certain gaps in understanding spiritual truth concerning people who have died never hearing the gospel message of Jesus Christ. The only way that reincarnation would be contradictory to the truth in the Holy Bible is if it were used to replace the need for the shed blood of the *only-begotten* Son of God as the only means for salvation. To be sure, we must reject any such erroneous assertion.

The Apostle John heard and saw many truths, but he was not permitted to record all of them for others to know. *For example,* he recorded the following:

> When the seven thunders had uttered their voices, I was about to write, but I heard a voice from heaven saying to me: "Seal up those things which the seven thunders uttered, and do not write them."
>
> *Revelation 10:4 KJV Paraphrase*

Revelation 10:4 illustrates that, although the Holy Bible contains everything that human beings really need to know for salvation and sanctification, the Holy Bible does not contain every single spiritual truth or fact. I am not trying to suggest here that the concept of reincarnation was revealed by the Creator-God to the Apostle John in Revelation 10:4. I am merely stating that there are some truths and facts that are neither recorded nor represented in the Holy Bible.

Certainly, an understanding or belief in reincarnation was never, is not now, and will never be required for the salvation and sanctification of one's soul. Unfortunately, in many instances, a superficial understanding of reincarnation distracts souls from their real purpose. That is one reason that the construct of reincarnation was not introduced in the Holy Bible. Another reason is that the primary focus of the Holy Bible is the deliverance and salvation of the Creator-God's chosen people through their faith in the God of the Holy Bible alone and not postponing salvation for some speculated future incarnation.

## IV.

*Heaping their grief* — that is, widening their separation from the Creator-God — some reincarnation cultists espouse the transmigration of souls from one biological species to another. Although human beings are animals *(Homo sapiens),* they are the only creatures that: (1) have individual souls, (2) possess elevated consciousness (i.e., a higher order awareness of who they are), and (3) are free-will agents that make moral decisions. Souls are *not* appointed by the Creator-God to inhabit any earthly creature other than the human creature. To be sure, Christ Jesus cast out unclean spirits (i.e., fallen souls beyond divine reclamation) from a possessed man and gave them permission to enter the bodies of nearby swine *(Matthew 8:28-33; Mark 5:1-13; Luke 8:27-33).* However, the transmigration of human souls to other animals, including pigs, does not occur as part of the Creator-God's plan for salvation, spiritual development, and spiritual advancement.

# V.

Reincarnation is meant for the purpose of spiritual development and advancement; it is not meant for the purpose of retrogression and/or devolvement. If the ember of the Creator-God's Life in us is not rekindled in a soul during its sojourn on Earth, then the soul simply turns into another human creature. This, of course, does not happen if the soul refuses to re-enter corporeality. Then, the soul becomes an unclean spirit, demon, or devil (all three terms are used synonymously here and throughout various versions and translations of the Holy Bible).

Reincarnation plays a major role in the pattern of the Creator-God's Justice. It provides opportunities for fallen souls to progress in spiritual awareness so that they can eventually make an informed decision concerning their acceptance or rejection of Jesus Christ as Lord, Personal Savior, and Sovereign King. (The Creator-God requires that such an informed decision be made during our sojourn on Earth.)

Without an understanding of: (1) salvation through Christ Jesus alone and (2) sanctification only by the Creator-God's Holy Spirit, reincarnation cultists have both romanticized reincarnation and inflated it to the position of an end-in-itself rather than the means to an end.

The most important moment in each soul's existence is the one in which it either completely accepts or completely rejects Jesus Christ as Personal Savior. After that moment, the most important moment is the one that is occurring right now and not in some distant past incarnation or some imagined future incarnation.

# VI.

Some well-intentioned students of the Bible who embrace the concept of reincarnation like to refer to comments by the Jewish historian Titus Flavius Josephus (born in 37 A.D. as Yosef ben Matityahu) that are seemingly supportive of reincarnation. Unfortunately, when comments by Josephus about people receiving a new body are contextualized (or even recontextualized), the comments are ambiguous, to say the least, or point in a direction away from a doctrine of reincarnation. *For example,* Josephus remarked that the Pharisees of his day (of which he himself was one) took the position that the souls of righteous people receive another body after they die. Of course, most Bible-taught Christians understand that the souls of righteous people receive a new body either (1) at the time of the pre-Millennial Rapture (i.e., *the first Resurrection)* or (2) at the time of the post-Millennial Great White Throne Judgment (which, the present author posits, is part of *the second Resurrection). Resurrection* in the Bible never refers to *reincarnation* nor is *reincarnation* ever mentioned in the Bible. Of the thirty-nine times that the word *resurrection* has been used in the King James Version of the New Testament, it has been translated from the Greek word ἀνάστασις *(anastasis)* [G386], which clearly means "raised to a translated or transformed bodily life."

Author's Notes: In Book Two of Josephus' *The Jewish War* (Chapter Eight, Section Fourteen), he used the Greek phrase εἰς ἕτερον σῶμα *(eis heteron soma)* [G1519] [G2087] [G4983] — meaning, "into another (i.e., a different or new) body" — which does not require the level of inference for transmigration or reincarnation that would be indicated, *for example,* by the Greek words: (1) μετεμψύχωσις *(metempsuchosis)* [a blend of G3326 and G5591]; (2) μετενσαρκῶση *(metensarkosi)* [a blend of G3326 and G4561]; or (3) νέα ενσάρκωση *(nea ensarkosi)* [G3501 and G4561].

---

# Disclaimer

The incarnation of the Creator-God as Jesus Christ is not to be confused with reincarnation. Likewise, references to the pre-incarnate Christ and the post-incarnate Christ are not to be confused with reincarnation. The *only-begotten* Son of the Creator-God existed before "the Word *[Logos]* was made flesh" *(John 1:14 KJV)* — just as he continues to exist today as the Risen Christ in his post-incarnate state. Jesus Christ did not need to progress spiritually in order to become the Christ (the promised Messiah of Israel) and Savior of the world. Why? Jesus Christ is not only the *only-begotten* Son of the Creator-God, Jesus Christ *is* the Creator-God *(Colossians 2:9)*.

# Karma

When a soul (Greek *psuche*) saved from eternal condemnation is permanently denuded of its corporeality at the time of physical death, its spirit (Greek *pneuma*) is transported to experiential heights of *being* originally intended by the Creator-God for unfallen souls. Until that time, all souls in corporeality (saved as well as unsaved) are subject to spiritually-natural laws of cause and effect. Laws of cause and effect for human beings are expressed in the Bible by such statements as: (1) "whatever a person sows, that also shall he reap" *(Galatians 6:7 KJV Paraphrase);* (2) "he who kills with the sword must be killed with the sword" *(Revelation 13:10 KJV Paraphrase;* see also *Jeremiah 15:2 KJV* and *Matthew 26:52 KJV);* and (3) "it would be better for someone who harms little children to have a millstone hung about his neck and be drowned in the sea" *(Matthew 18:26 KJV Paraphrase;* see also *Mark 9:42* and *Luke 17:2).* In common thinking, laws of cause and effect are often expressed by the plaintive question of "What did I do to deserve this?" and by the statement of "What goes around comes around."

Universal laws of cause and effect cover events that occur in the following realms (sometimes simultaneously, sometimes not): physical (corporeal), psychological (mental), psychic (electromagnetic), and spiritual (metaphysical). In other words, simply stated, whatever souls in corporeality sow physically, psychologically, psychically, and/or spiritually is tied to what they reap physically, psychologically, psychically, and/or spiritually — especially in the long term. To be sure, the consequences of an individual's salvation are more complex than a simple demonstration of good intentions and desirable actions immediately producing good results and desirable consequences. *For example,* Christ Jesus promised not only eternal redemption to saved human beings in their afterlife but also tribulation, persecution, hardship, rejection, and even murder for them while they are still on Earth.

Collectively, universal laws of cause and effect can be referred to as *karma*. *Karma* is not a paradigm, metaphor, or metaphysical position. *Karma* is a principle based on universal laws. The laws associated with *karma* are like the laws of physics that were originally put into effect during *the Big Bang* by the Creator-God to function without His active involvement except on a case-by-case basis, *for example,* through His intercession and intervention — especially in provisions, rewards, and blessings given by Him in response to our prayers, declarations of faith, and salvation.

Although based on universal laws, *karma* never cancels the Will of the Creator-God's grace, mercy, forgiveness, unforgiveness, Judgment, and/or Wrath (i.e., His justified Anger). The Will of the Creator-God always supersedes *karma. For example,* when accepted as the substitutionary atonement for one's own personal sin, the shed blood of Jesus Christ nullifies all eternal consequences for that sin. The eternal consequences of that sin are timelessly transferred to the crucified Christ at the time that we repent of our sin and make public confession of Jesus as our personal Savior. To be sure, however, laws of nature are still in effect for saved sinners who have not yet transitioned to incorporeality. *For example,* the physiologic effects of a sexually transmitted disease (STD) as a result of sexual sin will still be experienced by saved human beings even after their confession and repentance, and the disease may even be transmitted from infected parents to their unborn children. Metaphysically speaking, *karma* is like Einstein's relativity, which is best understood in general as well as special terms.

# Karmic Transferability

Not only does the shed blood of Jesus Christ nullify all eternal consequences for our personal sins, the substitutionary atonement of Jesus Christ also nullifies all effects of intergenerational sin (i.e., karmic transferability or ancestral karma) for human beings.

The concept of intergenerational sin is demonstrated in both (1) the Old Testament and (2) the New Testament:

(1a) In the Old Testament, the concept of karmic transferability is represented in statements concerning who pays for certain crimes against the Creator-God. *For example,* the Creator-God declares for people who worship false gods: "I will visit the iniquity of the fathers upon their descendants even to their third and fourth generations" *(Exodus 20:4-5 KJV Paraphrase;* see also *Exodus 34:7, Numbers 14:18,* and *Deuteronomy 5:9).*

(1b) In another example from the Old Testament, the Lord God Almighty declares that "a bastard shall not enter into the congregation of the Lord; even his descendants to their tenth generation shall not enter into the congregation of the Lord" *(Deuteronomy 23:2 KJV Paraphrase).*

(2a) In the New Testament, the concept of karmic transferability is represented by the statement from Christ Jesus that "the blood of all the prophets, which was shed from the foundation of the world, will be required of this [unsaved] generation" *(Luke 11:50-51 KJV Paraphrase).*

(2b) The concept is also represented in the New Testament by this question to Christ Jesus from his disciples concerning a man who was born blind: "Master, did this man sin or did his parents sin in that he was born blind?" *(John 9:2 KJV)*

To reiterate, the shed blood of Jesus Christ nullifies all consequences for the ancestral karma of Christian believers. Christian leaders who preach that a doctrine of intergenerational sin is still in effect for Christians: (1) are bored with the simplicity of the gospel of salvation; (2) are worried that their congregations might be bored, or become bored, by the simplicity of the gospel message; (3) are limited in their intelligence and/or understanding of overarching salvation principles in the Bible; (4) are too legalistic (i.e., *pharisaical* or *sadducaical)* for their own good or the good of others; (5) have defaulted to extra-substitutionary academic thinking (i.e., that something else in addition to the shed blood of Jesus Christ must be required for the atonement of sin); and/or (6) are consciously or unconsciously seeking to control and manipulate their congregations by holding them in bondage to Old Testament legalism and, thereby, emotionally indenture them to their local church and its leaders.

Not only is karmic transferability represented in terms of specific curses in the Bible but also in terms of specific blessings. *For example,* it is clear in the Old Testament that the Creator-God promises temporal blessings to the people of Israel if they keep His commandments and not follow after other gods:

> And the Lord your God will make you the head and not the tail, and you will be above only and not be beneath, if you follow the commandments which I give to you this day.
>
> *Deuteronomy 28:13 KJV Paraphrase*

The Lord God Almighty also promises to bless all nations of the Earth that bless Israel by sharing their material prosperity with Israel (see *Genesis 12:3* and *Romans 15:27).*

# Rebirth

The general concept of karma is familiar to most people — even those who may not be familiar with the word *karma*. The general concept of karma is known to most Christians, Jews, Hindus, Buddhists, Jains, Sikhs, Daoists, and people from other religious, theological, and philosophical traditions. Except for the overwhelming majority of Christians and most contemporary Jews, the principle of karma is intertwined with a logical interpretation of the purpose for reincarnation. (If you are not reading the sections of this book as they are sequenced, please review the previous section for a discussion on the compatibility of reincarnation with Christianity and Judaism.) Some Jews, especially those who have been exposed to mystical interpretations of the Hebrew Bible and the Talmud (i.e., the Mishnah and Gemara) in *Kabbalism* (also spelled *Cabbalism* and *Qabbalism*) are familiar with the concept of soul recycling through human rebirth, sometimes referred to in Hebrew as *Gilgul Neshamot* or *Gilgul Nefeshot:*

| | |
|---|---|
| *Gilgul Neshamot* | גִּלְגּל נְשָׁמוֹת |
| *Gilgul Nefeshot* | גִּלְגּל נְפֵשׁוֹת |

Author's Notes: The *neshamah* (plural *neshamot)* is the highest graded component of the tripartite soul and, therefore, the *higher self* of an entity; and the *nefesh* (plural *nefeshot)* is the lowest graded component of the tripartite soul and, therefore, the *lower self* of an entity.

Although the lower self of each soul is capable of existing independently in human rebirths, in metaphysical reality the higher self of each soul (except for those who have damned themselves and no longer have a higher self) is part of a spiritual syncytium of souls (the *us all* about which I wrote in the section entitled *Identity and Consciousness* in Chapter One). This *spiritual syncytium* is a coalescence of living substance — in this case, not *protoplasm* or *cytoplasm* but *consciousness,* which is the substrate of the entire universe and the fundamental fabric of each tripartite soul. All unfallen souls together constituted the original composite Adam. As a result of the Adamic Fall, however, all souls became separated from one another as well as from the Creator-God. In order to completely rejoin their original spiritual syncytium, individual souls are tasked with overcoming the pulls and tugs of their lower, fallen self by learning to depend on their higher self — which, in the final analysis, is one's absolute identity in the Supraconsciousness of the Creator-God's divine Mind.

It is the Creator-God's Will for unsaved souls to reenter the earth plane of consciousness as human beings in order to improve and correct their character deficits as well as learn how to overcome the temptations of a carnal mind (i.e., the mind that operates in flesh through the lower self). The rebirth of a soul in human flesh is both a curse and a blessing: (1) It is a curse because it is a divinely-imposed consequence of one's original fall. (2) It is a blessing because it provides additional opportunities for each soul to receive salvation through the shed blood of Jesus Christ (except, of course, for those who damn themselves by willfully and knowingly rejecting Christ and, therefore, have no additional opportunities).

It is the Creator-God's Will that salvation can only be received by a soul during its sojourn in corporeality. Although a soul in an incorporeal state retains its free will, salvation cannot be received by it when it is in incorporeality *(for example,* in between incarnations). In contrast, eternal damnation can be received by a soul when it is in an incorporeal state. *For example,* a soul is in danger of becoming an unclean spirit if it refuses to reincarnate because, by doing so, it is willfully and knowingly transgressing the Will of the Creator-God for its spiritual progress.

## The Sum of the Matter

What can alter, mitigate, and/or cancel the results, consequences, and effects of karma? The results, consequences, and effects of karma can be altered, mitigated, and/or cancelled by physical, psychological, psychic, and spiritual interventions through medical treatments, psychological therapy, electromagnetic healing, meditation, hypnotherapy, past lives regression, requests for forgiveness from others as well as one's own forgiveness of others, prayer, authentic contrition, confession, repentance, and salvation.

The deepest and most profound understanding of spiritual matters for human beings is not to be found in their knowledge of karma, metaphysics, electromagnetic healing, spirit communication, psychic phenomena, reincarnation, esoterica, mystery religions, obscure philosophies, or arcane rituals. The deepest and most profound understanding of spiritual matters for human beings is to be found in the knowledge of their own salvation and eternal release from (1) condemnation and (2) karmic laws of cause and effect. So, do not be fooled into thinking, after you have been saved, that there are deeper, more mysterious meanings to life. No, anything else you can learn will not be able to go conceptually deeper than a solid, foundational understanding of salvation and spiritual freedom through Christ Jesus. Anything else we learn may (1) expand our horizons, (2) help to clarify meanings of global events and personal experiences, (3) reveal and unfold the layered complexities of general and specific psychism, and (4) provide additional understanding of the Creator-God and our life in and through Him. But all additional layers to our understanding will not be conceptually deeper than the knowledge of our own salvation and eternal release from condemnation: they can only be *surface* layers (but not necessarily *superficial* layers). Although they may be important, they are still *surface* nonetheless because they can never be or become more important than the knowledge of one's own salvation and the actualization of one's higher self through the shed blood of Jesus Christ.

People who have experienced genuine want, lack, or need in their lives or who have been victims of discrimination, rejection, and persecution are especially vulnerable to deceptions, obsessions, and compulsions about religious, theological, and philosophical *mysteries*. Why? We often want to understand these so-called mysteries in order to feel more important, more significant, and of greater value in the overall scheme of things. And we often want to explain that the causes of our discrimination, rejection, and persecution are a result of our own self-perceived sensitivities, susceptibilities, and global importance. To be sure, we each are already of great value to the Creator-God, most important to Him, and greatly loved by Him. Therefore, let us first learn to completely and fully understand the concept of salvation before we seek to understand other concepts.

# Chapter Four:

# Sickness and Health

# Accidents

More than once, the present author has heard and read the statement: "There are no accidents in God." Similar statements might be used by metaphysical practitioners, prosperity preachers, positive thinking proponents, "profess it and confess it" teachers of biblical truth, and idealistic optimists. I, too, believe the veracity of the statement: "There are no accidents in God." However, I do not believe that the statement means that there are no accidents in the physical universe, a place where the Creator-God's appearance (i.e., biblically speaking, His "face") is hidden from us. Rather, I believe that the statement means that, in the kingdom of the Creator-God, all things proceed in accordance with His Will and His Purpose. And I believe that the statement means that, in the Creator-God's spiritual universe, everyone and everything has its proper place "as it has pleased Him" *(1 Corinthians 12:18 KJV Paraphrase)*. Although there are no variables in the Creator-God's world, where all things are known to be good, there are numerous unknown variables within the physical state, which is a world set apart from Him. Here, on Earth, accidents *do* happen.

In the Old Testament, when the Philistines captured the ark of God and brought it from the city Ebenezer to Ashdod, then to Gath, and then to Ekron, it is recorded that many of the inhabitants of those cities died and that their survivors were afflicted with "hemorrhoids in their secret parts" — which is to say, "rectal hemorrhoids" *(1 Samuel 5:6, 5:9, and 5:12 KJV Paraphrase)*. In response, the priests of the Philistines — because they were unsure whether the affliction had come by the hand of the Lord God Almighty or by chance *(1 Samuel 6:9 KJV)* — gave instructions that the ark be placed on a cart pulled by two unattended milk cows to see if it would be drawn to the house of

Israel at Bethshemesh. Although the cart was pulled by the cows to Bethshemesh (proving to the Philistines that the plague was a result of their having captured the ark and, thus, was not by chance), the Philistines had at least considered the possibility of chance being the cause of their malady, such possibility overlooked by many Christians today concerning the cause of some common circumstances and physical conditions. (Another Old Testament example, citing Deuteronomy 19:4-5, is given in the section entitled *The Role of Uncertainty* in Chapter Three of this book.)

To hear many Christians tell it, one might conclude that the Creator-God is interested in mundane things. They forget that He is primarily interested in one thing and one thing only: the salvation of fallen souls and their restoration to Him. Yet people profess that the Creator-God has helped them find a watch, has caused them to win a lottery, or has stopped an insurance company's computer from cancelling their policy after an automobile accident. And, when something unpleasant happens to them, some of the same people wonder why the Creator-God has been unjust, why He is testing them specifically, or why He has cursed them. To them, I say: "Yes, the Creator-God has an eye for detail, but only if it serves His purpose." Christians need to recognize that there is a difference between circumstance and blessing, just as they need to recognize that there is a difference between circumstance and curse. We need to be able to separate magical thinking, voodoo, and animism from the way we approach the Creator-God and the way we think the Creator-God approaches us.

Regarding corporeality, there are many accidents that can happen. There are accidents intrinsic to our physical nature — meaning, genetic accidents or accidents of heredity. There are accidents extrinsic to our physical nature, such as those caused by exposure to toxic chemicals or infectious agents or by traumas — all of which, while possibly intended by criminal perpetrators *(for example,* terrorists), are certainly accidental to their victims. For those who believe that thoughts are things and that things are thoughts, it is important to emphasize that the simple admission that accidents happen does not mean that, in so doing, we permit them entrance into our experience, give them reality, or grant them power over us. Rather, the admission gives us a better view of how to work with the details germane to each particular problem. Recognizing where we are and what we are subject to as corporeal beings helps us to: (1) not blame, accuse, or rail against the Creator-God; (2) turn to His wisdom and strength to override our own erroneous interpretations of earthly events; and (3) be healed of accepting false burdens as well as avoiding responsibilities. To be sure, this is not a rejection of the Creator-God's ability to intercede on our behalf. Rather, it is an acceptance of the number of variables that we encounter outside of the Creator-God's spiritual universe. In other words, causality in the physical universe is multivariate.

Relative to psychism, the following inferences can be drawn concerning accidents: (1) accidents occur in the physical universe; (2) accidents do not occur in the spiritual universe; (3) accidents happen to corporeal beings; and (4) accidents do not happen to incorporeal beings.

Author's Notes: For additional insights on chance as well as an introduction to the Creator-God's *guided chance,* read the author's book entitled *Intelligent Evolution* (Copyright 2022, United States Copyright Office TX-0008-869-477, ISBN 978-0996222426).

# What the Old Testament says about Sickness and Deformity

In general, accounts of physical illness and deformity in the Old Testament are linked with transgressions of the Creator-God's laws, spiritual uncleanness, and dependence on a false sense of self.

Concerning physical maladies, the following accounts are reported in the Old Testament:

(1) The Lord God Almighty plagued pharaoh and his household because pharaoh lusted after Sarai, Abram's wife *(Genesis 12:17)*.

(2) Because of Abimelech's lust, the Lord God Almighty "closed up all the wombs of the household of Abimelech" *(Genesis 20:18 KJV Paraphrase)*.

(3) The Egyptians were plagued because pharaoh would not let the children of Israel leave Egypt *(Exodus 7:17-12:29)*.

(4) If the children of Israel failed to obey His commandments, the Creator-God would appoint over them "terror, consumption, and fever" *(Leviticus 26:16 KJV Paraphrase)*.

(5) The children of Israel were plagued when they doubted that the Creator-God would provide for them *(Numbers 11:33)*.

(6) The Lord God Almighty made Miriam leprous because she spoke out against Moses *(Numbers, Chapter Twelve)*.

(7) Ten of the twelve men sent out to evaluate the promised land were struck dead because they brought back a false, unfavorable report — which had caused the children of Israel to doubt the real nature of their inheritance *(Numbers 14:36-37)*.

(8) The wrath of the Creator-God broke out in a plague killing 14,700 people because they rebelled against Moses and Aaron *(Numbers 16:46-50)*.

(9) Twenty-four thousand people died from a plague that punished Israel for worshiping false gods *(Numbers 25:1-9)*.

(10) Disobedience to the Lord God Almighty by the children of Israel would result in their being struck with the following afflictions from which they would not be healed: "inflammation," "extreme burning," "blight," "jaundice," "boils," "hemorrhoids," "the scab," "the itch," as well as "every sickness" and "every plague" *(Deuteronomy 28:21-22, 27-28, 35, 60-61 KJV Paraphrase)*.

(11) The first child of King David's adulterous relationship with Bathsheba was struck ill and died *(2 Samuel 12:15-18)*.

(12) Seventy thousand men died from a pestilence sent because of King David's sin in ordering a census of Israel *(2 Samuel 24:13-16; 1 Chronicles 21:11-14)*.

(13) Elisha's servant Gehazi was struck with leprosy because of his greed *(2 Kings 5:27)*.

(14) Jehoram, King of Judah, was struck in his bowels with an incurable disease because of his evil reign; and his people were plagued because of the evil they did under his influence *(2 Chronicles 21:11-20)*.

(15) Uzziah, King of Judah, was struck with leprosy because he tried to usurp the God-appointed functions of the priesthood *(2 Kings 15:5)*.

(16) The Lord God Almighty promised that He would consume "by the sword, and by famine, and by pestilence" all who forsake Him *(used in numerous verses throughout Jeremiah and Ezekiel)*.

Concerning physical deformities, the following is written:

> And the Lord spoke to Moses, saying: "Speak to Aaron and say: 'None of your descendants who have any blemish should function in the capacity of priest. Whoever has a blemish shall not serve the Lord in His ministry, including: the blind, the lame, those who have facial deformities, those who have deformities in an extremity, those who have an injured or deformed foot, those who have an injured or deformed hand, those who are hunchback (i.e., with kyphosis), dwarves, those who have impaired vision, those who suffer from psoriasis, those who have scabs, or those who have imperfect or crushed testicles.'"
>
> *Leviticus 21:16-20 KJV Paraphrase*

The sixteen passages from the Old Testament referencing plagues, pestilences, and death punishments convey the following principles: (1) When we reject the Creator-God's laws, we bring judgment as a just recompense upon ourselves. (2) As we sin, we heap our grief. And, (3) for every sin or crime against the Creator-God, there is a fitting punishment. That sometimes such punishment is outwardly apparent in a physical illness, disease process, or death is not irreconcilable with the fact that the Creator-God is Goodness-in-itself. As to the actual cause of the ailment or problem, this question posed by the Holy Spirit through the Prophet Jeremiah settles it once and for all: "Why do you commit this great evil against your own souls?" *(Jeremiah 44:7 KJV Paraphrase)* In other words, why do you rebel against the Will of the Creator-God and open yourselves up to such pain and sorrow? In effect, then, it is we who bring judgment upon ourselves. It is we who punish ourselves. And *sometimes* our punishment comes in the form of disease, anatomic anomaly, impaired function, or even death.

Regarding the Old Testament restrictions on those who had physical deformities or disabilities, such restrictions are but a typology whose meaning becomes clear only in the light of understanding the requirement by the Creator-God of a perfect sacrifice for sins. That some physical deformities and disabilities are a result of one's past sins in prior lifetimes is always a possibility. And that some physical deformities and disabilities are intended for the glory of the Creator-God should not be doubted *(for example,* see *John 9:1-3).* However, many deformities are coincidental to our being in corporeality and are a result of chance due to corporeality's imperfect nature.

That punishment only sometimes manifests itself as physical illness, disability, or death, and that not all physical problems are a direct result of sin, are important facts to remember. Why? (1) So that we are not deceived into thinking of ourselves as free from sin if we are (a) in good physical condition, (b) free from physical imperfections, and/or (c) physically attractive; (2) so that we are not too hard on ourselves when we are (a) physically ill or (b) in an accident that incapacitates us; and (3) so that we not think unjustly about, or act uncompassionately toward, those suffering physically, mentally, or emotionally from an abnormal condition.

Metaphysically speaking, the human condition itself is abnormal and unnatural for those who "live and move and have their being in Christ Jesus" *(Acts 17:28 KJV Paraphrase).* True sickness is absence from the Creator-God, real deformity is being bent out of shape from His complete image and perfect likeness, and actual disability from the Creator-God's perspective is the inability to love. When comprehended and remembered, such truths help us to keep physical sickness, deformity, and disability in proper perspective when they are confronted in ourselves and others.

Again, sin does not always result in physical difficulty. If it did, we would be increasingly exposed to stench from infected flesh as well as continually surrounded by encumbered physical shapes. No, there are many wicked people who have a strong physical constitution, who thrive on the activities of evil, and who threaten to overpower gentle men and women. Indeed, if sin always resulted in physical illness or deformity, fewer would be sinning.

Relative to psychism, the following inferences can be drawn concerning sickness and deformity: (1) the presence of iniquity within one's soul deforms one's spiritual being; (2) metaphysically speaking, corporeality is the visible sign of iniquity; (3) all sinful acts represent spiritual sickness and result in spiritual deformity; (4) the spiritual sickness and deformity of one's spiritual being are not always reflected in one's personal physical form; (5) the shed blood of Jesus Christ metaphysically removes iniquity and sin from one's soul when that soul acknowledges that Jesus Christ is Lord; and (6) physical deformity and sickness can occur in physical beings as a result of genetic inheritance, abnormal personal biochemistry, microbial agents, accident, sin, mechanical wear and tear, and/or appointment by the Creator-God (given by Him to us either as a specific personal challenge or as a part of a divine chastening).

# On Suffering and Affliction

Would you make Christ Jesus a liar? Then, why do you try? He did not say that our sojourn on Earth would be trouble-free. In fact, he said that we would have tribulation in this world *(John 16:33)*. The promised Messiah did not say that his followers would be cherished by humankind. No, he said that they would be "the most hated of all people" *(Matthew 10:22 KJV Paraphrase)*. The Anointed One did not say that the prophets and gifted people he would send would be received with open arms. He said that they would be killed, crucified, scourged, and persecuted from city to city *(Matthew 23:34)*. Moreover, Christ Jesus said that, especially during the end-times (specifically, before *the Millennium*), authentic believers would be so hated by all nations that they would be delivered up to be afflicted and killed *(Matthew 24:9)*. He said that they would be betrayed by parents, children, siblings, and friends *(Matthew 10:21)*.

Christ Jesus himself suffered rejection and abandonment from both friends and foes. He felt scorn. And he knew humiliation. Why is it, then, that so many of his followers expect their acceptance and reward to be given here on Earth? Our Master said: "The servant is not greater than his Lord. If they have persecuted me, then they will persecute you" *(John 15:20 KJV Paraphrase)*. And "They shall put you out of the synagogues and churches; yes, the time is coming that whoever kills you will think that he is doing the Creator-God's service" *(John 16:2 KJV Paraphrase)*. Yet there are those who would have us believe that suffering is not meant to be a part of the Christian experience. They ignore the Christian tradition and legacy.

Suffering is part of the Christian tradition and legacy. I write not only about suffering due to physical illness and thorns of the flesh but also about suffering due to emotional, mental, and physical stress that comes from choosing to do the right thing when tempted to do the wrong thing and when everyone else is doing the wrong thing. Also, those born "after the Spirit" always take heat from — which is to say, are continually abused by — those born "after the flesh" *(Galatians 4:28 KJV)*. Regardless of what anyone says, it is not easy to know rejection, scorn, and shame. Those who say it is easy have not suffered in such ways. No, they have only thought about such suffering theoretically. It is one thing to suffer for one's own sins; it is another thing entirely to suffer as the object of someone else's sins.

Like King David, we should fear pathogenic microbes less than humankind. Such primordial animalcules and crystallizations of unclean thought can nowhere come near the power of evil that can be generated through, and subserved by, human beings who have given themselves over to malice and avarice. Pathogens do not have the same capacity to act as vessels, channels, or conduits for evil that human beings have. Why "like King David"? When King David sinned against the Creator-God by commissioning an unordained census of his subjects, he was given three choices concerning the form in which his divine retribution would be meted out. Prophet Gad, King David's seer, came to him and said:

> "Shall seven years of famine come to you in your land? Or will you flee three months before your enemies while they pursue you? Or shall there be three days of pestilence in your land? Advise me now so I may provide an answer to the Lord God Almighty, who sent me."
>
> *2 Samuel 24:13 KJV Paraphrase*

David responded:

> "Let us fall now into the hand of the Lord because His mercies are great. Let me not fall into the hand of man."
>
> *2 Samuel 24:14 KJV Paraphrase*

---

Then, it is recorded that:

> The Lord sent a pestilence upon Israel from the morning to the time appointed: and there died of the people from Dan to Beersheba seventy thousand.
>
> *2 Samuel 24:15 KJV Paraphrase*

King David was no fool. He knew there might have been no end to the violence and destruction wrought by human beings intent on doing evil. He knew that tender mercy does not come from the hand of warriors. Unfortunately, however, because many souls in dust now live amidst the illusion of grandeur wrought by technology and electronics, they have falsely concluded that the human mind is less gross than it was during King David's time. They have not fully scaled the mount and looked about. They have not allowed themselves to see the darkness that haunts and impels them.

Truly, this Earth is the furnace of which Prophet Isaiah spoke. It is a "furnace of affliction" *(Isaiah 48:10 KJV)*. It is here that souls are exposed to all sorts of ills. However, that is not to say that souls in dust must be consumed by the heat from this furnace because its heat, like the hot coal delivered to the lips of Isaiah by the heavenly seraph, may be used instead to purge them of iniquity and sin.

In 1977, I heard a voice from Heaven saying to me: "Remove the tarnish." At that time, I did not understand its full import. However, through diligent Bible study, I finally understood a fuller sense of its intended meaning. I understood that the voice was referring to the purification of my spiritual mettle — which substance, metaphysically speaking, is faith. How is it that I arrived as such an interpretation? In searching the Scriptures (the Holy Bible is the only Scripture), I came to see that a fully-ripened faith in the Creator-God is the only substance of the real, spiritual person because it is the only substance capable of metaphysically reflecting the Creator-God completely and perfectly. Thus, I have also come to see that the soil of selfishness must be smelted from the stuff of the Creator-God that is in us — if we are ever to be recreated, or renewed, in His complete image and perfect likeness. In short, I now know that this world and its carnal mind must be washed from our senses if we are ever to see the Creator-God face-to-face and, concomitantly, that it must be washed from our souls if we are to be remade crystal clear and shine forth as the spiritual stars in His heavens. All souls must be refined and polished in order for them to be able to stand in the Fiery Presence of the Creator-God and reflect His holy light (as well as not perish because of its glory).

Yes, we are tarnished. It is our having first turned from the Creator-God that is responsible for this curious meld of spirit to earthly flesh. Our spiritual silver and gold — our faith and trust — is soiled by self-pride and self-will.

All things told, suffering and affliction do have a place in the lives of Christians. How? Suffering and affliction cause us to seek, see, and cling to (in that order) the Creator-God. The Lord God Almighty said:

> "I will go and return to My place (i.e., I will hide Myself) until they acknowledge their offense against Me and seek My face. In their affliction, they will seek Me quickly."
>
> *Hosea 5:15 KJV Paraphrase*

We know from the Bible that it is through suffering and affliction that we learn patience and obedience to the Creator-God:

> We glory in tribulation, knowing that tribulation imbues us with patience.
>
> *Romans 5:3 KJV Paraphrase*

Although Jesus was the Son of God, yet he learned self-discipline in the flesh by the things that he suffered.

*Hebrews 5:8 KJV Paraphrase*


It is through suffering and affliction that we serve as examples of the Creator-God's love, thereby helping to make Him a tangible reality to those about us:

> If we are afflicted, it is for your consolation and salvation because it is helpful to your enduring the same suffering that we suffer.
>
> *2 Corinthians 1:6 KJV Paraphrase*

> We who live are always delivered to death for the sake of Jesus that the life of Jesus might be made manifest in our mortal flesh.
>
> *2 Corinthians 4:11 KJV Paraphrase*

> For this were you also called because Christ suffered for us, leaving us an example of how we will follow in his footsteps.
>
> *1 Peter 2:21 KJV Paraphrase*


It is through suffering and affliction that we are brought to perfection and united to the body of Christ:

> As Christ has suffered in the flesh for us, prepare yourselves likewise with the same expectation because the person who suffers in the flesh has ceased from sin that he no longer should live the remainder of his time in the flesh to the lusts of men but to the Will of God.
>
> *1 Peter 4:1-2 KJV Paraphrase*

And, finally, it is through suffering and affliction that we are again made *white* — which is to say, completely purged of the dross of iniquity and sin:

> And some of those who have understanding shall fall in order to try them, to purge them, and to make them white.
> *Daniel 11:35 KJV Paraphrase*

> And one of the elders responded, saying to me: "Who are these that are arrayed in white robes? From where did they come?" And I, John, said to him: "Sir, you know." And he said to me: "These are they who came out of the great tribulation, and have washed their robes, and made them white in the blood of the Lamb."
> *Revelation 7:13-14 KJV Paraphrase*


Relative to psychism, the following inferences can be drawn concerning suffering and affliction: (1) spiritual suffering and affliction always result — either immediately or eventually — when one disobeys the Will of the Creator-God; (2) while in human form, spiritual suffering and affliction are sometimes reflected in emotional, mental, and/or physical suffering and affliction; and (3) physical suffering and affliction can occur as a result of genetic inheritance, abnormal personal biochemistry, microbial agents, accident, torture, torment, trauma, victimization, oppression, persecution, abuse, mechanical wear and tear, and/or appointment by the Creator-God (given by Him to us either as a specific personal challenge or as a part of a divine chastening).

# The Earliest Christian Healings

It is recorded in the Holy Bible that Christ Jesus:

(1) healed a man of leprosy by touching him and commanding: "Be clean" *(Matthew 8:1-4; Mark 1:40-45; Luke 5:12-15)*.

(2) healed a centurion's servant of palsy, saying to the centurion: "Go your way; and, as you have believed, so shall it be done to you" *(Matthew 8:5-13; Luke 7:1-10)*.

(3) healed Peter's mother-in-law of a fever by touching her and rebuking the fever *(Matthew 8:14-15; Mark 1:30-31; Luke 4:38-39)*.

(4) healed a man of his palsy by forgiving him of his sins *(Matthew 9:1-6; Mark 2:1-2; Luke 5:18-26)*.

(5) raised Jairus' daughter because of the faith of her father *(Matthew 9:18-19 and 23-26; Mark 5:22-24 and 35-43; Luke 8:41-42 and 49-56)*.

(6) healed a woman who had a "flow of blood for twelve years," proclaiming: "Your faith has made you whole" *(Matthew 9:20-22; Mark 5:25-34; Luke 8:43-48)*.

(7) healed two blind men by touching their eyes and saying: "According to your faith shall it be to you" *(Matthew 9:27-31)*.

(8) healed a man with a withered hand by commanding him to "stretch it forth" *(Matthew 12:10-13; Mark 3:1-5; Luke 6:6-10)*.

(9) had compassion on the blind who requested healing, saying: "Go your way; your faith has made you whole" *(Matthew 20:30-34; Mark 10:46-52; Luke 18:35-43)*.

(10) healed a deaf man by commanding that his ears: "Be opened" *(Mark 7:31-37)*.

(11) healed a blind man who sought his touch *(Mark 8:22-26)*.

(12) raised a widow's son from the dead *(Luke 7:11-18)*.

(13) healed a man of edema *(Luke 14:1-6)*.

(14) healed ten lepers at their request, saying to the one who returned to offer thanks: "Arise, go your way; your faith has made you whole" *(Luke 17:11-19)*.

(15) healed the severed ear of the servant of the high priest in defense of peace *(Luke 2:50-51)*.

(16) healed, from a distance, a nobleman's son of fever *(John 4:46-54)*.

(17) healed a man, crippled for thirty-eight years, after asking him if he wanted to be made whole, and later telling him to sin no more "to prevent something worse from afflicting him" *(John 5:1-16)*.

(18) healed a beggar, who had been born blind *(John 9:1-38)*.

(19) raised Lazarus from the dead *(John 11:1-46)*.


In addition to the specific instances just cited, it is also recorded that others were healed of "all kinds of sickness and all kinds of disease" *(Matthew 4:23 KJV Paraphrase)* and that, in one location, Christ Jesus "did not perform many mighty works because of the unbelief of the people who lived there" *(Matthew 13:58 KJV Paraphrase)*.

After studying the biblical accounts of healing done by Christ Jesus, it is clear that he relieved individuals of suffering and affliction: (1) sometimes to reward their faith (or the faith of their loved ones), (2) sometimes to cultivate faith, and (3) sometimes to do both. Also, it is clear that, without even the rudiment of faith present, Christ Jesus refrained from healing. Why? He knew that faith is a sign of penitence and that without penitence not only could there be no faith but no salvation as well. He understood that, although the suffering and affliction of the impenitent person might be great, they are not great enough as long as the person remains impenitent. Christ Jesus will not relieve from suffering those who refuse to flee to the Godhead for healing. He does not waste his energies on self-indulgent people.

In summary, then, what was necessary for Christ Jesus to effect the healing of physical bodies? We can infer that the following were requisite: (1) the holiness of the Lord Jesus himself; (2) the yielding of his spirit to allow the Godhead's Will to work through him (keeping in mind that Christ Jesus is God Incarnate); (3) the presence of the power of the Lord God Almighty; (4) the needs of people requiring healing as a proof of the Creator-God's presence; (5) the needs of people requiring healing as a relief from their suffering and affliction; (6) a basic belief in the Creator-God by the people desirous of healing; and (7) the Creator-God's love extended to unredeemed souls, such love demonstrated through His grace, or unmerited favor.

Concerning healings effected by his followers, it is recorded that, while yet on Earth, Christ Jesus commissioned, first, the twelve Apostles *(Matthew 10:1-8; Mark 3:13-19, 6:7-13; Luke 9:1-6)* and, later, seventy disciples *(Luke 10:1-9)* to give witness to the word of the Lord God Almighty through the sign of healing. Both groups of men were given "power from on high" *(Luke 24:49 KJV)* in order that they might prove their words with works *(Matthew 10:1; Luke 9:1; Luke 10:19)*. And, following Christ Jesus' departure from this earthly realm, additional acts of healing were performed by his continuing followers as well as new followers.

Concerning healings by the followers of Christ Jesus, it is recorded that:

(1) Peter healed a man who had been lame for forty years *(Acts 3:1-11, 4:22)*.

(2) the Apostles healed multitudes *(Acts 5:12-16, 14:3, 19:11-12)*.

(3) Stephen worked "miracles among the people" *(Acts 6:8 KJV)*.

(4) Philip cured "many taken with palsies, and that were lame" *(Acts 8:7 KJV)*.

(5) Ananias touched Saul to heal him of his God-afflicted blindness *(Acts 9:17-18)*.

(6) Peter proclaimed to Aeneas, a man who was sick of the palsy for eight years: "Jesus Christ makes you whole. Arise and make your bed" *(Acts 9:34-35 KJV Paraphrase)*.

(7) Peter raised the body of Tabitha (Dorcas) from death *(Acts 9:40)*.

(8) Paul and Barnabas wrought many miracles among the Gentiles *(Acts 16:12)*.

(9) Paul healed the father of Publius and others who came to him because of that healing *(Acts 28:8-9)*.

Invariably, the acts of healing performed by the Apostles and early disciples helped to convert many people to Christ Jesus and establish communities of Christian faith. Here, it should be emphasized that the Scriptures indicate that the healing of the physical body through spiritual means is only a sign of the presence of the Creator-God and not the fullness of that presence. In other words, although physical healing may be greatly desired by those who suffer and are afflicted (understandably so), unless it helps them effect a changed mental state (from thinking unholy thoughts to thinking holy ones) and prepare a suitable habitation within themselves for the Creator-God's Holy Spirit to indwell them, it can be of no real benefit to them. Thus, without the presence of the Creator-God within, a well-functioning human body is of null importance spiritually. Though the straightening of a kyphotic spine to an upright position may be a miraculous sight to behold, it is far surpassed in splendor by the straightening of a twisted soul to righteousness (i.e., right-standing with the Lord). Why? It is the latter that most glorifies the Creator-God.

Then, where does all of this place modern Christians in relation to the promises of Jesus Christ that "these signs shall follow those who believe: they shall lay hands on the sick and the sick shall recover" *(Mark 16:17-18 KJV Paraphrase)*. It places us within reach of that promise as long as we maintain, cultivate, and profess our faith and as long as we do not "ask amiss" *(James 4:5 KJV)* — meaning, as long as we do not pray for things that are not in keeping with the Will of the Creator-God in the restoration of souls to His Kingdom *(not* in the restoration of mortal bodies to His Kingdom).

Relative to psychism, the following inferences can be drawn concerning healing: (1) the greatest kind of healing is spiritual healing — which is to say, the healing of one's soul in its separation from the Creator-God (i.e., through salvation/redemption); (2) the greatest kind of healing (i.e., salvation/redemption) is solely effected by personally accepting the shed blood of Jesus Christ as the only atonement for one's iniquity and sins; (3) physical healing may or may not occur as the result of one's salvation/redemption; (4) there are no limitations to what Christ Jesus can do relative to the removal of suffering, affliction, sickness, and deformity; (5) just because Christ Jesus *can* perform miracles for us personally does not mean that he *will* perform miracles for us personally (other than the miracle of salvation, which is always freely given to those who confess and profess him); (6) whether Christ Jesus heals us physically or not depends on the multivariate nature of the identified problem *(for example,* we may have a physical problem because it is meant to challenge us spiritually — or someone close to us — in addition to challenge us physically); (7) the followers of Christ

Jesus can impart physical healing to individuals through electromagnetic means either by touching the sick and afflicted (through the "laying on of hands") or without touching the sick and afflicted (through distance healing); (8) there are no spiritual or physical barriers for Christ Jesus; and (9) there are some spiritual and physical barriers for the followers of Christ Jesus relative to healing.

# The Many Causes of Disease

Although the cause of a disease need not always be sought for psychic, electromagnetic, metaphysical, declarative, and/or prayerful forms of healing treatments, sometimes the cause should be sought if the healing treatments are to be more efficacious. *For example,* if the cause of an individual's disease is due to a particular sin or fear, healing treatments will not be as effective until the individual ceases from involvement in that particular sin or from entertaining that particular fear.

## Sin

Different forms of disease are associated with transgression, or trespass, against the spiritual laws of the Creator-God. However, students of truth should not conclude that all sin results in disease or that all disease comes from sin. To be sure, there is a relationship between sin and disease but only in these instances: (1) the general existence of sickness and death on Earth because of the Adamic Fall; (2) sickness manifested in the physical bodies of souls who, though intent on doing good, have done wrong; and (3) the visitation of the Creator-God's Wrath on humankind because of its continued practice of idolatry and willful rejection of Christ Jesus. (For the sake of clarification, *practice of idolatry* here refers to worshiping anything other than the God of the Holy Bible.)

In the first case, the presence of disease on Earth reflects the Creator-God's curse because of our original error of turning from Him *(Genesis 3:17).* In the case of souls inclined to do good, such souls go against their own grain of better judgment when they do wrong, thus creating conflicts within themselves and, until resolved through penitence and the Creator-God's immediate forgiveness, the resulting tension weakens their physical bodies, allowing them to become increasingly susceptible to certain ailments. And, in the case of the Creator-God's Wrath, souls intent on doing evil may be plagued by an angel of the Creator-God in an attempt to correct them, as a deterrent to keep them from harming others, and/or as a judgment for their sins.

Here, it should be made clear that it is not within the Creator-God's Will to use His power to force lost souls to return to Him. If any are to return to Him, they must do so of their own free will. However, that is not to say that a just recompense isn't due those who continue to live after the flesh and the carnal mind that directs it. All souls who surrender to carnal mind must eventually receive punishment. And retribution in the flesh for those who campaign against the Creator-God is one way that such punishment may be administered. *For example,* at the time of the end of *the Millennium,* when the "noisome and grievous sore" *(Revelation 16:2 KJV)* falls upon those who have the mark of the Islamic beast and worship his image, that disease will be a just recompense. In this case, punishment is not a form of correction.

To keep one's interpretation of disease in proper perspective relative to sin, we must *not* labor under these assumptions: (1) that physical disease is not in keeping with the spiritual laws of the Creator-God; (2) that every time we are diseased we have sinned; or (3) that every time we sin we will be stricken by disease. Why? These are not absolute truths. Laboring as if they are absolute truths will distort your vision and prevent you from seeing the true cause of various physical problems as well as their individual resolution.

# Fear

Fear is related to disease in two possible ways: as its perpetrator or as its perpetuator. How? Fear robs a soul of its inner peace and harmony, thereby weakening the soul's ability to protect its physical body from the ravages of carnal mind and mortal mind. What kinds of fear? Fear of inadequacy. Fear of others. Fear of loneliness. Fear of disease itself. And fear of death. When fear governs, the Kingdom of God is far from us and we fall victim to all sorts of ills.

Does that mean that we should fear nothing? No, we should fear ignorance and pride in ourselves. However, all other fears are not of the Creator-God but are imposed on us by the "spirit of error" *(1 John 4:6 KJV)*. Daily, we are tempted to fear for the safety of the false image we have of ourselves or of the one we would like others to have of us. To conquer those fears through Christ Jesus provides us with an escape from the diseases they may produce. That is not to say that all fearless and physically strong people are in right-standing with the Creator-God. Indeed, there are many selfish and willful souls in dust who are quite fierce and fit, afraid only of not getting what they want.

What directions are there from Christ Jesus concerning fear? He commanded: "Do not fear those who kill the body but are unable to kill the soul; rather, fear the one who is able to destroy both soul and body in hell" *(Matthew 10:26 KJV Paraphrase)*.

# Entertaining Unhealthy Thoughts

There are many whose thoughts dwell on the myriad forms of sickness in fear of contracting them. And there are those who purposely set themselves up for certain ailments or at least try to fool others into believing that they have them. Why? To gain the pity and sympathy of others. To attest to their own nobility by establishing themselves as martyrs. To feel less alone. To divert their own attention away from more serious matters, including the unhealthy condition of their own souls. Any one — or any combination — of these possible reasons can provide the explanation. Each case must be examined separately. But, whatever the reason, too much or too little emphasis on the human body can produce negative side effects.

Hypochondria and Munchausen syndrome are two conditions in which individuals place undue emphasis on their physical health. In hypochondria, although the hoax may also be on himself or herself, the primary design of the sufferer is to fool others into believing that he or she is too frail, in poor health, and prone to illness. However, a hypochondriac is rarely ill because he or she recognizes that to be so would take too much time and energy away from their schemes to manipulate and exploit others. Munchausen syndrome goes a step or two beyond imaginary illnesses. In Munchausen syndrome, symptoms indicative of particular disease processes actually appear. Named for Baron Karl Friedrich von Münchausen (1720-1797 AD), a German soldier and adventurist well known for his tall tales, it is the condition in which symptoms of various physical ailments are consciously or subconsciously reproduced in the body through self-infliction or self-deception (i.e., pathomimicry). Difficult to diagnose, Munchausen syndrome takes imagined illness to the extreme that, in bizarre forms of masochism, individuals are willing to suffer physically in order to capture the attention — that is, parasitize the energies — of others.

## Heredity

Depending on how you look at it, heredity can be either a legitimate or an illegitimate cause of disease. If you look at it from the standpoint of corporeality, it is legitimate. If you look at it from the standpoint of Christian metaphysics, it is illegitimate — just as all corporeality is illegitimate (because it is not our *first estate)*. However, regardless of standpoint, the unfortunate fact is that souls in dust are born into this world with bodies that are subject to the genetic directions of a biochemical machinery that is faulty by nature.

To help provide an antidote for bitterness and remove false pride, it is important for us to understand and remember that the physical characteristics unique to each one of us have not been specifically imposed on us by the Creator-God. Rather, the physical inheritance of individuals is almost always coincidental to their being in corporeality. The coefficient of existence is responsible for the particular set of genetic circumstances that each one of us is in. That means that the dominant and recessive traits that cause certain physical abnormalities, or predispositions to them, is not linked to the Creator-God but to mortal man. That is not to say they cannot be overridden by the Creator-God. No, it is within the scope of His grace to bless what does not deserve to be blessed. Fortunately, although chance has no memory, the Creator-God does. He is able to re-member us to the body of His Christ through salvation.

And, concerning changing our appearances, it was once told to me from Heaven: "It is easier to change appearances when dealing with the reflection." In other words, it is easier to transmute and transmogrify our appearance when using the power of the Creator-God to reflect His complete image and perfect likeness in our thoughts, words, and deeds.

## Infectious Agents and Toxins

Metaphysically speaking, viruses are the crystallizations of unclean thought, pathogens are lies, and toxins are the scum of the Earth. Infectious agents and toxins can be either the primary or secondary causes of disease — which is to say, they may adversely affect a healthy body because of their highly contagious or poisonous nature or so affect a body that has already been debilitated by another cause (psychological, physical, and/or spiritual) and has, therefore, been rendered more vulnerable to attack.

An analogy and typology for better understanding the relationship of potentially-harmful infectious agents to sin — and the diseases they secondarily cause as a result of sin — can be found in biblical ordinances about leprosy. In Chapters Thirteen and Fourteen of Leviticus are found various rules and regulations for the diagnosis and treatment of leprosy, the ancient scourge of the sinful. It is stated there that leprosy was to be diagnosed by its spreading, or contagious, nature and that the leper was to be separated from the rest of the camp until he or she was healed — after which time the person would be cleansed through the priest's sacrifices to the Lord God Almighty (Yahweh). The exact progression of events included: (1) the diagnosis of the disease; (2) the separation of the diseased person from the rest of the people; (3) either the festering ("fretting") of the disease to a worsened state or the healing of the disease; and (4) based on the just-mentioned turn of events, either the leper's continued separation from his family and friends or his rejoining them after ritual cleansing, which took place through the making of guilt, sin, and burnt offerings on the diseased person's behalf by the priest.

What is strongly implied in the previously-mentioned chapters of Leviticus is that the condition of leprosy was drawn to individuals who knowingly sinned. This connection of sickness to sin is substantiated in two ways: First, because a special guilt, or trespass, offering was required in addition to the usual sin and burnt offerings. And, second, because cleansing of the diseased person is discussed separately from healing.

When disease is a result of sin (and, remember, not all disease is), the disease may be healed ("may" and not "always will be"). However, the healing of the diseased person depends on the admission of his or her guilt, request for forgiveness in the name of Christ Jesus, and absolution of the sin by the Creator-God (such absolution occurring as soon as the first two conditions are met). The worsening of an illness or disease does not necessarily mean that a healing did not take place because of a patient's impenitent heart. Remember, some debilitating conditions fall within the Creator-God's permissive Will. And, although no one wants it, even pain can be permitted by the Creator-God.

Concerning poisonous and toxic substances, the few biblical accounts of their removal or neutralization and the healing of their side effects provide us with enough information on how they should be viewed and treated. Moses detoxified the waters of Marah *(Exodus 15:23-24)*. Elisha cured Jericho's waters of their evil *(2 Kings 2:19-22)*; and he rendered poisonous food harmless *(2 Kings 4:38-41)*. Budding metaphysicians need to recognize that poisonous substances and toxins exist. To say that they don't exist is foolishly stupid. If they did not exist, there would have been no need for Moses' or Elisha's detoxifying and curing the waters or for Elisha's neutralizing poisons in food. And there would have been no need for Christ Jesus' healing individuals of fever, one effect of toxin accumulation within the body. (Christ Jesus healed Peter's mother-in-law of fever as well as the son of the nobleman at Capernaum.)

Just because poisonous substances and toxins exist does not mean that we must be servants to them. No, those who believe in Jesus Christ have power over substances that are poisonous or toxic to the physical body. Christ Jesus said: "And these signs shall follow those who believe... they shall take up serpents and, if they drink any deadly thing, it shall not hurt them" *(Mark 16:17-18)*. Are we to believe that the statement just quoted is literally true? Yes, Paul witnessed its truth for us. When a poisonous snake bit him, "he shook off the beast into the fire and felt no harm when he should have swollen or fallen down dead suddenly" *(Acts 28:5-6 KJV Paraphrase).* And, when Publius' father lay sick of a fever, "Paul entered in, and prayed, and laid his hands on him, and healed him" *(Acts 28:8 KJV).* If the promise of power over poisonous substances and toxins was made good for Paul, then why not for us if we have surrendered ourselves to Christ Jesus? That is not to say that we should test the Creator-God's power or tempt Him by consciously placing ourselves in jeopardy or reject using common sense in order to testify of our desired victory over evil.

Although it is impossible to always keep infectious agents at arm's length, it is always possible to keep them at bay and to expel harmful substances from the temple of our body if we cultivate and maintain a gratitude for salvation through Christ Jesus. Such gratitude lifts us up to the Creator-God for His blessing, the showers of which can wash even the pestilence of pustulants from our earthly flesh. If the Creator-God is our habitation, then we can trust in His promise that "no evil shall befall us nor plague come near our dwelling" *(Psalm 91:10 KJV).*

## Ongoing Stress

Stress, in this context, is the physiologic response of an individual to stressors. And stressors are the agents or stimuli that produce the response. Scientific research has shown that some forms and episodes of different diseases — such as hypertension, arthritis, psoriasis, arteriosclerosis, nephrosclerosis, gastrointestinal ulcers, chronic migraine, and asthma — are reactions to continued physical and/or psychological stress. If stress is the culprit, wouldn't it be best to avoid it (as well as the diseases caused by it) by removing ourselves, as much as possible, from all stressors? No, isolating ourselves is not the answer because, quite simply, that is not why we are here — and, besides, contact with stressors is hardly avoided. Even a prolonged absence of normal stimuli can be stressful.

What is important is not our avoidance of stressors but our avoidance of continued stress by being able to interpret the changes, real or imagined, in our physical surroundings and psychological environments. Why? Generally speaking, people are distressed when they perceive that their security is threatened. And they react to threatening changes in their surroundings or environments by becoming fearful, anxious, angry, bitter, hateful, grief-stricken, and/or depressed. Clearly, what security it is that they are worried about is not their spiritual security but their earthly security. And that, in itself, is futile because there will never be an extended period of time on this Earth when our physical, emotional, and mental well-being is not threatened. In fact, with worldwide economic and social upheaval at our front doors, it is inevitable that things will become increasingly worse. However, being able to interpret changes indigenous to our corporeal experience (i.e., the human condition) can help us to react to stressors in ways less injurious to our psychological and physiological health.

If we wish to avoid continued stress and the diseases caused by it, what is important is that we not become choked by the cares of this world and that our hearts not fail us because of our fears of tomorrow. However, refraining from giving power to earthborn cares and earthbound fears can only be achieved through the casting of our burdens on the Lord God Almighty as the only provider and sustainer that there really is and depending solely on His Holy Spirit to comfort us. Only within the context of His Christ do the barbs and arrows of this life sting less. Then, let us pray that we might be like the early Christians who were "troubled on every side, yet not distressed" *(2*

*Corinthians 4:8 KJV).*

# Old Age

There is a natural tendency for the physical body to corrupt, decay, and perish from mechanical wear and tear in addition to traumatic life-threatening injuries. The physical body cannot last forever. It was not meant to. It is not immortal nor can it ever become immortal. Therefore, except for those who have an untimely death, everyone in corporeality has a time of old age. That, however, does not necessarily preclude the existence of older physical bodies in a healthy state. Old age does not have to mean the all-out collapse of these carcasses that we haul about. Although "Moses was a hundred and twenty years old when he died, his eye was not dim nor his natural force abated" *(Deuteronomy 34:7 KJV).* Yes, Moses was an uncommon man because he "was more humble than all other men who were on the face of the Earth" *(Numbers 12:3 KJV Paraphrase).* But that does not mean that we cannot also walk so closely to the Creator-God that the light within us dispels what, in His reality, is the myth of decrepitude. Christ Jesus freed the woman from her infirmity (perhaps rheumatism) even though she had been bound for eighteen years *(Luke 13:16).* Although bent, she straightened up to greet him *(Luke 13:13).*

It is recorded in the Bible that Yahweh said: "My Spirit shall not always strive with man because he also is flesh; yet his days shall be one hundred and twenty years" *(Genesis 6:3 KJV Paraphrase).* And, recognizing our decreased life span, King David wrote this proclamation: "The days of our years are seventy" *(Psalm 90:10 KJV Paraphrase).* However, also recorded is that there have been men and women who exceeded those figures for longevity. *For example,* the following ages are given in the Bible for these antediluvians at the time of their passing: Adam (930), Seth (912), Enosh (905), Kenan

(910), Mahalel (895), Jared (962), Enoch (365), Methuselah (969), Lamech (777), Noah (950), and Shem (600). And these ages are given for the following postdiluvians: Arphaxad (438), Shelah (433), Eber (464), Peleg (239), Reu (239), Serug (230), Nahor (148), Terah (205), Sarah (127), Abraham (175), Ishmael (137), Isaac (180), Jacob (147), Joseph (110), Levi (137), Kohath (133), Amram (137), Moses (120), Joshua the son of Nun (110), Eli (98), Jehoida (130), Job (140), and the prophetess Anna (over 100).

Whatever age we live to should not matter. What should matter is whether or not a faith in the Creator-God has taken hold of us sometime during our sojourn here. What should matter is whether or not we have given our lives over to Christ Jesus. Perhaps King David said it best when he said to Solomon just before his passing: "I go the way of all flesh" *(1 Kings 2:2 KJV Paraphrase).* No one can escape the end of their pilgrimage on Earth regardless of opportunities lost or challenges met. Our appointed times always draw nigh to us. (The last statement does not mean that the Creator-God never alters someone's appointed time.)

During *the Millennium*, or final 1,000 year period of time before there is "a new heaven and a new earth" *(Revelation 21:1 KJV),* the Holy Spirit teaches us through Prophet Isaiah that human life spans will be extended:

> [During *the Millennium*] there will no longer be an infant who lives only a few days or someone who does not live out his or her full life span; in fact, someone who dies at the age of one hundred will still be a child and anyone who dies earlier than one hundred will be thought to be under a curse.
>
> *Isaiah 65:20 KJV Paraphrase*

Life spans will be longer during *the Millennium* because the electromagnetic presence of Christ Jesus on Earth will impact human beings in the following beneficial ways: (1) the structure of chromosomes, including their end portions *(telomeres),* will be more stable and fragment less easily; (2) the number of generations that individual cell types can reproduce, or undergo cell division, will be greater; and (3) mechanisms for biological defense will be stronger and, therefore, more resilient in maintaining and mounting nonspecific and specific responses to life-altering and potentially life-threatening physical changes — in other words, our immune systems will receive a sustained, powerful boost.

# On the Spiritual Treatment of Disease

## Keeping Things in Proper Perspective

There is "sickness unto death" and there is "sickness not unto death" *(John 11:4 KJV)*. The latter can be healed, but the former cannot. Why? "Sickness unto death" is the end of the appointed time that one has on Earth. That is not to say that some people have not died prematurely because they failed to call upon the name of the Lord. That is not to say that some have not died untimely deaths due to accident, manslaughter, or murder. And that is not to say that some have not had their stay extended because of the Lord's intercession.

It is written: "And the time drew near that Israel (i.e., Jacob) must die" *(Genesis 47:29 KJV Paraphrase)*. Also, "Now the days of King David drew near that he should die" *(1 Kings 2:1 KJV Paraphrase)*. Job said: "All the days of my appointed time will I wait, then shall my change come" *(Job 14:14 KJV Paraphrase)*. Of what change was Job speaking? The time which "is soon cut off, and we fly away" *(Psalm 90:10 KJV Paraphrase)*. The time when souls must leave their earthly flesh behind.

In treating illness, it is important to keep in mind that there is both "sickness unto death" and "sickness not unto death." And it is important to keep in mind the Creator-God's Will and the time that is appointed for individual souls to remain in corporeality so that, in desiring healing for ourselves or those about us, we will not presume to know what is best or what the Creator-God has in store for us. No, regardless of which treatment modality we use to try to effect a healing, we should always want to defer to the Creator-God's Will. It is not necessary for us to be in control of life or death. That is not our job. It is not within our purview.

---

## Determining the Cause

Although there is a cause for every physical problem, not every physical problem need have its cause sought in order to determine how to treat it. Determining how to best treat the sick largely depends on how the sick want to be treated. Do they want to be victims or victors? Those who want to be victims are difficult, although not impossible, to treat. In fact, sometimes the best treatment for them is nontreatment. On the other hand, those who want to be victors are easy to treat. Such desire already puts them on the road to recovery (if, of course, recovery fits into the Creator-God's plan for them). Then, ascertain first what it is that the patient wants. Christ Jesus himself asked the crippled man: "Do you desire to be made whole?" *(John 5:6 KJV Paraphrase)* Strange as it may seem, not everyone wants to be made whole physically, psychologically, or spiritually.

## Pharmacopoeia

The Greek word for "sorcery" is *pharmakeia* (φαρμακεία) [G5331], from which we get the words *pharmacy* and *pharmacopoeia*. A *pharmacy* makes and dispenses prescribed drugs and medicines. A *pharmacopoeia* is a compendium of drugs and medicines. People who use prescribed drugs are not bewitched nor is someone who prescribes them a sorcerer. However, one need only look through the latest copy of the yearly-published *Physicians' Desk Reference* (PDR) to find that there is a negative side to every drug and medicine prescribed. It is most unfortunate that the negative side is not recognized by many people because, for as long as their faith is placed in drugs and medicines, it is displaced from the Creator-God. Yes, that is a strong statement but consider the mentality that exists today: Most sick people expect to be handed the solution to their problems in a bottle or a vial. And most medical practitioners, even though they know better, are willing to comply in order to assuage their patients' ignorance or satisfy their own greed.

Yes, we should treat matter as matter and not as spirit, but that does not mean always treating matter with matter — unless, of course, one is not grounded in spiritual truth. Those who have not yet accepted Christ Jesus do not have the foundation necessary to lean on the Creator-God completely for physical healing without drugs. To be sure, such leaning is not easy and someone who relies on prescribed medication should never be shamed. It can take years for an individual to develop not only an aversion to material remedies above spiritual remedies but also to develop a fuller comprehension of spiritual healing. It can take years to turn to the closet of one's soul rather than the medicine cabinet in times of physical need. But it can be done. The children of the Creator-God should anticipate much through Christ Jesus.

It is important for those who decide not to use pharmaceuticals to not make that decision for someone else. Each soul must work out its own healing, just as each soul must work out its "own salvation" *(Philippians 2:12 KJV)*. No one can force another person to give himself or herself up to the Creator-God. And, from a Christian metaphysical practitioner's standpoint, we are able to include others within the Creator-God's consciousness only to the degree that they will allow themselves to be included.

## Intercessory Prayer

Prayer is a state of supplication. It is the bending of our will and the bowing of our souls to the Creator-God. It is worshipful adoration, meditation, and telepathic communication. It is the state of our being receptive to the Creator-God's thoughts. It is a form of holy communion. It is our drawing nigh to the Creator, the Lord God of all.

Intercessory prayers are prayers made to the Creator-God on behalf of others. They are made with the intent of helping others to have a closer walk with Him. They are made that others might learn to know Him — and, thus, themselves — better.

The following things should be remembered when we pray for those who need to be healed physically, psychologically, and/or spiritually: (1) We must keep in mind that the primary healing is salvation/redemption. (2) We must be careful not to treat all effects as more important than their causes. (3) We must maintain a more enlightened view of what being made whole really is.

What heals? The balm of Gilead and the salve of salvation — Christ Jesus himself, from whom all virtue proceeds.

## *Laying-On of Hands*
### (Electromagnetic Healing)

There are individuals who have a special, spiritual gift for healing through *the laying-on of hands.* The Holy Spirit operates through them, using them as conduits for divine energy. However, these gifted people must first have surrendered themselves to the Creator-God for His use.

Of course, in the Holy Bible there are precedents for such healing. Multitudes sought healing through the touch of Christ Jesus "because *virtue* went out of him and healed them all" *(Luke 6:19 KJV).* It is no mere play on words to add that such virtue can only be imparted through those who are virtuous, or true to the Creator-God's image and likeness.

What is the nature of *healing virtue?* It is electromagnetic in nature (i.e., in essence). Christ Jesus demonstrated his awareness of its substantiality when he was thronged by many and yet felt especially touched by one person:

> And Jesus said: "Who touched me?" When all denied, Peter and they that were with him said: "Master, the multitude surround you and press upon you, and you say 'Who touched me?'" Jesus responded: "Somebody has touched me for I perceive that *virtue* has gone out of me."
>
> *Luke 8:45-46 KJV Paraphrase*

It should be remembered that Christ Jesus commissioned his Apostles and disciples to heal the sick and that the resurrected Christ specifically stated that one of the signs that would follow those who believe on him would be the recovery of the sick through the laying-on of hands *(Mark 16:18 KJV)*.

The Apostles were commanded by Christ Jesus to tarry in the city of Jerusalem after he was received up into heaven so they might "be imbued with power from on high" *(Luke 24:49 KJV Paraphrase)* and, as a result, give witness of him "both in Jerusalem and in all Judea and Samaria and to the uttermost parts of the Earth" *(Acts 1:8 KJV Paraphrase)*. It is further recorded: (1) that "through the laying-on of the Apostles' hands, the Holy Spirit was given" *(Acts 8:18 KJV Paraphrase)*; (2) that Paul wrote to Timothy: "Neglect not the gift that is in you, which was given to you by prophecy with the laying-on of hands by the elders" *(1 Timothy 4:14 KJV Paraphrase)*; and (3) that the healing of the sick through the laying-on of hands is one of the works of a living faith *(Hebrews 6:1-2)*.

Here, so that we do not lose sight of the fullness of the Creator-God, whenever we consider "the laying-on of hands" as a method for treating illness, we should remind ourselves that the healings effected during the earliest Christian ministries were used to punctuate, promote, and prove the gospel of salvation, not replace it.

# Metaphysics

No contemporary dictionary definition of *metaphysics* elucidates its historical importance as much as the definition given by Dr. Noah Webster in his 1828 edition of *An American Dictionary of the English Language:*

> Metaphysics, noun. [Greek *meta,* after (beyond), and *phusikay,* physics (nature). It is said that this name was given to the science by Aristotle or of his followers, who considered the science of natural bodies, *physics,* as the first in the order of studies, and the science of mind or intelligence to be the second.] The science of the principles and causes of all things existing; hence, the science of mind or intelligence. This science comprehends *ontology,* or the science which treats of the nature, essence, and qualities or attributes of being; *cosmology,* the science of the world, which treats of the nature and laws of matter and motion; *anthroposophy,* which treats of the powers of man, and the motions by which life is produced; *psychology,* which treats of the intellectual soul; *pneumatology,* or the science of spirits or angels, etc. *Metaphysical theology,* called by Leibnitz and others *theodicy,* treats of the existence of God, his essence and attributes. These divisions of the science of metaphysics, which prevailed in the ancient schools, are now not much regarded. The natural division of things that exist is into body and mind, things material and things immaterial. The former belong to physics, and the latter to the science of metaphysics. (Parenthetical inclusions from the present author.)

Today, largely due to the influence of Cartesian-based and Kantian-based philosophies, most people who have any notion at all of metaphysics regard it as the science of the conditions of knowledge or the science of pure *(a priori)* reason. However, there are still a few — most notably, Christian Scientists — who consider metaphysics as the humanly practical science of divine Mind in relation to spiritual being.

The errors of Christian Science include:

(1) the conceptual separation of "Jesus" from "Christ" — with "Christ" primarily receiving a metaphysical inference representative of the consciousness associated with divine Mind;

(2) ambiguity in acknowledging and explaining Christian mainstream understanding concerning the sacrificial atonement of Jesus Christ;

(3) not accounting for the multivariate nature of illness and physical abnormalities and the normalcy of biomechanical wear and tear on the human body or the normalcy of physical death;

(4) not utilizing all of the knowledge that the Creator-God has given to human beings for the treatment of illness, disease, and biomechanical failure;

(5) rejecting medical treatment for the children of Christian Scientists;

(6) not acknowledging the existence of evil in order to effectively combat its insidious nature; and

(7) establishing an organization: (a) that purposely separated itself from mainstream Christianity; (b) that ceased to develop and mature beyond the thinking of its leader, who died in 1910; and (c) whose primary purpose became the perpetuation of its own organizational existence (such is the nature of all human enterprises).

Briefly stated, the metaphysics used to treat physical ailment is "beyond physics" — which is to say, above physical operation in effecting changes in the corporeal condition. Besides employing supplication to the Creator-God, Christian metaphysical practitioners depend on understanding the true nature of reality and applying that understanding to help determine the cause — as well as the treatment — of illnesses. Christian metaphysical practitioners try to recognize who and what we are in the Creator-God's reality and then apply that recognition to the physical experience by seeing through the illusions of physical sense and laying claim to what is true in the One in whom we "live and move and have our being" *(Acts 17:28 KJV)*. Such Christian metaphysical demonstration rests ultimately on principles, or truths, that are self-evident to the practitioner in the light of Christ Jesus. Picturing oneself and others in the light of Christ Jesus is used to help purge physical bodies of unhealthy conditions. Therefore, a true metaphysician is a practitioner of truth who lays claim to man's God-given dominion over Earth through Christ Jesus and rebukes the powers of darkness through the power of the Creator-God's glory and Holy Spirit.

As used in its spiritual sense, *metaphysics* is best capsulized in the following statements by Mary Baker Eddy in *Science and Health with Key to the Scriptures* (Christian Science Publishing Society, Boston, 1934):

> The Principle of divine metaphysics is God; the practice of divine metaphysics is the utilization of the power of Truth over error; its rules demonstrate its Science.
>
> *Science and Health 111:11-14*

> In metaphysics, matter disappears from the remedy entirely and Mind takes its rightful and supreme place.
>
> *Science and Health 156:29-31*

Metaphysics is above physics, and matter does not enter into metaphysical premises or conclusions. The categories of metaphysics rest on one basis, the divine Mind. Metaphysics resolves things into thoughts, and exchanges the objects of sense for the ideas of Soul.

*Science and Health 269:11-16*

Our system of Mind-healing rests on the apprehension of the nature and essence of all being, — on the divine Mind and Love's essential qualities.

*Science and Health 460:5-8*

To bring conceptual understanding of divine metaphysics (i.e., Christian metaphysics) into the third millennium of the Christian era (i.e., *the Millennium* that Christ Jesus rules on Earth), the author of *The Biology of Psychism from a Christian Perspective* has elucidated the following six guiding principles:

(1) Divine metaphysics for the third millennium of the Christian era is a way of looking at life that recognizes and acknowledges the existence of a supernatural reality and a spiritual universe in addition to the existence of a corporeal reality and a physical universe. However, divine metaphysics employs the understanding that a supernatural reality and its accompanying spiritual universe supersede any and all corporeal, physical, and material realities.

(2) Employing divine metaphysics during the third millennium of the Christian era does not mean pitting it against the best practices of medicine, psychology, or other established healing arts; rather, it means seeking to complement, enhance, and work alongside those practices.

(3) Divine metaphysics for the third millennium of the Christian era does not do away with relying radically on the Creator-God for healing to the exclusion of all other practices. It just includes the recognition that employing such reliance varies based on time, place, condition, and situation. To be sure, we are always to trust in the Creator-God completely for all healing, but divine metaphysics for the third millennium of the Christian era includes the understanding that God works at times not only in mysterious ways but also in different ways for different conditions in different people in order to address mental, emotional, physical, and spiritual healing not in just one individual but in us all, collectively and corporately.

(4) Divine metaphysics for the third millennium of the Christian era includes the understanding that multiple variables are involved in human conditions and, for that reason alone, men and women with God-given intelligence try to use all that the Creator-God has revealed to humanity through His goodness.

(5) Divine metaphysics for the third millennium of the Christian era is completely compatible with biblical Christianity and the millennial rule of Jesus Christ on Earth.

(6) In their application of divine healing principles, authentic practitioners of Christian metaphysics during the third millennium of the Christian era always defer to the sovereignty of Jesus Christ and the supremacy of his absolute truth.

## The Role of Faith in Healing

Without faith in the Creator-God, there can be no true healing of the physical body through spiritual means. Even when the Holy Spirit heals one person based on another person's prayerful intercession, faith is required in the intercessor. Of course, there may be healing of the physical body though physical means, but that is not miraculous. No, that does not evidence trust in the Creator-God. The Scriptures declare: "Faith is the substance of things hoped for and the evidence of things not seen" *(Hebrews 11:1 KJV Paraphrase).* And "the person who comes to God must believe that He is and that He is a rewarder of those who diligently seek Him" *(Hebrews 11:6 KJV Paraphrase).* Doesn't it make perfect sense that we cannot depend on the Creator-God for healing unless we first believe that He exists and that He is who He says He is?

There are those who shudder when they hear the expression "blind faith" because they think it is descriptive of how an imbecile would live or how a fool would approach the Creator-God. However, as we come to understand the basics, we recognize that blind faith is where faith in the Creator-God actually begins for those who are in corporeality. Remember, the Lord God Almighty said to Moses: "You cannot see My face (i.e., the fullness of My presence) because no human being shall see its fullness and live" *(Exodus 33:20 KJV Paraphrase).* Remember, also, that Christ Jesus declared: "God is a Spirit" *(John 4:23 KJV).* No mortal can see the Creator-God. Yes, we must be blind to this world if we are to see beyond it to the next and, yes, our true sight is spiritual and not physical, but, if we are to pass through our darkest hours successfully by meeting the tests, trials, and tribulations that we have here on Earth, we must first have blind faith. Blind faith is the faith that helps us make it through the very times we have no glimpse of the Creator-God's truth or His spiritual light. That is why we must be willing to learn to "walk by faith and not by sight" *(2 Corinthians 5:7 KJV).*

To be sure, spiritual sight is more desirable to have than blind faith. However, from where do you think such vision comes? (1) Without a childlike (not *childish* but *childlike*) faith in the Creator-God when we are unable to see the outcomes of earthly events, (2) without faith in

His ability to lead us, and (3) without faith in His supremacy over all things, spiritual sight simply will not develop. Moreover, without faith there can be no understanding. If any believers are the least bit bright concerning spiritual things, it is only because the Lord God Almighty has shone on their faith and, thus reflecting Him, they are enlightened. True brilliance does not come to those who are without a faith in the Creator-God. And, make no mistake, superior cognitive ability is not equivalent to having the wisdom of the Creator-God.

Who is it that really heals? When the lame man at the temple gate was healed, the Apostle Peter was quick to point out to the crowd that gathered that the man had not been healed through his or the Apostle John's own power or through holiness but through faith in *the name* (that is, *the identity*) of Christ Jesus *(Acts 3:16)*. Such a *name* is *the name* of the Creator-God: As surely as the "angel of the Lord" had *the name* of the Lord God Almighty in him, so does Christ Jesus have His identity in him. To say (1) that Elijah or Elisha raised the dead, (2) that Peter and John cured a lame man, (3) that "by the hands of the Apostles were many signs and wonders wrought among the people" *(Acts 5:12 KJV)*, or (4) that "Paul healed" *(Acts 28:8 KJV)* is alright as long as we understand that it is the Holy Spirit of the Creator-God that performs miracles in response to our faith in Christ Jesus. That the Creator-God alone heals does not negate the action and power of the Creator-God within us through Christ Jesus and His Holy Spirit.

## Who Governs?

The physical body, earthly personality, human emotions, and cerebral intellect are all governed by carnal mind unless they are made subject to the Creator-God's Will.

It is counterproductive for souls in dust to labor on the premise that matter does not exist because, although matter can have no absolute reality in the eternity of the Creator-God, it is the condition over which we, as children of God, must demonstrate our dominion. Then, rather than working to deny the existence of laws of physical nature, we should accept that they work for the majority of those in flesh yet, at the same time, not acquiesce to them nor count them as more powerful than the spiritual laws of the Creator-God. To become better Christian healers — that is, to become channels more open to, and expressive of, the ineffable Creator-God — first, we need to recognize that physical laws are in operation and, second, that spiritual laws can supplant them, supersede them, and overpower them. This recognition is required if the Creator-God's Will is foremost on the minds of those who focus their attention and concentrate their energies on disarming and dispelling the errors engendered by the mortal state itself. Keep in mind that it is not the Will of the Creator-God to exalt anything from the physical condition of being except its resident souls in whom humility has become an obsession.

What about our mortality? All souls in corporeality are mortal in the sense that they inhabit earthly bodies. But, through the shed blood of Jesus Christ, some have reclaimed their immortality in the Creator-God and have been raised back up to Him through their "adoption as sons and daughters" *(Galatians 4:5 KJV Paraphrase)*. However, those who do not claim their spiritual heritage in Jesus Christ are no more than who they think they are. Therein lies self-judgment and its just desserts. If we see ourselves as devils, or agents of evil, then evil works through us, its works become our works, and we are indistinguishable from its spiritual darkness. In contrast, if we see ourselves as saints of the Creator-God, or agents for His good, then goodness itself works through us, its works become our works, and we regain our real identity — as well as true individuality — in its spiritual light. Concerning that last point, however, the following qualification is required: Heaven does not open itself up to, nor express itself through, those who have simply deluded themselves into thinking that they are worthy to do the Creator-God's work. Such delusion is a fool's haven and no Heaven at all. It would be unseemly for the Creator-God to express Himself through those who have not sufficiently prepared themselves to receive Him graciously, humbly, and obediently.

Each day, every one of us has an opportunity to praise the Lord God Almighty in what we think and do as well as in how we act and react by thanking Him, exalting Him, adoring Him, witnessing of His gospel, proclaiming His omnipotence and grace, demonstrating our trust in Him, exercising our faith, and manifesting His love toward others. However, if we choose to exalt a false self — what the Apostle Paul called "the old man" *(Ephesians 4:22 KJV* and *Colossians 3:9 KJV)* — we will be left wearing only the ashes of humility in penitence.

There should be no doubt in your mind that the Creator-God alone governs. The following question remains for each reader of this book: Have you made the Creator-God the Sovereign of your life?

# Bibliography

American Psychiatric Association. *Diagnostic and Statistical Manual of Mental Disorders DSM-5* (Fifth Edition). Washington, D.C.: American Psychiatric Publishing, 2013.

Aristotle. *Metaphysics: Translated with an Introduction by Hugh Lawson-Tancred*. New York: Penguin Books, 2004.

Beier, HT, GP Tostykh, JD Musick, RJ Thomas, and BL Ibey. "Plasma membrane nanoporation as a possible mechanism behind infrared excitation of cells." *Journal of Neural Engineering* Volume 11 (6), 2014: 66006.

Berry, George Ricker. *The Interlinear Literal Translation of the Hebrew Old Testament*. Grand Rapids: Kregel Publications, 1979 (Reprinted from the 1897 Edition).

Brenton, Sir Lancelot C.L. *The Septuagint Version: Greek and English*. Grand Rapids: Regency Reference Library, 1990 (originally published by Samuel Bagster and Sons, London, 1851).

Bull, Caroline and Michael Fenech. "Genome-Health Nutrigenomics and Nutrigenetics: Nutritional Requirements or 'Nutriomes' for Chromosomal Stability and Telomere Maintenance at the Individual Level." *Proceedings of the Nutrition Society* Volume 67, 2008: 146–156.

Bullinger, E. W. *Figures of Speech Used in the Bible*. Grand Rapids: Baker Book House, 1968 (Reprinted from the 1898 Edition).

Bullinger, E. W. *The Companion Bible* (Facsimile Edition). Grand Rapids: Kregel Publications, 1922.

Cloud, John. "Beyond Drugs: How Alternative Treatments Can Ease Pain." *Time* Volume 177, March 7, 2011: 80-88.

Comer, Ronald J. and Jonathan S. Comer. *Abnormal Psychology* (Tenth Edition). New York: Worth Publishers, 2017.

*Comparative Study Bible: A Parallel Bible (New International Version, New American Standard Bible, Amplified Bible, and King James Version)*. Grand Rapids: Zondervan Bible Publishing House, 1984.

Devitt, Michael. "Needle manipulation may hold the key to acupuncture's effects." *Acupuncture Today* Volume 03, Issue 02, February 2002: 1-4.

Eddy, Mary Baker. *Complete Concordance to Miscellaneous Writings and Works other than Science and Health*. Boston: Trustees under the Will of Mary Baker G. Eddy, 1915.

Eddy, Mary Baker. *Concordance to Science and Health with Key to the Scriptures*. Boston: Trustees under the Will of Mary Baker G. Eddy, 1933.

Eddy, Mary Baker. *Prose Works other than Science and Health with Key to the Scriptures*. Boston: The First Church of Christ, Scientist, 1953.

Eddy, Mary Baker. *Science and Health with Key to the Scriptures*. Boston: Christian Science Board of Directors, 1906.

Fawcett, Don W. *Bloom and Fawcett: A Textbook of Histology* (Twelfth Edition). London: Hodder Arnold Publishers, 1997.

Felsenthal, Edward (editor). *The Science of Memory*. New York: Time Books, 2018.

Fox, Douglas. "The Limits of Intelligence." *Scientific American* Volume 305, July 2011: 36-43.

Gardner, Howard. *Frames of Mind: The Theory of Multiple Intelligences.* New York: Basic Books, 2011.

Goldman, Lee and Andrew I. Schafer. *Goldman's Cecil Textbook of Medicine* (24th edition). Philadelphia: W. B. Saunders Company, 2011.

Gosling, J. A., P. F. Harris, J. R. Humperson, I. Whitmore, and P. L. T. Willan. *Atlas of Human Anatomy with Integrated Text.* Philadelphia: J. B. Lippincott Company, 1985.

Gardner, David G. and Delores Shoback. *Greenspan's Basic and Clinical Endocrinology* (Tenth Edition). New York: McGraw Hill, 2018.

Haushalter, Walter M. *Mrs. Eddy Purloins from Hegel.*[27] Boston: A. A. Beauchamp, 1936.

Hall, John E. *Guyton and Hall Textbook of Medical Physiology* (Thirteenth Edition). Philadelphia: W. B. Saunders Company, 2015.

Haqq, Christopher, Chih-Yen King, Etsuji Ukiyama, Sassan Falsafi, Tania N. Haqq, Patricia K. Donahoe, and Michael A. Weiss. "Molecular Basis of Mammalian Sexual Determination: Activation of Müllerian Inhibiting Substance Gene Expression by SRY." *Science* Volume 266, December 2, 1994: 1494-1500.

*JPS Hebrew-English Tanakh* (Second Edition). Philadelphia: The Jewish Publication Society, 2000.

Kant, Immanuel. *Prolegomena to any Future Metaphysics Which Will Be Able to Come Forth as Science (translation from 1783 edition).* New York: The Liberal Arts Press, 1950.

---

[27] The inclusion of Haushalter's book in this bibliography should not be construed as an endorsement by the present author because its major premise is contrived and supported by specious arguments.

Kant, Immanuel. *Prolegomena zu einer jeden künftigen Metaphysik die als Wissenschaft wird auftreten können* (Erstdruck: Riga 1783). Berlin: Berliner Ausgabe, 2 Auflage, 2013.

Kant, Immanuel. *The Metaphysical Foundations of Natural Science.* Lexington: Translated by Ernest Belfort Bax, 2015.

Kimura, Doreen. "Sex Differences in the Brain." *Scientific American,* September 1992, page 119-125.

Kushner, Lawrence. *The Book of Letters: A Mystical Alef-Bait.* New York: Harper and Row Publishers, 1975.

*Layman's Parallel Bible: King James Version, Modern Language Bible, Living Bible, and Revised Standard Version.* Grand Rapids: Zondervan Bible Publishers, 1973.

LaVay, Simon. "Brain Structure Difference Between Heterosexual and Homosexual Men." *New England Journal of Medicine,* Vol. 162, Issue 9, 1995, pages 145-167.

Leonhardt, Helmut. *Innere Organe.* Stuttgart: Georg Thieme Verlag, 1991.

Luther, Martin. *Die Bibel oder die ganze Heilige Schrift des Alten and Neuen Testaments.* Deutschland: National Verlag Kompanie, 1967.

McMinn, R. M. H. and R. T. Hutchings. *Color Atlas of Human Anatomy* (Second Edition). Chicago: Year Book Medical Publishers, Inc., 1988.

Meyer-Bahlburg, Heino, Anke A. Ehrhardt, Laura R. Rosen, Rhoda S. Gruen, Norma P. Veridiano, Felix H. Vann and Herbert F. Neuwalder. "Prenatal Estrogens and the Development of Homosexual Orientation." *Developmental Psychology* 31, 1995: 12-21.

Miller, Madeleine S. and J. Lane. *The New Harper's Bible Dictionary*. New York: Harper and Row, 1973.

Nelson, David L. and Michael M. Cox. *Lehninger Principles of Biochemistry* (Seventh Edition). New York: W. H. Freeman, 2017.

*New King James Version Holy Bible*. Nashville: Thomas Nelson, 2006.

Park, Alice. "Healing the Hurt: Finding New Ways to Treat Pain." *Time* March 7, 2011, Volume 177(9): 64-71.

Patterson, Charlotte. "Sexual Orientation and Human Development: An Overview" in *Developmental Psychology*, 31, 1995, page 3-11.

Piel, Jonathan (editor). "Mind and Brain: Special Issue." *Scientific American*. Volume 267, Number 3, September 1992: 1-159.

Platzer, Werner. *Bewegungsapparat*. Stuttgart: Georg Thieme Verlag, 1991.

Poncé, Charles. *Kabbalah: An Introduction and Illumination for the World Today*. Wheaton: The Theosophical Publishing House, 1978.

Purves, Dale, George J. Augustine, David Fitzpatrick, William C. Hall, Anthony-Samuel LaMantia, Richard D. Mooney, Michael L. Platt, and Leonard W. White (editors). *Neuroscience* (International Sixth Edition). New York: Oxford University Press (Sinauer Associates), 2019.

Quimby, Phineas Parkhurst. *The Quimby Manuscripts (1846-1865)*. London: Forgotten Books (Classic Reprint Series), 2015.

Rahlfs, Alfred (editor). *Septuaginta*. Deutsche Bibelgesellschaft Stuttgart, 1979.

Senior, Donald and John J. Collins (editors). *The Catholic Study Bible* (Second Edition). New York: Oxford University Press, 2006.

Sharot, Tali. "The Optimism Bias." *Time* Volume 23, June 6, 2011: 40-46.

Singer, Isidore. (editor) *The Jewish Encyclopedia: Volumes 1-12.* New York: Funk and Wagnalls Company, 1944.

Stern, David H. *Jewish New Testament.* Jerusalem: Jewish New Testament Publications, 1989.

Suddath, Claire. "Living with Pain: What Happens When You Can't Make It Go Away?" *Time* Volume 177, March 7, 2011: 72-79.

Strong, James. *Strong's Exhaustive Concordance of the Bible.* Nashville: Crusade Bible Publishers, Inc., 1890.

Strong, James. "Dictionary of the Hebrew Bible" and "Dictionary of the Greek Testament" in *Strong's Exhaustive Concordance of the Bible.* Crusade Bible Publishers, Inc., Nashville, 1890.

Teilhard de Chardin, Pierre. *Christianity and Evolution: Reflections on Science and Religion.* Orlando: A Harvest Book · Harcourt, Inc., 1974.

Teilhard de Chardin, Pierre. *Le phénomène humain.* Paris: Editions du Seuil, 1955.

Teilhard de Chardin, Pierre. *The Phenomenon of Man.* New York: Harper Perennial Modern Thought, 2008.

*The Comparative Study Bible: A Parallel Bible: New International Version, New American Standard Bible, Amplified Bible, King James Version.* Grand Rapids: Zondervan Bible Publishing House, 1984.

*The Layman's Parallel Bible: King James Version, Modern Language Bible, Living Bible, Revised Standard Version.* Grand Rapids: Zondervan Bible Publishers, 1973.

Tortora, Gerard J. and Sandra Reynolds Grabowski. *Principles of Anatomy and Physiology* (Seventh Edition).[28] New York: HarperCollins College Publishers, 1993. [See also Tortora, Gerard J. and Bryan H. Derrickson in this Bibliography]

Tortora, Gerard J. and Bryan H. Derrickson. *Principles of Anatomy and Physiology* (Thirteenth Edition). New York: HarperCollins College Publishers, 2011. [See also Tortora, Gerard J. and Sandra Reynolds Grabowski in this Bibliography]

Walvoord, John F. and Roy B. Zuck (editors). *The Bible Knowledge Commentary: An Exposition of the Scriptures by Dallas Seminary Faculty* (New Testament Edition). Elgin: David C. Cook, 1983.

Walvoord, John F. and Roy B. Zuck (editors). *The Bible Knowledge Commentary: An Exposition of the Scriptures by Dallas Seminary Faculty* (Old Testament Edition). Colorado Springs: Cook Communications Ministries, 2000.

Vine, William E., Merrill F. Unger, and William White. *Vine's Complete Expository Dictionary of Old and New Testament Words*. Nashville: Thomas Nelson, Inc., 1985.

Webster, Noah. *Noah Webster's First Edition of An American Dictionary of the English Language* (Facsimile Edition). Anaheim: Foundation for American Christian Education, 1967.

---

[28] Joseph Adam Pearson is listed in the Preface, page xxiii, of *Principles of Anatomy and Physiology* by Tortora and Grabowski as a "Seventh Edition Reviewer." The present author's responsibilities as a paid reviewer included carefully reading the entire manuscript that eventually became the 1,000-page textbook, reviewing it for scientific accuracy, and submitting written comments with recommendations for change directly to the editorial staff of the publisher.

*Webster's II New Riverside Dictionary*, Riverside Publishing Company, 1984.

Wyngaarden, James B. and Lloyd H. Smith, Jr. *Cecil Textbook of Medicine* (Seventeenth Edition). Philadelphia: W. B. Saunders Company, 1982. [See also *Goldman, Lee* in this Bibliography]

Young, Robert. *Holy Bible: Young's Literal Translation* (Reprint of 1898 Revised Edition). New York: Covenant Press, 2017.

*Zondervan Parallel New Testament in Greek and English*. Grand Rapids: Zondervan Bible Publishers, 1975.

# Books by the Author

*As I See It: The Nature of Reality by God* by Rev. Joseph Adam Pearson, Ph.D., Christ Evangelical Bible Institute, Copyright 2022. ISBN 978-0615590615.

*Classroom Version of As I See It: The Nature of Reality by God* by Rev. Joseph Adam Pearson, Ph.D., Christ Evangelical Bible Institute, Copyright 2022. ISBN: 978-1734294705.

*God, Our Universal Self: A Primer for Future Christian Metaphysics* by Rev. Joseph Adam Pearson, Ph.D., Christ Evangelical Bible Institute, Copyright 2022. ISBN 978-0985772857.

*Divine Metaphysics of Human Anatomy* by Rev. Joseph Adam Pearson, Ph.D., Christ Evangelical Bible Institute, Copyright 2021. ISBN 978-0985772819.

*Hello from 3050 AD!* by Rev. Joseph Adam Pearson, Ph.D., Christ Evangelical Bible Institute, Copyright 2022. ISBN 978-0996222402.

*Christianity and Homosexuality Reconciled: New Thinking for a New Millennium!* by Rev. Joseph Adam Pearson, Ph.D., Christ Evangelical Bible Institute, Copyright 2022. ISBN 978-0985772888.

*The Koran (al-Qur'an): Testimony of Antichrist* by Rev. Joseph Adam Pearson, Ph.D., Christ Evangelical Bible Institute, Copyright 2020. ISBN 978-0985772833.

*Telugu Version of Quran: Testimony of Antichrist* by Rev. Joseph Adam Pearson, Ph.D., Christ Evangelical Bible Institute, Copyright 2020. ISBN 978-0996222457.

*Urdu Version of Quran: Testimony of Antichrist* by Rev. Joseph Adam Pearson, Ph.D., Christ Evangelical Bible Institute, Copyright 2020. ISBN 978-0996222440.

*Revelation of Antichrist* by Rev. Joseph Adam Pearson, Ph.D., Christ Evangelical Bible Institute, Copyright 2021. ISBN 978-0996222488.

*Intelligent Evolution* by Rev. Joseph Adam Pearson, Ph.D., Christ Evangelical Bible Institute, Copyright 2022. ISBN 978-0996222426.

*The Biology of Psychism from a Christian Perspective* by Rev. Joseph Adam Pearson, Ph.D., Christ Evangelical Bible Institute, Copyright 2022. ISBN 978-0996222464.

*The Threeness of God* by Rev. Joseph Adam Pearson, Ph.D., Christ Evangelical Bible Institute, Copyright 2021. ISBN 978-1734294729.

*The author may be contacted at*

*drjpearson@aol.com*

*and*

*drjosephadampearson@gmail.com*

*Visit the author's legacy websites at*

*www.dr-joseph-adam-pearson.com*

*and*

*www.christevangelicalbibleinstitute.com*

www.ingramcontent.com/pod-product-compliance
Lightning Source LLC
Chambersburg PA
CBHW080454110426

42742CB00017B/2891